RANCH WIFE

Ranch Wife
by Jo Jeffers

with a foreword by Katherine Jensen

ILLUSTRATIONS BY ROSS SANTEE

The University of Arizona Press
Tucson

The University of Arizona Press
www.uapress.arizona.edu

© 1993 The Arizona Board of Regents
All rights reserved. Published 1993

Printed in the United States of America
19 18 17 16 15 14   6 5 4 3 2

Originally published by Doubleday & Company, Inc.,
© 1964 Jo Jeffers.

Library of Congress Cataloging-in-Publication Data
Jeffers, Jo, 1931–
Ranch wife / Jo Jeffers ; with a foreword by Katherine Jensen ;
illustrations by Ross Santee.
p. cm.
Originally published : Garden City, NY : Doubleday, 1964.
ISBN 978-0-8165-1386-4 (alk. paper)
1. Jeffers, Jo, 1931– . 2. Ranchers' wives—Arizona—Biography.
3. Ranch life—Arizona—Social life and customs. I. Title.
CT275.J45A3   1993
979.1'05'092–dc20
[B]   93-23764
CIP

For Cooney

Contents

Foreword

Jo Jeffers' story of her first years on an Arizona ranch combines the romance of a Midwestern girl gone to the wide open Southwest with the hard, clear realism of ranching on the high desert. What appear at first glance to be contradictions reflect instead the complexity of that peculiar occupation "ranch wife." Her telling also reflects the complexity of people who occupy that position and write about it. While protesting her ill-fitting Stanford education, Jeffers not only peppers the book with literary allusions but writes with the grace of a well-trained author. She may not have felt personally comfortable in the rarified atmosphere of Palo Alto, but she ably uses scholarly tools to portray a different world.

Having grown up in the orderly, fenced confines of a Midwestern small town, Jeffers brings an outsider's perspective to the landscape, work world, and interpersonal relations of Southwestern ranching, taking much less for granted than a native viewer might. But she also writes the book half a dozen years into a ranch marriage and cattle work with a real depth of experience that informs her images of people, land, and social and economic process.

I grew up on a ranch on the northern edge of the Black Hills of South Dakota, left in 1964 for the mostly urban world of academia, spent several years in the early 70s in northern Arizona, had two babies there, and returned to the high plains of Wyoming to teach, research, and write, in part about rural women; I lived many of the same experiences described in *Ranch Wife* but from the opposite direction. I find Jo Jeffers' viewpoint discerning, faithful, and remarkably similar to that of Linda Hasselstrom, who writes, "I was not born on the land; I was reborn here when I moved from a small city to a ranch at the age of nine. I was adopted by the land, and began developing a personal land ethic the first time I looked out on the empty, rolling prairie around my home."[1]

Jeffers' book, written thirty years ago, has a quality of timelessness about it. It describes a life that some might think resonates of a Western life of the 1920s and 30s. As a comparison to Hasselstrom's current work suggests, it could also have been written in the 1990s. Demonstrated by both daily responsibilities and the political and economic issues these authors address, a persistent continuity endures in ranch work and in the situations of women whose work is on the land.

Some feminist scholars may wince at the book title (and an editor in the 1990s would probably encourage the

---

1. Linda Hasselstrom, *Land Circle: Writings Collected from the Land* (Golden, Colorado: Fulcrum Publishing, 1991), flyleaf.

choice of "Ranch Woman" or simply "Rancher"). I think, however, of an article I published in 1982 called "Mother Calls Herself a Housewife, but She Buys Bulls,"[2] which explored problems of nomenclature and identity among women in agriculture. What do people whose work is the unpaid and varying but essential contribution to a family enterprise call themselves? What if you are, in addition, the female partner of the prototypical American cowboy? The naming and crediting of this kind of work life have been generally ignored, both culturally and legally, although somewhat clarified theoretically with our exploration in the last decade of the unpaid work of rural women worldwide. Even though they may produce more than half the world's food, they are rarely called "farmers" or "ranchers" but more often "wives." That unarticulated position of ranch women prepares us for the first chapter, "The West," which begins with Jo's childhood, mentions a great aunt who went to Fort Apache to teach school, but in the end focuses on a portrayal of the cattleman—whom we know will be personified by Cooney Jeffers, the author's husband.

In describing the West and its prototypical representative, Jeffers uses familiar characterizations of freedom and individualism, of tenderhearted toughness and weather-beaten sensitivity. She focuses on the theme of risk taking among Westerners. Though not inaccurate, those descriptions are perhaps less telling than Cooney's uncertainty about whether he would be able to leave his cows for his wedding and honeymoon until after a July rainfall ensured a sufficient water supply in the stock tanks.

---

2. In *The Technological Woman: Interfacing with Tomorrow*, Jan Zimmerman, ed. (New York: Praeger, 1983), pp. 136–144.

Chapters two and three recount events of the wedding and Jo's early cooking and cleaning errors, but the first real description of the ranch partnership does not come until chapter four, titled, ironically, "Branding." Jeffers begins that chapter by describing a successful rancher's wife in northern Arizona as necessarily a combination of "Rebecca of Sunnybrook Farm . . . , Nanook of the North . . . , and Lawrence of Arabia . . . , with the patience of Griselda, the empathy of Florence Nightingale, the strength of an Amazon, the equestrian skill of a Valkyrie, and the intuition of the Hound of the Baskervilles."

More seriously, she suggests that too much extraneous activity is demanded of women (generally) these days and that a wife must be all things to all people.

> While a rancher's wife escapes, physically, from some of the absurd burdens society places on the suburban woman, she is still expected to do more than keep house, wash, and cook. If she has children in school, she must drive them tedious distances back and forth every day and participate in their school activities after the ranch chores are over. (p. 64)

It was, finally, the chore of branding which Jeffers describes as not only getting her "'broken in' to ranch life, but also in getting [her] broken down to some extent." And it is in "Branding" that she speaks most clearly with a female partner's voice. Relating in graphic detail the branding, vaccinating, dehorning, and castrating procedures, she says, "Branding is the one job I shall never really reconcile myself to." Sick from the odor of burning hair and the knowledge of a fundamental cruelty, she concludes that it was better to be out helping at the chutes than inside listening to the noise of calves, men, and dogs. Exploring unsatisfactory alternative procedures for marking owner-

ship while hoping for better techniques in the future,
she also relates the danger and fatigue of the branding
roundup.

More than any other writer, Jeffers helped me realize
that I dutifully risked my shinbones in running calves
down the alley to the chute as a child, patiently accepted
the "woman's" job of vaccinating and keeping records as
an adult female, but managed somehow to absent myself
from branding after I became a mother and could not stand
the sight and smell and sound of burning flesh on perfect
babies. If not their mother, Jeffers takes the view of surro-
gate mother when she returns to the subject of branding
in a later chapter on the vulnerable orphaned "dogies."

> Instead of breaking free with its hind legs kicking in de-
> fiance and bellowing for its mother, the dogie walked
> out, dizzily and slowly, not knowing what had happened
> or why it had to happen to him. It shook its head a few
> times and wandered over to the feed trough, because it
> had no mother to run to.
>
> And we went on, shouting and swearing and working
> as fast as we could, because we were not sure what was
> happening or why it had to happen, either. (p. 134)

The Cooney Ranch lies adjacent to the Navajo Reservation, and Navajos figure several places in the volume in
the context of their participation in the life of the ranch.
Jeffers describes a ceremony on the Hopi mesas and the
connection between "man and nature" in that context, but
the Navajos we meet are part of the personal cultural in-
teractions of Anglos ranching on the high desert which the
Navajos would surely call Dinetah, Navajoland.

Again, while in the 1990s a writer might not begin a
chapter on the Navajos with a story of Sam Roanhorse's
extended and unannounced absence from the ranch or his

wife's request for a loan, those are familiar experiences to
Anglos living in Navajoland. No disrespect is intended.
The author makes it clear that Sam, before Jo arrived, was
part of the ranch and the occupant of the bunkhouse; it
was Jo and Cooney who slept in the Ford station wagon for
two weeks until the bunkhouse could be expanded. Jeffers
ultimately offers an understanding of cultural difference
and an appreciation of Navajo values. In contrast to the
Anglo myth of the self-made man, Jeffers speaks of the Navajos who "live with the centuries, . . . time only the continuation of life processes—the eternal, unending harmony
of the universe, the balance of Nature, the changing of the
seasons." And of relations with the Anglo world, she says,

> . . . the Navajo is free. He will not respect us because
> we have education or large houses or credit at the bank.
> He will not be treated as anything other than an absolute
> equal. If he grew up secure in the affection and inter-
> dependence of his own clan, he really feels, in his heart,
> that he is among the chosen people—the Dineh—he is a
> Navajo. (p. 103)

Beyond that general view, the Navajos Jeffers describes
possess different personalities and exhibit a variety of
strengths and weaknesses. Navajo women as well as men
figure in her reflections—from Grace, the excellent student whom Jo regretted seeing go to beauty school rather
than university, or Sam's daughter Pauline, who describes
her Kinaalda (puberty ceremony) and survives open heart
surgery with humor and toughness.

Jeffers gives three chapters seasonal names, and she de-
votes ample description to the land, the seasons, and the
weather, the parameters shaping any rancher's life. Few
other occupations depend as much on the vegetative pro-

duction of terrain, the changes in work according to time of year, or the wealth or devastation that rainfall, wind, or blizzards can bring. Although my own livelihood has long been independent of the weather, I still cannot escape the visceral response I have to any rain shower. A vestige of my growing up, when rain meant a years' crop, my father's mental health, and maybe going to town for a movie, the smell of rain always produces psychic euphoria, and I see it through the wipers, hear it on the roof of our 1948 Dodge. Jeffers says,

> No words can ever express the elation in a rancher's heart when a long dry spell is finally broken by a good rain. I can still remember how I felt one summer day, after our first rain of the year, standing out in the corral when it was over, smelling the strong, pungent earth and watching a bunch of young bulls we had just bought run across the pasture, throwing up their heads, while behind them, from one end of the ranch to the other, stretched a double rainbow, unspeakably beautiful. (p. 234)

It was not far north of there in the middle of the Navajo Reservation that I saw my first double rainbow just a few years later, spanning the red rocks of the high desert, as a Princeton friend explained why that was optically impossible.

But the wonder of the Southwest comes in large measure from its harshness. Winter at an altitude of a mile or more is real, with snow and cold, with danger to livestock and a sharp beauty that reminds the author of the Navajo Night chant:

> I am walking on the tops of mountains.
> The Gods are before me.
> The Gods are behind me.
> I am walking in the midst of the Gods. (p. 182)

Summer is the hot, dry wait for rain, which the Hopi ceremonials may produce, or at least celebrate, in the snake
dances through which Jeffers contemplates the power of
sex and reproduction and the cycle of birth, death, and
rebirth in the beauty and order of Creation. Spring in the
desert is not so much about pastel flowers as it is about
blowing sand, not only in the huge outdoors but through
any building, leaving dunes under the doors, on the win-
dowsills. But spring also includes "the wonder of life,"
which appears and reappears in Jeffers' descriptions—of
the ranch woman herself, of the experience of delivering a
calf and persuading the heifer to take on the job of mother-
ing, and even, in her older, stronger self, refusing to watch
the old cows shipped off.

In a chapter on "Enemies," Jeffers is clear from the beginning that while cattlemen have natural enemies, the
ones we would expect on the desert (coyotes, gophers,
wild dogs, rattlesnakes, and loco weed), the man-made
ones are harder to cope with—from human vandals to
hunters, the economy, and the government. Just as Linda
Hasselstrom writes currently about a land ethic in the con-
temporary world when rightful ownership, livestock grazing, and even eating meat are matters of heated public
conversation and policy debate, Jeffers wrote thoughtfully
nearly thirty years ago about ranching responsibility and
the ranching way of life.

Ranch Wife makes an important contribution to the understanding of the lives of rural women in the American
West. Personal accounts provide the best means we have
so far of perceiving lives and work of women who fit so
poorly into our general categories either of work or of
"women's work." Ranch women are people who do valued
work without measurable pay, women whose work is more

likely to be outside than inside. Marxist analyses try to distinguish between productive and reproductive activity, but these women who do work in which the delineation is even more obscure than for most women probably make those analyses transparent for their irrelevance. A few rare writers, Jo Jeffers among them, have had the combination of experience and time to be able to write about the women who are the counterparts to the cowboy whom we have made a worldwide archetype of American durability. Ranch wives, too, endure.

Katherine Jensen

Laramie, Wyoming

"I did not wish to live what was not life, living is so dear; nor did I wish to practise resignation, unless it was quite necessary. I wanted to live deep and suck out all the marrow of life, to live so sturdily and Spartan-like as to put to rout all that was not life, to cut a broad swath and shave close, to drive life into a corner, and reduce it to its lowest terms, and, if it proved to be mean, why then to get the whole and genuine meanness of it, and publish its meanness to the world; or if it were sublime, to know it by experience and be able to give a true account of it in my next excursion."

HENRY DAVID THOREAU in *Walden*

RANCH WIFE

1

The West

Has there been, in the last hundred years, a boy born who did not at one time or another want to be a cowboy? Hero of the Great American Dream, most inexorably western of all westerners, his way of life and code of ethics are familiar and enduring. Enchanted word—"cowboy." Visions of fast horses, wide open spaces, and the desire for freedom that is in the heart of every boy. Every boy and, once in a while, a little girl.

At the age of five, I was the two-gunned scourge of Brown County, Minnesota. I gulped down Ralston every morning because it sponsored Tom Mix. On the radio and in the comic strips, I followed the Lone Ranger and Tonto ("Hi ho, Silver, awaaay!") in their relentless pursuit of the Bad Men. I spent those dreadful mornings in kindergarten thinking about the next Saturday afternoon Gene

Autry movie. My favorite book was a dog-eared volume called, simply, *The Book of Cowboys*.

Many were the days and nights I spent in bed, gasping with asthma and wheezing merrily as I read my cowboy book and one called *Little Rose of the Mesa*. During the long, northern winter nights, with the snow piled up against the window, as I lay restless, choking for breath, honestly fearful lest I might die before morning, I promised myself that one day I would be strong and healthy. One day I would ride horses and walk in clean, sunlit air. "When I grow up," I thought to myself, "if I ever do, I shall go to Arizona and be a cowboy."

At the long family dinner table in the dining room of the hotel owned by my father's family, chin in hands, I sat fascinated by my Grandfather Johnson's tales of Jim Bridger the Indian Scout, and cunning old Chief Rain-in-the-Face. Grandpa called me "Little Kickapoo," which I liked very much. Often, someone would tell the blood-curdling saga of the last great Sioux uprising against the settlers in the Minnesota River Valley. My grandma's family had used their old Dacotah Hotel as a hospital to treat the wounded in the massacre. I could never decide whether I was on the settlers' side or the Indians', but my sympathy leaned toward the Indians.

One day I would be quite taken by the idea of living in the forest, Hiawatha-like, hunting deer and catching fish. The next day I was equally intent on riding the range under the blazing desert sun.

Grandpa loved Nature (in the abstract), but was appalled at the thought of getting dirty. Somehow he had managed to plant trees and flowers all over the town of New Ulm in a pleasant, well-ordered European fashion, in parks and boulevards. I have often imagined Grandpa in a white starched shirt, tie, immaculate gray suit, clutching a cigar and sporting a cane, gingerly patting manure on his rosebushes.

He always talked about the Great American West and I think he might have gone one day if he had not thought it sounded a bit dangerous. Grandpa was fond of farming, also in the abstract. He had a notion that my father should be a gentleman farmer. My father didn't even want to be a gentleman, particularly. But, perhaps, listening to Grandpa, I developed the passion for livestock which has been with me since childhood. In those days it usually took the form of cats, dogs, and Easter ducks. How I loved animals—any size, shape, color, or species! The hours I spent in Grandfather's museum of natural history, my nose against the glass cases, eye to eye with eagles, hawks, and stuffed owls.

The fact that my grandfather had built parks, boulevards, a fine library, a historical and natural history museum, or that his brother had been Governor was continually being impressed upon me by The Family. The only thing that did impress me was that Grandpa had known the old Sioux chiefs, Jim Bridger and the mountain men. I was almost grown before I realized, to my grave disillusionment, that Jim Bridger had lived long before my grandfather's time.

Grandpa loved freedom, too. Freedom and good German beer. Unfortunately, the two are not compatible. He often talked about going to Tahiti, but never seemed to get farther than Turner Hall. His daily constitutionals took him over the Old Indian Trail. He was the only person alive who knew where the trail had been and it was a remarkable coincidence, we thought, that it passed every tavern in town.

Often, on lazy summer afternoons, we would sit together drinking beer, Grandpa and I. Mother thought that I should have a "near beer" instead, but Grandpa would say, "Pooh! How do you expect her to drink that stuff?" and he would pour some Haunstein's or Schell's into my mug.

He would talk in his flowing rhetoric about noble Indians, brave soldiers, French fur traders, rugged mountain men, and wild cowboys. I would half-listen, studying his long Swedish head, his clear blue eyes, and his slender, sensitive hands. Although Grandpa began his life in poverty, he was the true aristocrat of the family . . . one of those rare natural aristocrats who accept, with grace, being alone, aloof, and never understood as their portion in life. I looked at him as a sort of human Mount Everest, towering, challenging, but always inaccessible. He was justly proud of being a self-educated man. His mother was a hard-working Swedish woman. Her husband, a jovial, boisterous, hard-drinking man, had left her frequently, out of his compulsion for wanderlust and his necessity for being unfettered. She supported her children by taking in washing.

Grandma's family were solid, practical German burghers, all of them heartily and unabashedly bourgeois. I don't believe Grandma cared much about freedom or libraries or Indians. She was more interested in whether her angel food cake raised or not. She laughed from the very depths of her soul. When she laughed, the whole house seemed to vibrate with warmth and reassurance.

Oh, how she could laugh and cook and eat! Her world was her kitchen and all the good things of that microcosm were hers . . . the fine china, silver, linen, and crystal; the rich butter and cream; the old friends who came to gossip over coffee and *kügelhopf*. She was the confidante of everyone from the laundress to the mayor. Everyone but Grandpa.

When I was very small, she taught me to knit and work needlepoint. In her sunny kitchen I would stand on a stool, cutting homemade noodles into long, crooked strips. "Ach, Jody," she would say, looking at my Levi-Strauss overalls, "don't you ever want to grow up to be a lady?" Grandma was a lady. Her dresses were silk or wool, always simple and well-made. She liked good substantial clothes and tasteful jewelry. She had been a beauty in her youth and never let anyone forget it.

There is a German word which, alone, describes the state my Grandma strived for: *gemütlichkeit*. It is a condition more sensuous than mere contentment; warmer than mere satisfaction. Her home was always a kind of haven . . . sunny, cheerful, filled with people and the smell of *kaffeekuchen* in the oven.

Grandma and Grandpa Johnson never quite managed to reach each other. Instead of advocating "togetherness" they lived in a kind of marital *apartheid*. And yet there was mutual respect and a curiosity about when the balance of power might suddenly shift.

These things have been with me from the beginning: my grandpa's love of learning, of freedom, of Nature; my grandma's love of comfort, of friends, of a home well-kept.

On my mother's side, there were the peculiarly English combinations of sense and sensibility, wild imagination and strict resourcefulness. There were bountiful Thanksgivings overrun with cousins at Grandmother Scofield's frame house. When we visited them in Neligh, a small Nebraska prairie town, there were the moonlit nights listening to the coyotes howl on the outskirts of town.

There was the icy morning dash down to the kitchen and the huddling in front of the big black cookstove where Grandmother burned the prairie fuel, corn cobs. There was the infamous cat, Tom Peedle, who slept in the ash box and had perpetually singed hair. And there was Duke, the collie, who arose early in the morning to gather the overshoes from all the neighbors' porches and bring them home. Most vivid of all, in my memory, were the mourning doves who sang so sweetly and sadly on mild spring days, for all the disillusionment and lost love in the whole world.

Grandmother Scofield had come West with her mother and father in a wagon. They settled on the Nebraska prairies and lived for a time in a sod shanty. In spite of that, she had acquired a good education in the East. Grandmother Addie had a wry wit and loved to memorize poetry. I think she would have become an actress if she hadn't fallen in love with "Ern." She would sometimes stop in her work, cup her hand behind her ear, and say silly things like, "Hark! I hear footsteps approaching on horseback!"

Grandmother had a cousin Claire, who, as an adventurous young lady had come to the Territory of Arizona. She taught school for a time at Fort Apache, then a remote cavalry outpost. In those days the schoolteachers spent their summers cutting wild hay (and I suppose sowing wild oats) for the winter. How strange it seemed to me, half a century later, when I found myself living on the same Apache Reservation with a friend who taught school there.

And so it was that all these people were a part of me.

I was them, but I was something else, too. I was one enormous appetite—physically, mentally, and spiritually. In me was a continuing, insatiable hunger—for love, beauty, learning, wisdom, freedom, and all the good things of this earth. At twenty, I wanted to do everything, see everything, know everything, love everyone. Compared with me, Faust was lackadaisical. And always, *always*, there was my uncompromising will bent toward the West.

All the time I was growing up we moved . . . farther south, farther west. When my parents moved to Arizona in 1949, I knew I was home. For the first time in my life, I was home. From that moment, I have never really been satisfied away from the vast windswept glory that is northeastern Arizona.

I had spent my first two years of college at Stanford, where I had been absorbed by English Literature and the ratio of three men to every woman. But while I loved learning, something vital was missing. The ivory tower was too lofty for a being whose feet loved the naked earth. There was something vaguely unreal and sterile about the intellectual life. Somehow, I was geared to a rural, nineteenth-century world, while my friends were quite at home in their psychologically, sociologically oriented world. I was stifled and restless, dissatisfied and rebellious. I did not belong at Stanford any more than an eagle belongs in a cage, even though the cage was gilded.

For one happy and unforgettable year I had studied at the University of Nottingham in England. There, in the heart of the Midlands, I had lived with an English family and had known and loved them as my own. England's pleasant green farmlands and ancient wooded hills will

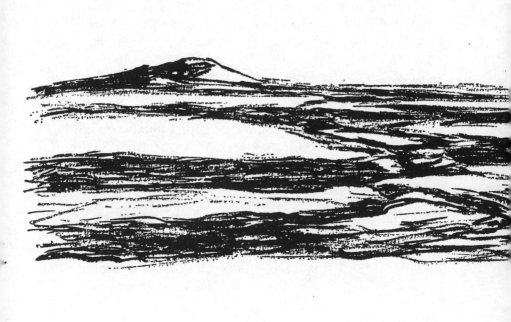

forever be a part of me. Perhaps I might have stayed, had not the openness and stillness and overpowering expanse of northern Arizona drawn me home again.

Like Dr. Jekyll and poor Mr. Hyde, there would always be two conflicting sides to me. One loves a just, peaceful, orderly, reasonable life. The other is still wild, free, half-civilized and unscrupulous. An English fellow student once said to me, "You are a child of Nature with the dust of the world in your eyes." Victorian as it sounded, he was right. And I knew that wherever I happened to be, I was a Westerner, because being a Westerner is not a geographical entity as much as it is an outlook on life.

Think of the American West and you think of Francis Parkman's *Oregon Trail* with its smoky Ogallalla Sioux camps and perilous buffalo hunts. You think of Mark Twain's and Bret Harte's gold rush humor; of J. Frank Dobie's indomitable Texans and long-horn cattle; of Owen Wister's Virginian. You think of Frederick Remington's unsurpassable horses, straight-backed Cavalry soldiers and his Plains Indians in their buckskins and beads; of Charlie Russell's unforgettable starving, half-frozen cows and howling lobo wolves, his hard-faced cowboys and lean, despairing Indians; of Will James's bowlegged waddies and half-broke broncs. You can see Peter Hurd's clean, sunlit New Mexico landscapes with their lonely windmills and fences stretching to eternity.

If you think of Arizona, you remember Ross Santee's immortal sketches: his cowponies, who always look as if they have been "rode plumb down"; his lone riders and endless distances; his ramshackle cow camps and, most of all, his cowboys and Apaches, who look and act, walk and ride, even think and smell, like cowboys and Apaches.

The American West. The words evoke prairies, mountains, buffalo, mustangs, Indians, cowboys, Mexican vaqueros, saloons, and six-shooters. There is a sound of youth, strength, courage, and raw humor about those words . . . a song of triumph; a note of grief. To the Westerners, life was a challenge to their inherent abilities. They worked hard, accepted the risks, and felt entitled to anything they could buy. Security, to them, was synonymous with wealth. The devil take any man who tried to deprive them of their rights to life, liberty, and the pursuit of happiness. They remembered, as we tend to forget, that the pursuit was all they had been promised. They took on life's vicissitudes like some heavyweight boxer saying, "Bring on the contenders, I'll fight 'em as they come."

The American West has fostered and attracted all sorts of people: mountain men; trappers; adventurers; Franciscan priests; artists; gamblers; scouts; former soldiers; Southerners who had no home to return to after the Civil War; drifters; escaping outlaws; blacksmiths; horse traders; bankers; buffalo hunters; railroaders; Indians being driven out of their tribal hunting grounds; homesteaders; cattlemen; sheepmen; gold seekers; Mormons fleeing religious persecution; frontier doctors; lawmen; land promoters; immigrants; schoolteachers; fancy ladies; itinerant laborers; musicians and actors; peddlers of patent medicines; wide-eyed Midwestern farm girls hired as Harvey House waitresses along the Santa Fe line; traders to the Indians; gunmen.

They were the discontented, the disillusioned, the disenchanted, the ambitious, the unwanted, the disgraced, the curious, the lost, the idealists, the romantics, the unadjusted, the "beats" of a former generation. All these diverse people had some intangible thing in common. They were all searching for a life new, different, preferably better than the one they had left. They were men and women of action, not content to dream, but fired with the ambition to find whatever they sought or escape from whatever fact or fantasy pursued them.

As civilization, in its infancy, encroached upon the wilderness, the West shifted again and again. Territory after territory gained statehood. Still, there was a West. There remained in the Rocky Mountain states and the Southwest, great regions still hostile to the plow, aloof to the stranger, and indifferent to the world of men.

This West is an elusive place. To quote Raymond Carlson's Foreword to *Gallery of Western Paintings*:

> "It is more than a matter of geography. . . . Where the plains break off and the land gets rough and unruly, that's where you find the West. It is a lonely land not gentled to the plow. It is distance spanned but not yet fettered by ribbons of steel and asphalt. It is bigness scarred only by the wind and weather, full of sun and silence and peace. It is serenity drenched in extravagant colors."

The Westerner, as well, is an elusive person. Being a Westerner, to me, is having a soul soaring and free as the wind, a mind stimulated by discontent and unimpressed by convention. Although they were not of the West, Robert Louis Stevenson, Joseph Conrad, and Herman Melville were Westerners; and perhaps so were D. H. Lawrence and Ernest Hemingway. They were aware of all of life and hungry for it.

The traditional Westerner believes in taking calculated risks and some uncalculated ones. He is not only prepared to lose, but when he loses, he is willing to roll up his sleeves and start all over again with a curse on his lips and a grin on his face. There are few Westerners who cannot remember the misery of being "broke" or the triumph of having made it. He is probably the only man on earth who will break his back and risk his life's savings to make money, then turn around and lend it or give it to somebody who doesn't have any. This is called private enterprise and he believes in it.

More than anything else, a Westerner is himself. He is himself because he does not know how to be anything else and does not care to learn. He does not think that he is better than anyone else, but he knows that he is the equal of any man on earth. His social code leaves little room for doubt or anxiety: the Westerner treats ordinary people as if they were very important and important people as if they were very ordinary.

There is perhaps no Westerner as western as the cattleman. His heritage goes back to that brief period in American history when the great cattle empires flourished and the long-horned steer ruled the economy of the West. This period, roughly the 1870s and 1880s, is the best-remembered and most frequently evoked period of history and legend America or the world has ever seen. Perhaps it is because this history was not made by emperors, conquerors, archdukes, kings, or even presidents. It was made by ordinary men who rose out of oblivion to mold a completely new world with their own calloused hands and hindquarters. With an ordinary man's strength, intelligence, and courage, in an atmosphere of unparalleled freedom, they built where they might have destroyed, giving to the world a new set of values and a moral code to match the new land—a moral code as well-known to every schoolboy as that of King Arthur's knights. And these men were knights, indeed—ragged knights, smelling of leather and horses and cow manure. They were as loyal to their families and neighbors as they were hostile to intruders and thieves. They hadn't much time for courtly manners, but they gave, instead, kindness and a helping hand.

According to Edward Laroque Tinker in his book *The Horsemen of the Americas,* one early-day critic described the cowboy as "Nothing but a bunch of blasphemy, a horsy smell, a busted collarbone and a pair of spurs." Although that statement contains elements of truth, there is a certain lack of finesse about the description.

The North American rancher is not entirely like anyone else who has ever walked the earth. If the Spanish Sin is Pride, the Anglo Sin is Greed. The rancher has his share of each, but they are tempered with a Scotch-Irish sense of humor. You can recognize him almost as far as you can see him. Boots and a stetson are not a prerequisite, because he always seems to be wearing boots, whether he is or not.

He may be short and stocky, but he is more likely to be tall and lean, with a perpetually hungry look about him, like Melville's Dr. Long Ghost. He may be slow and languid or quick and sanguine. He may be quiet and reserved or loquacious and flippant. But there is something about him that distinguishes him from other men. Once you have known him, you can pick him out of a crowd as easily as you could see a Mexican steer in a herd of registered Herefords.

There is a straightforward yet distant look in his eyes. He seems to be listening for something, looking for something far away. His eyes may be gently humorous, but they are observing. Even in a dim room, they seem to be squinting against the sun they are so accustomed to. They seem to be saying, "Now, look here, I don't take myself too seriously and I'm damn sure not going to take you too seriously."

His hair, if he has any, is dry and of indeterminate color. It looks lonesome without a hat. His face and neck are wrinkled from the sun and wind. If he lives in the Dakotas, his face is ruddy. If he is from the Southwest, his complexion is dark and leathery. His mouth is hard and his lips are inevitably dry, as well as his throat. His wide mouth says, "I'll go along with you as far as I can, mister, but you'd better not try to run over me."

You can tell a cattleman by the way he stands, walks, and sits. He is as ill at ease in low-quarter shoes as if he had been caught walking down the street in a pair of run-down house shoes. When he is walking, he looks put-upon, as if the world really owed him a horse or pickup or Cadillac. He has been, from the beginning, more of a quadruped than a biped.

He has a great deal of difficulty standing upright, firmly, on his two legs. You usually find him leaning against some convenient structure. Where none is available, he rocks back and forth on his boot heels, his arms folded across his chest. Sometimes he will perch like a rooster, first on one foot, then the other, casting furtive glances in the direction of a far-off post all the while.

It is equally impossible for him to sit squarely in a chair. Either he slumps back with his feet propped up or he slumps forward, his elbows resting on a table. In the presence of his lawyer, banker, accountant, or a beautiful woman, you never saw a more miserable human. He scrooches up his shoulders, crosses his legs and wraps

them around each other, folds his arms into strange con-
tortions, and fidgets like an old maid aunt, all the time
wishing he were hunkered down on the ground against
a barn door or a fence post, in the sun.

For that matter, a cattleman doesn't even smoke like
anyone else. Watch him. In the best restaurant in Phoenix
or Tucson, he will cup his hands to light a cigarette as
if the wind might blow out the match any second. He
holds a filtered cigarette with his thumb and all four fingers, as if it were made of brown cigarette paper and
Bull Durham. He flicks the ashes in the palm of his hand,
over his shoulder, on the carpet, or in his pants cuff because he is not used to an ash tray on the open range.

He will hold a Wedgwood demitasse cup as if it were
a tin mug and eat lobster thermidor the way he would a
plate of *frijoles*. If he has lived long in Mexico, he might
even roll up his bread and consume it like a *tortilla*. He
likes beef and hot black coffee, with whiskey before and
after. When he lights up a cigar after dinner, it is with
the assurance of a man who has just made a killing on
the stock exchange. But somehow, his manners seem appropriate. They are easy, natural, quiet, courteous, with
the absence of self-consciousness that marks a sophisti-
cated man.

Writers of fiction have made him the most highly ro-
manticized man who ever lived, and he is probably the
least romantic. Like an Episcopal priest, he never *seems*
to be married. When you see a group of cattlemen sitting
around the lobby of the Paso Del Norte in El Paso or the
Hilton bar in Albuquerque or the Adams in Phoenix, you
think to yourself, "There's a fine-looking group of bache-
lors." Other men *look* married. Cattlemen don't.

Why? For one thing, the cattleman is probably one of

the most intractable human beings on earth. Then, too, by the very nature of his work, he is more accustomed to the company of cows, horses, and men than that of women and children. There is a free and easy manner about him that cannot be subdued by petticoats and perfume. This may very well be the secret of his attractiveness. Men admire him and women want to change him.

He is loyal, but dislikes obligations. No matter how attached he may be to his family, he lets nothing interfere with his freedom and individuality. He works hard to take care of a couple of thousand head of cattle, a wife, and several children, and feels he is entitled to spend his free time as he damn well pleases. His duty to his family includes the provision of food, shelter, clothing, recreation, and transportation for each of them. From there on out, they are on their own and to hell with the P.T.A.

The cattleman considers it his privilege, if not his sacred duty, to gripe continually about the weather, the cattle market, the price of feed, his taxes, or the way the government is being run.

He is the kind of man who is strongest in adversity. He dislikes and distrusts any show of emotion, and constantly steels himself against the worst that can happen. When the worst does happen, he is prepared for it—like a cowboy Andy Adams wrote about who, after braving Indian attacks, drouth, stampede, thunderstorms, river currents, and quicksand, can hold up his head and say, "Have not got the blues, but am in a hell of a fix."

Such a man was Cooney Jeffers the first time I ever saw him, my youthful head full of romantic notions and my heart full of love for the West.

2

The Rib

The first time I ever saw James Claxton Jeffers, tall and lean and brown from the sun, I felt as if I had been asleep all my life and had only just awakened to a real world. I was filled with those strange illusions which accompany that indescribable, complex, and peculiarly human state called "love." Somehow, the Arizona sky seemed never to have been as blue, the air as clear, the sand as red as they had lately become. Things that I had overlooked before were suddenly very important and things that had been very important to me no longer mattered.

When Chaucer's Crisseyde looked down from her window and saw Troilus for the first time, she turned pale and whispered, "Who gave me drink?" In an unguarded moment, like Crisseyde, I had fallen hopelessly, helplessly, and haplessly in love. No doubt about it, I was smitten.

Oh, I had been in love, all right. In fact, I don't remember ever having been out of love. Once I had over-
heard some acquaintances at Stanford discussing me and
another girl. They said, "Neither Jo nor Podie will get
married for a long time. Podie, because she doesn't love
anybody and Jo because she loves everybody." I had
loved people heartily, the way I had loved dogs and cats
and sunsets and books and good things to eat. But I trembled at the thought of marriage.

And then I met this rancher from Arizona, much older
than myself, at a Christmas party. He had gentle hazel
eyes and looked just about the way I thought a man
ought to look: I knew that I had found the man to whom
I wanted to belong.

The Greeks believed that love was a sort of disease
which entered a person first through the eyes. Symptoms
ranged from depression, loss of appetite, giddiness, sleep-
lessness, nausea, faintness, fever, and palpitations of the
heart, to temporary insanity. Since I was stricken with all
of them, I recognized the disease at once and set about
to cure it. The harder I tried, the more intense was my
affliction. O Misery!

To my dismay, I discovered that in the 1950s it was
no longer fashionable to fall passionately in love. With a
firm background in English Literature, I began asking
myself one day, "Bless us, whatever happened to Love?"

It seemed that "normal" people didn't fall in love any
more. They adjusted themselves to each other. They met
in college and if their parents had acquired about the
same number of automobiles and the same sized houses,
they became engaged. After several preparatory courses
in "Marriage and the Family," and after it looked as if
they might graduate some day, they had a large wed-

ding ceremony at which time they were given all the
things they would need in order to live the good life for
the next twenty-five years, by people who hadn't seen
them since their christening and who probably wouldn't
see them again until their funeral. They then purchased
some books on "Modern Sex Techniques" and "How to
Achieve Mutual Satisfaction in Marriage" and lived happily ever after, with the help of their analyst and an occasional martini.

The numerous marriage counselors, clinical psychologists, newspaper oracles, and clergymen agree that one
should seek a partner of similar age, race, social background, education, interests, and religion. Of course.

Can't you just see some Egyptian "Dr. Crane" telling
Cleopatra that she should forget about Mark Antony,
who is, after all, a Roman barbarian, and join an Egyptian bowling league where she could meet a nice young
man of similar background? Or a Veronese "Dear Abby"
saying: "Dear Juliet: Take your clergyman's advice and
tell your mother and father about your secret meetings
with Romeo. They will understand. In a few years, when
you are more mature, you may consider marriage, if
Romeo is not murdered by your cousin first." And there
was always Phaedra. Now there was a woman who believed in "togetherness." Unfortunately, her prig of a
stepson, Hippolytus, repulsed her advances and nothing
would do but she had to go hang herself. Imagine Desdemona complying complacently with the paternal advice, "Now what's all this nonsense about marrying a
Moor? A Moor, of all people! You really must take up
bridge, dear, and don't bother me any more about that
old black man."

What could be more sensible? After all, where did love

get Juliet, Cleopatra, Desdemona, Isolde, Dido, and all the rest? Dead, that's where. The point is that no power in Heaven or Hell can move a woman in love from her choice, even though it leads to destruction. And perhaps, just perhaps, those short tragic loves were worth as much as a lifetime of well-fed boredom.

I unburdened myself upon the sympathetic shoulders of my cousin, Herb, whose maturity, sobriety, and good sense I had always admired.

"You've been acting strange, lately," said Herb. "Are you sick?"

"Well," I swallowed, "it's like this . . . I'm in love with a cattle rancher twice my age . . ."

"You get yourself into the damndest things. What's his name?"

"Cooney."

"Nobody's named Cooney."

"Yes they are, too."

"The trouble with you, Jo, is that you have always been an incurable romantic."

"I know it," I said.

"Are you sure you don't just love the idea of him?"

"I don't think so."

"It's not unusual for a young woman to become infatuated with an older man. If you just stay away from him long enough, you'll forget him."

"No I won't either," I said.

"You have just idealized him . . . because you're so crazy about cows and horses and things like that. One of the first things sociologists say about choosing a marriage partner is never to marry your ideal. You're always disappointed in him and trying to reform him."

"He's my ideal, all right, but I have down-to-earth ideals."

"I know. He's your tall, rich, handsome cowboy and you have visions of living on a ranch and writing the Great American Novel."

"That's not it at all. I just want to be with him."

"Look at it this way . . . what do you love about him?"

"I don't know. I don't love anything about him. I just love him." I realized that sounded fairly silly, so I quit while I was ahead. I sat there looking sappy and calf-eyed while Herb proceeded to point out the Freudian implications of such a match.

The outcome of all this well-intentioned advice was that the next time I saw Cooney, he asked me to marry him and I accepted.

I thought my mother and father would be relieved. For years, people had been asking them embarrassing questions like, "Isn't Jo ever going to get married?" In Twentieth-Century America, it is a Sin to remain single. There I was, an unmentionable twenty-five, having failed in my filial duty to marry a rosy-cheeked, chubby-bottomed, bright-eyed young college graduate. What was wrong with that girl? All this nonsense about writing. Instead of wasting her time studying English in England (of all places!) why didn't she take Nursing or something Practical?

My father had a peculiar notion that, after spending his life's savings on my higher education, I should be self-supporting if not yet world-famous. On the one hand, he felt some relief at the transference of responsibility for my physical welfare. On the other, he questioned the necessity of four years of college to clean out a chicken coop.

Grievous doubts began to enter my mind. I knew that marriage to Cooney would not be easy. I had been a frail child and might not be able to stand the simple physical strain of ranch life. His family would probably think of me as the proverbial educated fool and his friends might not accept me because of the difference in our ages. I wondered what Cooney would think about my artistic friends and whether I would have to give up everything I had worked and studied so hard for all those years, because of the demands of ranch life.

The Jeffers family, like many Westerners, were traditionally suspicious of "book learning," but, paradoxically, proud of the members of the family who had acquired an education. Cooney relied on experience and observation instead of books. He believed that each situation was different and every man must be sized up carefully.

Shortly before we were married, an old friend of Cooney's said to him, sarcastically, "What's Jo going to do with all that education out there on the ranch?"

Cooney looked him in the eye. "She's going to sit and hold it," he said.

That summer of 1956 had been hot and dry. I went one day with Cooney to his Woodruff Well, where he was working on the pump jack. He was greasy and dusty and tired. When he finished, I leaned on his shoulder and he put his arm around me. Bess, the Australian shepherd, lay among the reeds and tamarisks at the edge of the tank, the dry wind ruffling her long white hair. She looked at us out of the corner of her blue eyes, not wanting to intrude on a serious and private conversation.

"You know," said Cooney, "in the old days, people used to say that each man has a lost rib, like Adam. When I met you, I felt like I'd found my lost rib."

That was probably the first and last romantic thing he ever said to me, but it did the trick.

"When can we be married?" I asked from the haven of his arms.

"I don't know when I'll be able to get away," he said. "We've had such a dry summer. I don't have anybody to take care of the ranch while I'm gone."

"Couldn't we get away for just a couple of weeks—"

"Couple of weeks! I may not be able to get away for a couple of days."

"But a couple of days isn't long enough to go anywhere. Besides, you need to rest for a while. You're so tired."

"I don't see how I can unless it rains," he said.

I looked up at the sky and there was not a cloud in sight. "If you can't leave the cows long enough to marry me, then maybe we'd better forget the whole thing."

"But, Jo, you don't understand. I can't just lock the gates and go whenever I want to. The cattle have to have water. If one of the gasoline engines breaks down or a well quits pumping, there's nobody else to fix it."

"But I wanted to get married right away so I could help you."

He sighed. "We'll see. If it rains, maybe I can take two or three days off."

"You don't think as much of me as you do of those cows!" I said.

"It isn't that. I have to make a living. I can't just get up and leave whenever I want to. You don't know all the things that can go wrong in two days! You're going to have to put up with a lot of things if you want to live on a ranch, so you'd better make up your mind."

By the middle of July it still hadn't rained, but somehow Cooney had let himself be persuaded to go to Albuquerque, which we thought was a pleasant place for a wedding, and Santa Fe for a honeymoon "If it rains while we're gone," he said.

If I had been uneasy before, I was lost now. Even though I had been in love, my consolation had been freedom. Dark suspicions crept into my mind that perhaps, like Grandfather, I really preferred marriage in the abstract. Now that precious freedom was to be sacrificed.

No more would I roam at will the unexplored corners of northern Arizona. No more would I spend leisurely hours shuffling through Mr. Henning's old Navajo County newspapers, gathering material for magazine articles. No more Hopi Katcina dances or frosty nights watching the Yeibechai dancers by Navajo campfires. No more spontaneous expeditions to Tsegi Canyon, Keet Seel, Betatakin ruins, or Canyon de Chelly. I might even miss plays, symphonies, and operas in San Francisco; cracked crab and abalone in Monterey. No more would my life and ambitions be completely my own, and the whole wide world mine to discover. From now on, I would belong to this man. I would know comfort, security, protection, love. I would help him and honor him and be a part of his life. But I knew, too, that the old rebellion and restlessness and longing for freedom would never entirely leave me.

In times of emotional crisis, which were rather frequent in my youth, I always had a strange compulsion. Heaven knows why, but as our wedding drew near, I had done it again. I had cut my hair off. It was some kind of great relief . . . off with her hair! A symbol of feminine emancipation! It left me feeling unfettered, reckless, devil-may-care, unburdened. It may even have been a harmless kind of self-destruction. While the emotional effects were stimulating, the visual results were less than appealing.

Once again, like Samson, my locks were shorn. People turned to stare at me on the street. They probably thought I had ringworm or had collaborated with the Nazis.

When Cooney saw me he said, "What happened to you?"

"I had my hair cut," I said.

"I see that."

"It was getting awfully long," I said.

"It was just right. You didn't have it cut, you had it butchered."

"You don't like it."

"It's all right, I guess. Nothing you can do about it now."

"Maybe it won't be noticeable with a hat."

"Can you find one that comes down over your whole head?"

"I have a good one. Hardly anything shows except my nose and it would be pretty hard to hide that."

He kept staring at me and frowning.

"Is it that bad?" I asked.

"It's just that . . . it makes you look like some little poor kid."

"When we go down the street, people will just think I'm your little girl," I said.

"They'll probably think you're my little boy."

My mother was being very efficient and arranging matters so that we could get the whole thing over with. Mother is always for getting things over with. She had called her brother in Nebraska who is in the newspaper business. Whenever something important happened, she called her influential brother in Nebraska. "He'll see that the announcements get here," she said confidently. She consulted Amy Vanderbilt's book, ordered a cake, bought a new dress, and generally attended to the mysteries accompanying that ancient and unfathomable rite.

My father was busy making certain that no one could possibly suffer from thirst during the proceedings. Helping him was a tall, rangy, former rancher named Roy Sommers, whom we had asked to be best man. Since he had known the manager of the Harvey House in Albuquerque for many years, he elected to make the arrangements. So conscientious about his new and delicate responsibilities was he that he had purchased a new pair of boots for the occasion. Still not entirely satisfied, being something of a perfectionist by nature, he went all out and was fitted for a brand-new, glowing set of teeth. At the time, nobody suspected how much human suffering they were to cause.

My father and Roy Sommers were filled with anxiety about the wedding. They journeyed to Winslow, thirty miles away, to buy new suits. Neither of them were what you might call Beau Brummels, and I would guess that twenty-five years had passed between suits for both of them. Papa had succeeded in locating a coat which buttoned across his vast midsection. Long Roy Sommers had tracked down a shirttail which stayed in. I wouldn't have told them for anything, but they kept reminding me of Laurel and Hardy.

Cooney was occupied with his cows and didn't have time to have a new suit tailored. I had turned suddenly practical and decided to wear a six-year-old blue linen dress instead of a long flimsy white gown that I would have to store in mothballs for my heirs to dispose of.

The family mood verged on hilarity, but I grew solemn and wary as a trapped lion as the fateful day approached. At last, Cooney was disposed to leave his cows and all was in readiness.

The Alvarado was a lovely place. There were freshly cut flowers and bowls overflowing with fruit in every room. Two of my friends flew in, ostensibly to be maids of honor, but in reality to get me through the ceremony somehow. In our room were three beds, side by side, and I was feeling for all the world like Goldilocks.

Roy Sommers and Cooney shared a room. I think Roy kept the key, just in case. The day of the wedding found their room strewn with exotic toiletries seldom seen since the days of Marie Antoinette. As my father remarked, it smelled like a tonsorial parlor. Father's room, on the other hand, was strewn with bottles of a different nature, odor, and function.

My mother followed me around, uttering words of encouragement. I believe she nursed a hidden fear that I might escape and join the Foreign Legion. Most comforting of all, Anne was there. Dear Anne. Quiet, sensible, honest Anne, friend of so many years. Anne, with whom I had stayed for a few months when she taught school at Fort Apache.

When Cooney and I went to the Bernalillo County Court House for the marriage license, we looked like the owl and the pussycat going to sea, only we had a tan Ford instead of a pea-green boat. I wore a scarf over my head so people wouldn't think I was wearing a Halloween wig. The woman behind the counter asked the necessary questions.

"And your birthplace, honey?" she asked me. Women are always calling me "honey." It makes me feel like a refugee.

"New Ulm, Minnesota," I said. The words sounded as unfamiliar as the vague remembrance of a long-ago dream.

"Date of birth?"

"April 28, 1931."

"I didn't know I was marrying an old maid!" said Cooney.

"That will be two dollars," said the clerk.

"Do you think it's worth it?" I asked him.

"That's a lot of money just to get married. If cattle prices don't come up this fall, I may have to come back and get a refund."

The clerk came over and shook our hands, smiled, and gave her little speech about luck and long life and all that. I suppose she thought we would need it.

From then on, details are hazy in my mind. I went into a sort of trance and must have been married in a state of suspended animation. Familiar faces hovered around me, hands nudged me here and there, putting hats on my head, keeping up with my belongings, and generally treating me as if I were the family idiot. Thus far I had done nothing to dispel that illusion.

The night before the wedding, there was a dinner in the Alvarado Dining Room. The-condemned-man-ate-hearty sort of affair. I have a blurred recollection of spotless linen, glistening silver plate, candlelight, gladioli, fragrant red wine, and filet mignons. Mother was there, I'm sure . . . she must have been . . . and Anne. Good Old Anne. The honorable gentleman I was going to marry sat at the end of the table in a white shirt and face. His collar must have had a lot of starch in it because he was very stiff-looking. Laurel and Hardy were there, too, with a glow that was not reflected from the candles.

Roy Sommers was in pain. His feet were killing him. There never, no never, was a cowman who would walk if he could ride a horse, mule, burro, or anything with four legs or wheels attached to it. During the day he had trod the hot pavements of Albuquerque in quest of various officials and corsages, and made countless trips to meet old friends who seemed to be arriving in all the wrong places at the wrong times.

As if that weren't punishment enough, I had seen him several times surreptitiously whittling on the pearly white set of teeth clutched in his hands. He sat there now, a Natural Man victimized by civilization. His filet mignon lay on the plate, taunting him. It spat at him from its metal platter. "Here," I thought, "is a man on the edge of defeat." When a man is unable to walk or eat, what does he do? Why, of course! He sits and drinks. That is exactly what Long Roy Sommers concluded.

"Say, would you please take that corn back?" he asked the waitress.

"Is something wrong, sir?" she asked.

"Corn is for horses," he said. And he sat and consumed corn in a more palatable liquid form, and looked down defiantly at the filet mignon, which by now had lost its sputter and grown docile.

Cooney's mother had insisted that she was too busy with her milk cow to come. However, some of his friends had abducted her. They turned the calf in to its mother, put out some hay and water, and grabbed Mrs. Jeffers' suitcase, which, for some inexplicable reason, was already packed.

Tall, straight, and rawboned, she marched into the Alvarado in her old-fashioned black dress, her pocketbook swinging from her arm. This was the first time she had seen any of her four children married and she wasn't sure she was going to like it.

More people had, by that time, arrived. The festivities were in full swing. In the cocktail lounge, the wedding party sang while the organist played old love songs. Father had his arm around Mother. Long Roy was captivated by the buxom organist's footwork and insisted to everyone present that she was waving to him with her feet. Everyone was enjoying himself immensely.

Everyone but me. Upstairs, I sat alone and dejected on one of the three beds. I had it in the back of my mind that maybe it would be better to wait another year or so before taking this serious a step. I hadn't been able to eat or drink. I put on my nightgown and crawled into bed, but found I could not sleep, either.

The door opened quietly and Anne came in. Sweet, comfortable Anne with the Boston accent. "What are you doing here all by yourself?" she asked.

"Anne," I said, "I'm scared."

"I know, but it will be wonderful. If you love Cooney, there's nothing to be afraid of."

"But it all seems so . . . permanent," I said.

"It is. You'll feel differently about it in the morning. Don't worry. Everything will be all right." She tiptoed out as if it were a sickroom. A few minutes later Cooney came in. He sat on the edge of the bed and looked at me for a long, long time. I put my arms around him.

"Have you changed your mind, Jo?" he asked.

"No," I answered shakily.

He got up. "Jo," he said, "it's not too late to back out. If you want to, we can wait another year. Then, if you still feel the same way . . ."

My doubts and fears suddenly seemed very childish. "Oh, I want to marry you . . . more than anything in the world. I want to be your wife. I don't know what was wrong with me. I wouldn't blame you for being disgusted."

"Sometimes you worry me," he said, shaking his head. He kissed me goodnight and I went to sleep.

We had arranged for an early morning Communion service before our civil ceremony. As we sat beside each other in the pew the next morning at St. Mark's Episcopal Church, I don't know which of us was shaking more. Solemnly, the service of Holy Communion proceeded. "Thou shalt love the Lord thy God with all thy heart, and with all thy soul, and with all thy mind."

The scent of roses clung gently to the morning air.

"Ye who do truly and earnestly repent you of your sins, and are in love and charity with your neighbors, and intend to lead a new life . . ."

A new life.

". . . following the Commandments of God and walking from henceforth in His Holy Ways . . ."

The morning breeze, warm but fresh, wafted through the open door of the chapel.

"Come unto me all that travail and are heavy laden, and I will refresh you."

Through the door and up the nave strolled a dog. A large, shaggy, yellow shepherd. He stopped, momentarily, stretching, while Cooney patted his head, then with great solemnity proceeded up the aisle until he reached the very altar of God. There he lay down as if it were the most natural place for him to be, crossed his forepaws reverently, and yawned a mighty yawn.

"We do not presume to come to this thy Table, O merciful Lord, trusting in our own righteousness, but in thy manifold and great mercies."

At the altar rail we knelt to receive the Body and Blood of Our Lord. The shepherd, lying still and calm, looked up at us with his golden eyes, assuring us that we all belonged there together, in humility.

"Look mercifully upon these thy servants, that they may love, honor, and cherish each other, and so live together in faithfulness and patience, in wisdom and true godliness, that their home may be a haven of blessing and of peace."

The civil ceremony, which seemed superfluous, took place in the garden of the Alvarado. Roy Sommers, manfully bearing his pain and the ring, got it into Cooney's hand. Cooney, with great difficulty, placed it on the appropriate trembling finger. Everyone kissed everyone else. In the confusion, my father and Long Roy almost kissed each other, murmured embarrassed apologies, and turned red in the face.

Rice, ancient symbol of prosperity and fertility, rained on us from hidden sources. It ran through my mind that it was a shame to waste all that rice instead of sending it to the starving hordes in India or someplace that had starving hordes. Shedding rice all the way to the dining room, we sat down to a wedding breakfast. I remember melon ball cocktails, champagne, a profusion of red carnations, and my mother looking very tired.

I remember showing off my bright gold wedding band to Mother Jeffers. She held out her hand to show me the dull, worn band there. "It's been on my finger for sixty years," she said. There were tears in her old fierce eyes.

Finally . . . finally . . . we were alone. I sat in the station wagon beside this perfect stranger whom I had known for so many years. He seemed bigger than he had been, somehow. His wide mouth was hard, stubborn, determined. But his eyes were the kindest, gentlest eyes in the world.

"You're awfully quiet," he said.

"I was just thinking," I said. "I'm not me any more . . . I'm somebody else, now."

"That's right," he said. "From now on, you're mine."

And I sat there quietly, thinking about the lost rib and God looking down at Adam and saying, "I will make him an help meet for him." That night it rained at the ranch.

3

Home on the Range

Our wedding trip had lasted ten days, and that was the longest vacation we have ever had. By the end of July 1956 we were home at the ranch and ready to start branding. I found myself in the midst of 150 square miles of land with a new husband, several thousand head of cattle, and no house. We were, quite literally, home on the range. Instead of renting a place in Holbrook, as Cooney suggested, I decided to "rough it" until we could build a house on the ranch. If I married a rancher, why, then, I would live in a cow camp.

There was a bunkhouse, loosely speaking. Two rooms, a bedroom and a kitchen which had been recognizable as a saddle shed some years earlier, stood in the midst of a corral, opposite the windmill. Since the camp was already occupied by Sam Roanhorse and another Navajo who worked for Cooney as cowhands, we chose to remain exclusive and set up light housekeeping in the back of the Ford station wagon.

For a couple of weeks we slept in the back of the Ford, making infrequent but necessary trips into Holbrook to use my mother's bathtub. Every morning we would awake with two dogs and several cats in bed with us. It was very cozy, for July. A horse was usually looking in the window, occasionally mistaking my hair for a pile of straw. About four o'clock, a gamecock with long, stringy tail feathers crowed from atop the hood ornament.

That first morning at the ranch, I discovered, rather abruptly, that the honeymoon was over.

"Wake up, sweetheart," I heard a voice say, remotely; indistinctly.

I opened one eye. "It's not time to get up yet," I said. "We only just went to bed."

"It's daylight, that's time to get up."

"It's not either daylight. It's still dark. I can't see a thing."

"That's because you have the quilt up over your head."

"Well, but what time is it?"

"It's four o'clock."

"Nobody gets up at four o'clock," I said, pulling the quilt back up over my eyes.

"How do you expect to get anything done if you sleep all day?"

"All day? I just want to sleep until six or seven."

"By god, we have work to do. I can't lie around in bed all morning."

"Well, just let me sleep ten minutes more."

"Come on, girl."

"Just five minutes more, then. I want to rest a little before I get up."

"What have you been doing all night?"

"That was sleep, not rest."

Cooney sighed and got out of bed. He grumbled as he was pulling on his boots. "People *die* in bed," he said.

"Yes, and I read that it's bad for your heart to just leap out of bed in the morning. You should get out gradually, like getting into cold water."

"I'll have to tell Maw. She's leaped out of bed every morning for the last seventy-nine years."

"Well, I'm not going to put any unnecessary strain on *my* heart."

"Never mind," said Cooney, with the look of a martyr. "I'm already dressed." He stalked into the bunkhouse kitchen. I didn't want to be disagreeable, so I went back to sleep. In what seemed like a matter of seconds, he was back with a cup of steaming black cowboy coffee in a white enamel mug.

"Thank you, sweet," I said. "Maybe now I can get my eyes open."

"Tomorrow morning you bring me my coffee in bed," he said.

"Husbands are supposed to make coffee in the morning for their nice little wives and bring it to them."

"That's what *you* think."

"You should be so thankful that I married you that you'd be glad to cook breakfast every morning."

"What the hell do you think I married *you* for?"

"I thought because I was so good-natured," I said.

The next morning I crawled out of bed about sunrise, groped my way to the kitchen, and put on the coffee. I don't see very well first thing in the morning and move around by touch for the first hour or so. While the rashers of bacon were sizzling in the skillet, I brought Cooney's coffee to him. I think he was miserable in bed, but he was determined to stay there until I finished breakfast.

"Here's your coffee, Claxton," I said.

"Oh, thanks," he said, pretending that he had been asleep. "Good little wife!" he patted me on the back the way he did Bess when she was a good dog.

"Don't you think it was awfully clever of me to get up so early?"

"Smart little wife," he said, patting me again as I dodged.

"I made the coffee with an egg, just like my grandma used to do," I said.

"That's fine," said Cooney. "There's just one thing wrong —you forgot to put the coffee in it."

"I did not! What do you want to do, eat it with a spoon?"

"Didn't anybody ever tell you that it doesn't take so much water to make good coffee?"

"Didn't anybody ever tell you not to look a gift horse in the mouth?"

"Hm. It's not bad. I guess I'm used to old Ceph's coffee."

"Who's old Ceph?"

"The old man who stays over at the West Camp."

"Well, tomorrow it's your turn."

Somewhere along the line, the system failed. Pity frequently melted Cooney's heart the first year we were married because I was so tired most of the time, and he often brought me coffee. But gradually, over the years, I have, by valiant efforts, struggled out of my esoteric half-consciousness to prepare juice, bacon, eggs, coffee, hot biscuits, and cereal for six or seven people, to say nothing of feeding the dogs, cats, building a fire in the fireplace, and putting hot water out for the chickens in the dead of winter. Oh, there have been the bad mornings when I burned the toast and let the coffee boil over, thinking about a poem by John Donne or wondering what makes animals' eyes glow in the dark when people's don't. One especially bad morning I made coffee and absentmindedly put the pot into the refrigerator.

"Is breakfast ready?" Cooney asked.

"Oh, you have time to shave," I said, frantically searching the kitchen all the while.

"I'm hungry this morning for some reason," he said. "Is the coffee made?"

"It will be in a minute."

He wandered out into the kitchen.

"Uh, it took me a long time to cut the bacon. Would you mind sharpening the knife?" I asked.

"I'll sharpen it later. Where's the coffee?"

"I lost it."

"You what?"

And so it went. In those halcyon days of early marriage, I cooked in the bunkhouse kitchen. It had wall-to-wall rocks on the floor. The moldings were decorated, at intervals, with mouse holes. An occasional lizard scurried in and out of the cupboards, which looked as if they had been built by someone with one eye lower than the other. We had cold running water, but had to heat water for dishes in the tea kettle. The refrigerator looked absolutely naked and shivering the first time I defrosted it. The small Butane stove had to be humored, but in its better moods was capable of producing corn bread, slightly scorched. At the time, I thought the kitchen was rather charming, although not entirely suitable for formal entertaining.

The only time I turned out a respectable cake in that oven, I was so elated that I left the removable bottom of one of my cake pans in between the two layers. When Cooney started to cut into it, there was an ominous "clunk."

In the ill-fitting drawers, there was some ancient silver plate which looked as if it might have been buried for a hundred years and dug up. I still use a large spoon with "Belle" engraved on the handle. Oh, Belle, how often I have wondered how your spoon found its way across the plains of northern Arizona and into my kitchen drawer.

I had rolled up my sleeves that first morning and gone to work with a broom and scrub brush, until the bunk-house smelled clean and soapy. The rock floor posed something of a problem, since Sam Roanhorse had been used to feeding the dogs on it and spots of a greasy nature lingered here and there.

Sam looked at me as something of a mixed blessing. True, he did not have to cook any more, but he had also lost his privacy. I had moved in on his bachelor establishment and thrown out all manner of comforting things that had been around for years, including some 1948 calendars and a dozen or so cracked tea cups. With a woman firmly entrenched at the ranch, he felt the necessity of washing before meals and wiping his feet before coming in. Instead of his traditional Navajo fare of fried bread, beans, and mutton stew, there were exotic dishes such as Swiss steak, scalloped potatoes, and green salad.

There is a widespread feeling among cattlemen that women perpetrate the misuse of water. There is too much wasted, not only in the coffee, but also on the house-cleaning. Long Roy Sommers, having kept some statistics over the years, claims that one woman uses as much water as fifty cows. Sam Roanhorse thought of the old days and sulked.

At first there was no porch or fence around the bunkhouse. The bulls would amble up to the corner of the building, stand in the sparse shade of the roof, and rub their rear ends against the wall. The saddle horses wandered around at will, looking in the doors or windows when they thought it was time for someone to feed them. When the wind blew, the sand piled up against the door.

The old two-room bunkhouse, with its sloped tin roof and board and batten walls, had been a haven for many a tired cowboy, Indian, and sheepherder. Inside, a potbellied stove warmed the weary and half-frozen feet of cowboys in from a long drive, or neighbors whose pickups had stalled.

In the summer, the cowboys would leave the doors open to catch the night breezes. A young cowboy who had worked for Cooney once told me about the time a horse named Shorty came in to water one hot summer night. As he stood there, drinking from the tub by the windmill, he heard Harold snoring inside. Being a curious horse by nature, he ambled over to the bunkhouse to see where the snoring was coming from. He walked quietly in the door, over to Harold's bed, and stood over his sleeping form, the water still dripping from his nose. When Harold felt that cold wet nose on his bare chest, he leaped out of bed, screaming. Shorty whirled around, jumped out the door, and took off running as far as they could see him in the moonlight.

For a number of months, Harold and another cowboy had been outsmarted by a large and cunning rat who had moved in on them. For a while they tried shooting at him with six-shooters, but the walls were getting bullet-ridden and noticeably drafty. They tried setting traps baited with cheese and bacon, but he was too crafty to fall for such an obvious plot against his life. One morning, Harold got up to cook breakfast and found, to his disgust, that somebody had left the dishpan full of dirty water. He began to clean it out. He was yawning and sleepy-eyed as he stood there trying to wring out the old dishrag that had been left in the bottom of the pan. As he squeezed the rag, it occurred to him that it felt unlike any dishrag he had ever used. When he looked down, he found, to his horror, that he was trying to wring out the rat. I've always considered myself fortunate for not having any encounters with irate descendants of Harold's rat.

Forming an el with the bunkhouse was a workshop, a dark conglomeration of rusty pipe fittings, tools, nails, pieces of pipe, iron, and other small treasures picked up alongside the Heber Road. Adjoining the shop was the barn where we kept feed, saddles, ropes, and other gear. The cats had dominion over the barn, but graciously allowed the presence of a handful of game hens who came in to cackle and lay eggs in the feed barrels when the spirit moved them.

Within sprinting distance of the new bunkhouse we eventually had built onto the end of the barn, there stands a picturesque relic of bygone days—a lopsided, unstable, but well-ventilated outhouse which has bravely withstood years of service to the Santa Fe Railroad, windstorms, blasts of lightning, cows rubbing against it, and two or three vital moves. I have complained and raved, given speeches about sanitation, social standing, the jet age, the habits of flies, and made mild threats, to no avail. There it stands to this day, in all its past glory

. . . a sentimental monument to the Old West and also a convenient refuge when the plumbing goes haywire.

When we were first married, my romantic view of life was dimmed somewhat by the fact that I had to trudge through two corrals to visit that venerable structure every morning when we were living in the station wagon. In my yellow peignoir with (of all things) ruffles on the bottom, I would make my way, haltingly but determinedly, down the well-trodden path as the rosy-fingered dawn broke across the east.

Among my newly acquired duties was taking care of the chickens. When we came, there were a few games who roosted and laid eggs according to the whim of the day, so that gathering the eggs was a task that required a certain amount of cunning, determination, and physical exertion. I wanted to build up a flock of chickens large enough to supply our eggs, at least, so Coonoy instructed me on the care and handling of chickens. They weren't accustomed to tender loving care, and there were times when a suit of armor would not have been superfluous equipment.

They fought and changed nests so often, we had to mark all the eggs we set under the hens with pencil marks and remove the unmarked eggs every day. When the chicks hatched off, I fed them dry oatmeal at first. Hens, like most animals, lose all fear and caution when their chicks are small. We had a brown, timid-looking hen I called Clara, who would have attacked an elephant if one bothered her brood. Before her eggs hatched, I would go in every day to take her grain and water and talk to her and stroke her feathers. The day her eggs began hatching, she ruffled up her feathers and made a low growling noise at me. One by one, she brought them down out of the nest, carrying them on her wing or back. She would strut around the corral, proud as any peacock, clucking to her eight little chicks, peeping and flapping their rudimentary wings around her.

She would fly in a rage at cows, bulls, horses, old Pooch dog or any person who ventured too close to her family. The best fight she ever fought, though, was the day she and Jack the Gander came to blows. He was a gray and white Toulouse gander with a bad disposition and a meddlesome nature. We kept two geese as watchdogs. If anything strange came near the ranch, even if an aircraft passed high overhead, Jack the Gander would stretch out his long neck and cry, "Waa, waa, waa, waa!"

Out of curiosity one day, he began following the new chicks around. Clara had always kept a respectful distance away from the geese and given up her place at the feed box when they came waddling over. This day, she stood her ground and squawked at Jack. He stuck out his neck, hissed, and backed away. She ruffled up her feathers, gathered her chicks under her wing, and growled. He began doing a little dance in front of her, stepping to one side, hissing, then shuffling to the other side. All of a sudden Clara decided to have it out with him. She jumped right up on top of his neck and clung for dear life, pecking at his head, beating him with her wings. The gander was running around in circles, his great wings flapping violently, uttering a wild assortment of squalls, hisses, and screeches, while Clara rode him around the corral, spurring him in the neck, like a rodeo cowboy on a bucking bronc.

Jack the Gander was hardly a lovable animal. He was, at times, unbearably quarrelsome, belligerent, stubborn, and, worst of all, snobbish. Our first confrontation had been unpleasant. No sooner had he emerged from his shipping crate than he ran toward me, hissing and snapping. I wasn't inclined to humor him, so I picked up a handful of snow and threw it at his head. He stood there a minute, shaking the snow out of his eyes, startled. Then he retreated and calmly waddled away, never bothering me again. I told myself that he was probably out of sorts after his long train trip from Iowa and that he was really a good sort of fellow at heart, but I never quite convinced myself.

Not until he hit the skids. Late one fall, he and his mate were drifting around the duck pond, dozing and napping in the moonlight. A lynx crept up to the water at the edge of the pond. When the gander was off guard, the cat grabbed the goose and carried her off down the arroyo, making short work of her. The next morning, we followed the tracks of the lynx cat and found the remains of the goose, lying in her own scattered feathers. Something had frightened the lynx and he had left without finishing his meal, but we thought he would be back that night and set a trap for him. Sam put the remains of the goose on the trigger and covered the trap with sand. To our dismay, we apprehended the wrong criminal. A swift, on his way to water, had come across the prize and walked right into the trap. As he lay there, helpless, with his leg caught, the lynx had come back to finish his meal. There had been a fight. The lynx easily killed the immobile swift and got away with his goose. Now the gander, who had been so proud, haughty, and bossy with his meek little mate, was in a state of shock.

It was sad to see him shuffling around the corrals, his head down. For several days he had called to his mate and at last had given up. He would take a few turns around the duck pond, clean his shiny feathers, and start on his daily constitutional. For a long time he would look around furtively, in hopes of hearing her or seeing her. In his loneliness, he began following us around as we did our work. When Cooney would come out in the morning, the gander would rush up to him, flapping his wings and honking in a joyful manner. Sometimes, we would start an argument with him, because he liked to argue. "You're just a bad old goose," I would say to him. He'd stand in front of me, honking and squawking and shaking his head just as long as I would talk to him, then turn and follow me. After a few weeks he even followed Cooney's jeep a little way when he drove off. Cooney could reach out and take hold of him and the old bully would tuck his head under Cooney's arm and stay quite still when Cooney stroked him. He talked to me and followed me, but would never volunteer to let me pet him, probably remembering the snowball.

In the spring, the ducks started laying and the goose seemed to be in better spirits. He still followed us and allowed Cooney to pet him, but his old depression was gone and some of his sassiness returned. I had noticed him, several times, settled down in front of the door behind which a duck was setting, but I thought he was just keeping her company. Then one day when I went out to water the setting duck, he raised to his full height between the duck and me, spread his wings, and began hissing threateningly. I moved to go around him, but he wouldn't let me pass. From behind the door came the guttural sound of the mother duck and the peeps of little ducklings. The gander had decided to adopt a family.

I never saw more tender care lavished on a brood than the old gander gave his ducklings. He would gather them all under his wings and take them over to the feed pan, hissing and shooing away all the other fowls in the vicinity. He led them out to the duck pond and gave them their swimming lessons, keeping the other ducks at a distance with threatening noises. If one of the ducklings rolled over on its back, he would carefully turn it right side up and wait for it to follow the others. He paid no attention to his human friends except to look up proudly and say, "Waa, waa, waa!" as he strolled by with his brood, the mother duck following dutifully at a respectful distance.

When at last we ordered another mate for him, in the summer, he had raised his family of ducks and become accustomed to his widower's state. We opened the crate at the edge of the pond, letting the goose out into the water. The first thing she did was take a bath, after her arduous journey. The gander had stopped dead in his tracks when he saw the goose preening herself at the water's edge. She made several tentative gurgles and swam around him, all the while casting brazenly seductive glances at him. No country boy in Las Vegas for the first time ever stuttered, blushed, and fumbled as the old gander did that first day. He tucked his head under his wing, every now and then hazarding a curious, precursory look at his new friend. For two days his shyness silenced him. Gradually the old bravado returned, and within a week or so he was strutting around the ranch, showing off his new bride, haughty as ever, with the humbled goose now following timidly behind him.

Not long after we were married I ran into the house one day, proudly holding up an enormous egg I had found. "Look!" I said to Cooney, "This is as big as a goose egg!"

Cooney looked up, unexcited. "Oh. That's just a rooster egg."

"I know I'm not very smart, but you can't tell me that roosters lay eggs."

"Well, not very often. I've only seen one before. Every once in a while a rooster will lay an egg. It's a freak of Nature."

"Really?" I said, my mouth open. "It must be like a hermaphrodite. Don't you think we ought to save it and send it to the University?"

I laid it carefully aside and thought all morning about the marvelous quirks of Nature and wondered, incidentally, how much the University might pay for a rooster egg. Hours later, Cooney came in and sat down, a guilty look on his face. "Jo," he said.

"What?"

"You know that rooster egg you found today?"

"Yes, what about it?"

"It wasn't a rooster egg. It was just a big double-yolked egg. I was kidding."

As if that weren't humiliating enough, a week or so later he asked me how many upper teeth a cow had.

"I suppose the same number as she has lower teeth," I said.

"You ought to know better than that," he said.

"Oh, about fifteen, I think."

He sighed. "Go count them when the milk cow comes in."

Not one to give up easily, especially when my curiosity was aroused, I spent a considerable time craning my neck that afternoon in a futile attempt to look inside a cow's mouth. Cooney and Sam were, all the while, watching me

from the window, not without amusement. At last I came
in. "I can't see their teeth," I said. "Tell me."

"Jo, they don't *have* any upper teeth . . . only jaw
teeth, way in the back. I thought college graduates were
supposed to be smart."

"For some strange reason, the English Department at
Stanford didn't offer any courses on animal husbandry the
years that I was there!"

My consolation was that I was not the only in-law of
the Jeffers family that had encountered similar experiences. When Nancy Jeffers first started seeing Bill, Cooney's cousin, she often rode with him to the ranch to
spend the day in the country. Nancy, from Illinois, discovered on one of these outings some lovely purple-hued
wild flowers and began to gather a bouquet of them. Bill,
quiet by nature, made no comment. When they returned
to Holbrook, they stopped for gas at Manly's station, then
a gathering place for ranchers who would stand around
and compare range conditions. Nancy proudly showed
her nosegay of purple flowers to the half-dozen cowmen
standing there. "Aren't they beautiful?" she said. When
they began to chuckle, she was hurt and surprised. "What's
the matter with my flowers, Bill?" she said.

"Nothing," Bill yawned, "except that that's loco weed."
Loco weed, a herb often deadly to cattle, is one of the
cowman's worst enemies.

Westerners seem to delight in practical jokes, especially
if they succeed in taking the stuffing out of stuffed shirts.
When we were first married, I knew a great deal more
than I do now and modesty about my vast store of information was not one of my greater virtues. One noon,
Cooney and I were sitting at the kitchen table having
lunch. I was discoursing in rather positive terms and at

some length about the ways ranching could be improved. All the while these helpful and intelligent suggestions were being put forth, Cooney sat quietly, with a somewhat disconcerting lack of interest and enthusiasm for my plans. "Please pass the peppers," I said, incidentally.

He passed them. I thought that they were Italian pickled peppers and popped one carelessly into my mouth, not bothering to interrupt the conversation. To my horror, I discovered that they were fiery Mexican jalapeño chiles. My forehead broke out in beads of perspiration, I choked, sputtered, coughed, and jumped out of my chair, tears filling my eyes, and ran to get a glass of water. My throat still felt as if it contained a glowing coal, when I stammered, "Why didn't you tell me those peppers were so hot?"

Cooney looked up innocently. "You didn't ask me," he said.

In those days I was always anxious about my cooking and afraid that it might not please everybody. Cooney was not hard to please except for his cattleman's natural aversion to anything connected with sheep or poultry. Whenever he smelled lamb or stewed chicken on the stove, he thought up some excuse to eat with his mother.

Striving desperately to please, I would ask him, "What do you want for supper?" or "Are you hungry for anything special?" That was before I was aware that the simple, unchanging answer would be "steak." But I suppose he was hesitant to declare his choice, so all he ever said was, "Oh, just something to fill up on."

No matter how much time and effort I put into a meal, the men ate it and left without a word of condemnation or praise. If I asked, "Was everything all right?" Cooney would say, "Sure."

Being young and sensitive and insecure about my home-making abilities, my feelings were hurt. One day when I had worked particularly hard and was feeling, in general, unloved, unappreciated, and unstrung, my patience deserted me. When the men came in for supper I had put a loaf of bread and some glasses of water on the table. I stood in the doorway, my arms folded, watching their mild surprise. "Well, you always say you just want something to fill up on. There it is," I said.

They exchanged amused looks, then sat down at the table as usual and began eating bread and water without a comment. "Is everything all right?" I asked, sarcastically. "Sure," said Cooney.

The next day, after dinner, the men got up from the table, carried their dishes out and one by one said, "That sure was a good dinner." Cooney came over and put his arm around me and patted me on the shoulder. "Good little cook," he said.

Most cowboys are easy to feed. They work hard and get hungry. When there is a lot of work around the ranch, we have three big meals a day with meat at every meal. During branding time or roundup, the usual routine is a large early breakfast, often before daylight, and another big meal at two or three o'clock. That is followed by a light supper around six or seven, just before bedtime. Like Cooney's friend, Dick Sellers, most cowboys claim, "I can eat anything that don't bite me first."

An example of the average cowboy's lack of epicureanism but abundance of humor was displayed by a good old cowhand who worked for us at one time. The first day he came in for breakfast, I asked him, "Dave, how do you like your eggs?"

He looked up at me from under his shock of light hair and said, laconically, "I like 'em fine."

"No, I mean how do you like them cooked?"

"Well," said Dave, "I like 'em better thataway."

In the old days, cowboy fare was not unlike a sailor's. Before barb wire, cowboys stayed with the grazing cattle day and night. They slept and ate at two or three wagons, which were scattered out over hundreds of miles sometimes. Perhaps twice a year they would make the long trip to a center like El Paso or Roswell—somewhere on a railroad or stage line. They would stay just long enough to go on a good drunk, spend most of their paycheck, and then drag home with the wagons loaded down with staples like bacon (what cowboys called "bacon" was usually salt pork); *frijoles* (Mexican pinto beans); one to two thousand pounds of flour; sugar; salt; barrels of Arbuckle coffee beans, which were ground fresh every day; corn meal; several five-gallon cans of molasses; dried fruit in twenty-five pound boxes; sometimes lard, if they didn't render out their own tallow from the beef they butchered. If they were lucky, the cattle were near some farming community in the mountain valleys or Rio Grande Valley. That meant an occasional treat of fresh fruit, cabbage, potatoes, sweet corn, turnips, green beans, wild greens, carrots, or onions.

Most of the meals on the wagons consisted of hot biscuits cooked in a Dutch oven, or sourdough bread, a "starter" of sourdough kept continually in a crock, for the next batch; steaks, roast, stews, soups, all of beef; gravy; sometimes vegetables; and steaming pots of black coffee. For breakfast there was usually a big kettle of "moonshine"—rice and raisins stewed together and sweetened. In the more colorful language of the cowboys clustered around the fire in the early morning, this mixture was known affectionately as "bear sign."

Men grew tall, tough, sinewy, and strong on this diet and way of life. Most of them rolled their own cigarettes or chewed tobacco, both of which, surprisingly, kept their lips from chapping and peeling badly in the sun and wind. They were not like today's youth; tall, healthy looking, tanned, and well built as some of our highly bred, over-fed, prize cattle, but vulnerable to disease and hardships. Cowboys of fifty years ago differed from today's breed as much as the tough, hardy little half-mustang cow ponies of that day differed from the big, smooth-muscled, perfectly proportioned, highly trained quarter horses of to-day. They look good in the rodeo arena, show ring, and on permanent pasture, but they don't have the endurance, stamina, and guts of the old cow ponies who carried their riders swiftly and surely over rough terrain, making thirty or forty miles in a day's drive.

Cowboys expect and need a somewhat specialized diet, the same way athletes do. It is usually high in protein and fat, low in rich or sweet food. His beloved sorghum mo-lasses gives him iron and satisfies his sweet tooth. We eat a lot of meat, green salads, and bread, but forsake the heavy rich food Midwestern farm wives cook for their threshing crews.

I made more than mere culinary mistakes that first year we were married. Many of our worst disasters were at-tributable to the fact that I am a good housekeeper. I don't mean to be neat, it's a trait I inherited from my Grandmother Johnson. She held a Germanic opinion that if one could not eat off the kitchen floor, it was not really clean. That theory, while admirable in Minnesota, leads to frustration and anxiety in northern Arizona. Especially

on a ranch which is inhabited by dogs, cats, cowboys, and
buffeted almost daily by dirt-laden winds. And then, in
the beginning, we had only three small rooms—the old
bunk room and kitchen plus a new room we had built
ourselves—in which to keep our clothes, wedding presents,
household goods, and Cooney's papers. Carried away by
a wave of enthusiasm one day, I threw out all of Cooney's
certificates for the government emergency drouth feed
program, thinking they were some old bills or circulars.
Since they were worth a couple of thousand dollars, he
was not overjoyed when he couldn't find them and I con-
fessed my dastardly deed. He had to go to Holbrook the
next day and explain to the proper authorities that he
had a new and incompetent wife who didn't understand
about things of that nature.

The next thing I threw away was a hat. A shapeless
felt, covered with the blood and grease of dozens of brand-
ings. It was on a closet shelf and, judging by the ac-
cumulation of dust, had not been worn for months. Without ceremony, I picked it up with my finger and thumb
and tossed it into the incinerator.

What I did not know was that, with the possible ex-
ception of his wife or horse, a hat is a cattleman's dearest
possession. He will uncomplainingly pay the price of a
yearling steer for it if it will turn water and hold its
shape in a rainstorm. He drinks out of it when he is
thirsty, he waves it at cattle to get them moving, or turn
them when they are coming down an alley. He uses it to
signal to his cowboys on a cattle drive. He wears it so
much that he feels naked without it. Any rancher's wife
can tell you that it is as difficult to throw away a battered, disreputable-looking, but cherished stetson as it is
to steal a bone from a dog.

There is some kind of extrasensory perception between a cattleman and his hat. That day I threw away Cooney's ancient and decrepit hat, I was shaken by a voice bellowing, "Where's my old branding hat?"

I stood trembling. "I don't know," I said. "Where was it?"

"In the closet. Did you throw that hat away?"

"Why?" I said.

"I *want* it, that's why."

Ever since then, when the closet becomes cluttered with the sacred relics, I gather my courage, carry the most venerable example to the incinerator in the most reverend manner I can assume, and burn it with military honors.

It was after a month of marriage that we completed another room. While Cooney was putting new steel cabinets, a sink and tile floor in the kitchen, Sam Roanhorse and the other Navajo had been building an adjoining room of old railroad switch ties. We chiseled flagstones out of a rock quarry on the ranch and laid them on the floor of the fourteen- by twenty-foot area. The ceiling was made of cedar beams, which we oiled. The walls were over a foot thick, stuccoed on both sides. Attached rather haphazardly to this room was a small tool shed which we had converted into that greatest of luxuries—a bathroom.

On one of those summer evenings, when we were tired from working on the house and had just settled down to a simple supper, the roar of a well-used engine proclaimed the arrival of Long Roy Sommers, come to pay us his first official visitation since the wedding ceremony. He stood in the kitchen, his head almost touching the low ceiling, holding his hat with the Montana crease in his long, slender fingers. He had come to apologize for reserving rooms with twin beds for us on our honeymoon

and had brought us two of his pencil drawings of yearling
colts, one named "Alvarado" and one "La Fonda," after
the hotels in which we had stayed.

Bess walked over to him, twisting and wagging her tail
for attention. "Hello, Bess," said Roy. "Let's go catch
a bull elk, should we?" Bess nodded and barked.

"Sit down and have supper with us," I said.

"No thanks, I'm getting too fleshy," said Roy, patting
his sunken diaphragm and bony hips.

"Oh, sit down. A plate of beans won't kill you."

"I just had a can of Vienna sausages. I'm not hungry,
thanks."

We sat in the flickering yellow light of the kerosene
lamps, talking about the old days of ranching when a
cowboy's home was all the way from the grasslands of
northern Mexico to the plains of Alberta, Canada. About
the days when Roy's and Cooney's families had controlled a good share of Texas and New Mexico. They
talked of the tough little cow ponies; of the Sioux ceremonies in which dogs were eaten as a great delicacy; of gun
fights and close calls along the Texas-Mexican border; of
the blizzards when whole herds of cattle were wiped out.
They remembered the drouths of the 1920s, when the
cattle were without grass or water and there were no
buyers for them or feed supplements . . . and the
times when ranchers had to go around killing every newborn calf to try to save the mother cows until it rained.
Roy Sommers had driven cattle for his father from the
Rio Grande to the Red River of the North. They had
summered huge herds on the Sioux reservation in South
Dakota. That was when he learned to know the Northwest and men like Charlie Russell—he had drunk with
Charlie Russell and acquired two of his priceless bronzes.

Roy was many things, but above all he was an artist. He was that paradox of the West . . . a man whose creativity and sensitivity are diametrically opposed to the stern, unyielding, hard-rock principles he was reared with. Pride and humility warred inside him, as well as unbending justice and compassion.

In one respect, he and Cooney were alike. Neither of them would, by nature, destroy or harm any living thing. Both had, of necessity, lived a life under the very severest conditions, where a man had to kill to live and destroy to build. Most ranchers thought no more of killing a lion or wolf or coyote than they would have of swatting a fly. With some people it is a pleasure, even a thrill, to kill. Most ranchers think nothing of killing their own beef, sheep, or chickens for food. With a few men, nothing can be killed without that swift dark cloud of conscience and doubt crossing their minds.

Long Roy Sommers sat languidly at the table, rolling a cigarette. Somewhere in the horse pasture, a couple of coyotes barked.

"Damn, I hate to kill a coyote," said Roy. He shook his head. "Cooney, dammit, he has as much right to live as I have, doesn't he?"

"By god, I don't think so," said Cooney. But I had watched him shoot at the coyotes and miss, and I thought of Robinson Jeffers' poetry and the line which went: "I had sooner, except the penalties, kill a man than a hawk."

"Let's play pitch to see who washes dishes," said Roy.

"The maid will wash them," I said, rolling up my sleeves. I heated the tea kettle of water on the stove.

"Well, if you insist," said Roy. "When you finish, let's whup the dogs and go to town."

"Thanks, Roy, but we have to brand in the morning," said Cooney.

"Say, Bess, old pal, old pal, how would you like to make a stew for the Sioux?" said Roy, scratching Bess under the chin. "Well, I'd better go back to town and see what's going on under the bright lights."

"Come back," I said. "Come back and I'll have a steak for you next time."

"No thanks. I'm getting too fleshy," he said.

He walked out to his car, loose and lanky as an old long-legged Chihuahua steer. He climbed in and slowly started off down the road, alone. In a few years, there would be no more men such as Roy Sommers in the world. Not ever again. He and all the hard-bitten, tender-hearted, weather-beaten cattlemen of yesterday were now as much of an anachronism as long-horned steers and Arbuckle coffee. Looking at him, tall, slightly stooped, narrow-hipped, with his steady, sad brown eyes, I thought of some lone, hungry lobo wolf, cautiously staying on the outskirts of the world of men—aloof, proud, knowing that when it is time for him to go, there will be no more of his kind.

4

Branding

A successful rancher's wife in northern Arizona needs to be a sort of combination Rebecca of Sunnybrook Farm (during the summer months), Nanook of the North (between November and February), and Lawrence of Arabia (in the spring). She should have the patience of Griselda, the empathy of Florence Nightingale, the strength of an Amazon, the equestrian skill of a Valkyrie, and the intuition of the Hound of the Baskervilles. Like the "Loathly Lady" of medieval legend, she must be "foule by daye and fayre by night." I didn't know all these things before I was married or I might have become an anthropologist or English teacher.

After the first few days at the ranch, I was inclined to suspect that married life consisted primarily of washing dishes. I thought of a little Scottish lady, an old friend of my mother's, who had once remarked, "I 'ad a difficult

time choosin' between Ted and my other beau, but my
mother said, 'Cum, Peg, choose one of them and make
the best of it. In the end, it will all cum to washin' pots
and mendin' socks.'"

Just about the time I began to believe the truth of
Peggy's theory I discovered, to my delight, that there was
more to ranch life than standing with my hands immersed
in hot water and bread dough.

No sooner had we finished the new room than we had
to start branding calves. Branding succeeded not only in
getting me "broken in" to ranch life, but also in getting
me broken down to some extent. Being five-foot-seven and
weighing in the vicinity of 122, I had been under the
illusion that I was reasonably strong, if not robust. But
although women may be healthier and live longer than
they did seventy years ago, they are certainly not as
tough. Perhaps that is because too much extraneous activity is demanded of women these days. A wife must
be all things to all people. While a rancher's wife escapes,
physically, from some of the absurd burdens society places
on the suburban woman, she is still expected to do more
than keep house, wash, and cook. If she has children in
school, she must drive them tedious distances back and
forth every day and participate in their school activities
after the ranch chores are over.

Her pioneering grandmother spent little time worrying
about her clothes, figure, face, business investments, social
graces, or educational accomplishments. It was sufficiently
satisfying for her to have lived with a man fifty years
and borne and raised children, grandchildren, and great-
grandchildren. She had fulfilled her purpose as a woman,
and done so amidst the easy company of female relatives
and childhood friends and neighbors. But she also missed

the exhilaration of being able to talk to intelligent people on their own level; the joy of having good books to read, fine porcelain to touch; the sense of belonging not only to her family, but the whole world.

At the turn of the century, genteel people generally agreed that there were two kinds of women—good and bad. When the clarion plea, "Go West, young man, go West!" rang forth, the "bad" women presumably heard it and followed the young men. The "bad" women were not always the wild, unscrupulous, hard hearted harridans fiction would have us believe they were. Frequently, a young woman of decent family and good reputation was "ruined" and came West to spare her relatives any humiliation. In those days, it didn't take much to "ruin" a young woman.

The "good" women were patient, devoted wives and mothers. In the country, women worked too hard to be anything *but* good. In most frontier towns, families who could afford to, sent their young ladies East or to California to instill in them certain social graces and preserve them from the ruinous company of their "inferiors."

There were, in fact, more than two kinds of women. The Greeks worshiped Hera, goddess of women, the home, and children. They also worshiped, without censure, Aphrodite, goddess of love and beauty. And from the very dawn of their tribal existence, they had worshiped a primeval, changeable, powerful moon-goddess, who later became associated with Artemis, the virgin huntress, goddess of wild nature, protectress of animals and women in childbirth. The American West seems almost to have been created for the Artemis-like woman.

She is not concerned with being a "good" woman or "bad" woman; only with the wonder of life. In her youth, she was a somewhat feral tomboy, usually her father's girl. In middle age, she is practical, energetic, inquisitive, of a liberal disposition. She seeks to please herself, and in doing so, pleases others. In old age she is known to have become a lovable, eccentric old tyrant.

In the comfort, leisure, and imposed security of civilized society, she often becomes overbearing, complaining, touchy, officious, and rebellious. Occasionally, she sublimates her drive and submerges her self-centeredness to become a dedicated teacher, nurse, artist, actress, or wife. She is most at home in the West, where there is an outlet for her vigor, where there are battles to be won, physical hardships to be survived, new challenges to be met and where there is space enough to absorb most of her ego.

In this confusing, chaotic, and personally ineffective culture we have created, in which the traditional roles of man and woman have become so hopelessly entangled, there is perhaps no relationship between a man and woman which remains as clear-cut and mutually satisfying as that of a rancher and his wife, if they choose to make it so. Ranching is a way of life that can be shared completely, and that is, in fact, noticeably incomplete without one or the other of the partners. That is not saying that it should deteriorate to the status of a business partnership. There are few other professions in this mechanized world of ours in which a husband and wife can find pleasure or pain in the same everyday things. But if a woman does not like the outdoors, animals, solitude, and hard work, she had better refrain from marrying a cattleman.

Ranch women come from every conceivable background and locality. I have known ranchers' wives from the English Midlands, the Pacific Coast, the North, the South, and the East. Whether they have studied at the Sorbonne (as a neighbor of mine has), or have no formal education at all, they have, of necessity, more than an average amount of common sense.

Although they are as individualistic as any group of women could be, they have certain characteristics in common. Like their husbands, they tend to be self-reliant, jealous of their independence, and, when the occasion demands it, stubborn as mules. They combine a capacity for hard physical work with a life-saving sense of humor and a down-to-earth set of values. They are seldom pretentious and find it difficult to tolerate pretentiousness in others.

Ranchers' wives are not toughened, gun-toting, hard-swearing masculine creatures, nor are they frail china figurines. They are plainly and incontrovertibly women.

Most of the ranch women I have known have, above all, been ladies. By "lady" I do not mean the standardized, well-coifed, polite-spoken, nail-polished, social conscious, bridge-playing variety, although there is nothing wrong with them. Webster's Unabridged Dictionary says: "lady . . . 1. obs.: . . . [obsolete indeed!] female head of a household. 2. a woman having proprietory rights, rule, or authority . . ." That is the way I mean "lady." The word comes from Anglo-Saxon "hlaf" plus "dige" . . . the kneader of the loaf. This ancient meaning is even closer to a ranch woman's definition of "lady." Woman's traditional role—the creatrix of the staff of life.

A true lady should have a spine of steel, although she may look as fragile as crystal. She is not easily shocked or provoked to anger. She is above snobbery and treats everyone with equal consideration and respect. In other words, a lady is a woman who is gracious. The rancher's lady is hospitable and enjoys people as only someone who is isolated from people much of the time can enjoy them. She may put on a pair of Levis, go with her husband to doctor a sick cow, repair a windmill, mend a fence, put out feed, or chop ice. She may don an apron and stay in the kitchen over a hot wood cookstove all day, preparing a meal for thirty men. She may live in town while the children are in school and only see her husband on weekends. She may or may not like to ride horses, but she knows a thing or two about a cow and that is what is important on a cow ranch.

Because she is sure of her innate womanliness, she is not afraid to do a man's chores when she has to. She doesn't mind getting dust in her eyes, mouth, and nose, having the wind knot her hair or wading in manure up to her ankles, when it is necessary. There are times when she gripes and complains, when she is woefully depressed, when she wonders idly what would have happened had she married that doctor or lawyer or bank clerk, but in her heart she knows that she would not trade places with any of her city sisters. She is awake to her life, and feels every minute of it, bad or good.

She has learned to live with herself and like it, because she has no alternative. Being on a ranch, twenty miles or more from the nearest town, she has found joy in simple things. She is aware of possessing an almost sacred knowledge of the living things around her. She suspects, although she may not admit it, that there is nothing on earth more pleasant than working all day at something you love, eating a simple supper, washing off the dust and grime in a hot bath, and sleeping soundly between fresh sheets, listening to the wind rustling the cottonwood leaves outside the window.

In the old days of ranching, the weak must have died young and only the strong survived. Children were made to work when they were very small. If there was a country schoolhouse nearby, they milked the cow, helped with the chores, then rode horseback or walked several miles to school. They ate plain, nourishing food—beef, pork, and chicken they raised themselves; fresh vegetables from their own garden, which they stored in a dugout during the winter months; clabber, cream, milk, buttermilk, and butter from the Jersey cow; eggs preserved in brine; sauerkraut made in huge stone crocks; wild berry preserves.

Shortly after we were married, Cooney and I were talking about our respective childhoods. There couldn't have been much more vast a difference between an Eskimo's and a Hottentot's. I had been frail, overprotected, and waited upon, with all the leisure anyone could desire to develop my imagination and little or no chance to develop my muscles. The sad truth is, I had no muscles worth mentioning until I started carrying around *The Complete Works of Shakespeare,* three volumes of Milton, and an *Oxford Anthology of English Poetry* several miles to class every day at an English university.

I remember asking Cooney one night, "What did you *play* when you were little?" He thought a moment and said, "I don't remember playing anything. I just worked. Papa made us get up about an hour before daylight to wrangle the horses. We'd have to walk out in the horse pasture and build a fire to keep warm until it got light enough to see the damn horses. I was just a button when they left me at a camp by myself with all the responsibility. Sometimes I'd be alone for a week or two at a time. We started riding about the same time we started walking."

It had made a man of him, but he had missed much of the beauty in life. On the other hand, I was a vast storehouse of worldly information, but something less than a whole human being. Fifty years ago, men and women of the West developed their bodies, their skill, their courage and resourcefulness, but neglected their minds. Now we have made, it seems, a complete and disastrous turnabout. People develop their minds and thoughtlessly neglect their bodies and senses. Perhaps one day we will realize, as did men of the Renaissance in Europe, that God made us whole.

Some of the women who grew up on ranches accepted the hardships as part of the routine of life. Many others considered it drudgery and anxiously awaited the day they would marry and be able to see the world or, at least, have the comforts of city life. To me, young and fresh and hopeful, it was a challenge—a new and exciting experience, this working with cattle. It was also the closest I had ever come to capitulation, but I developed a notion that if the strain killed me I would at least die with my boots on and a smile on my face. Whenever I admitted defeat, Cooney would say, "My maw always . . ." which made my hair bristle and got me back on my feet.

Riding was what I liked best and what was hardest for me, then. I didn't get particularly saddlesore, just tired —tired beyond words. I felt a little as if I were going through six weeks' basic training at a Marine base.

Since there had been sufficient rain in July to put out water in most of the dirt tanks, the cattle were scattered out all over the ranch. That necessitated making a drive every day for several weeks in order to pick up all the unbranded calves. Most of the drives covered ten to twenty miles.

That first year we were married, I couldn't bear to leave Cooney. I suppose I was very possessive and made him feel "hobbled" at times. Every morning I would grit my teeth and climb back on a horse, so I could be with him. Even though he thought the drives were too long for me, he let me go because he didn't want to leave me any more than I wanted to be left.

When the men split up to start the drive, I would go with Cooney, although it meant taking the outside circle which, roughly speaking, was the longest distance between two points. We would ride several miles straight west of the camp, then separate. Two men would take the strip a mile or so wide coming directly back toward camp. Two more would circle back from the north, and we would circle back from the south. Each day we made a slightly different drive in a counterclockwise direction from camp, until all the pastures had been looked over. It is extremely difficult to make a clean drive when you are working about seventy-five sections at a time, particularly if there are only three or four men on the drive, which has happened to us more frequently than not.

Until I helped with the drives that first year, I had not realized how vital every small piece of equipment is to a cowboy, nor how great a debt he owes to the Spanish Conquistadores, and later the Mexican vaqueros. In addition to his horses, which are originally of Andalusian descent, he copied the Mexicans' methods of breaking horses, working cattle, branding, roping, and his terms for cowboy equipment, slightly garbled.

The word "lariat" is a derivation of the Spanish "La Riatta." In the Southwest, most cowboys call it simply a rope, or riatta. His chaps are the vaqueros' "chaparreros." The taps on his stirrups are "tapiceros." The quirt he uses

on his horse was a Mexican "cuarta." The bronc he breaks
is from Spanish "bronco," meaning "wild." His string of
horses he refers to as a "remuda." His saddle is a modified form of the Spanish Conquistadores', large and
high-backed, greatly altered and padded to afford more
comfort for long hours of riding. The early-day cowboy
literally lived in his saddle, unless he was eating or sleeping, and he did that with his head propped up against it,
using it for a pillow. The American cowboy added a saddle horn for dallying, or holding the rope taut after a
calf had been roped. He girds his saddle with a cinch,
from the Spanish "cincha," and a "latigo" strap.

To protect his head from the sun, wind, rain, and cold,
he wears a modified "sombrero." In the 1880s, young John
B. Stetson, a frail tubercular, came West for his health.
He returned to Philadelphia in 1865 to continue his family
trade of making fine-quality felt hats. Weary of haggling
over prices in the Eastern market, he remembered the
cattlemen he had met in the West and began to design
and manufacture hats for the Western cattlemen. His
"Boss of the Plains" hats sold for five dollars. Ever since
then, the word "stetson" has been synonymous in the
West with the word "hat."

In July or August, when we have our biggest branding,
the southwesterly wind is hot and dry. The sun burns my
back through a long-sleeved cotton shirt. Even with a
wide-brimmed hat, my face gets sunburned. At night I
cannot get my fill of cool water and my lips remain
parched and cracked no matter how many times I stop
to smear lip cream on them during the day. I would set
out in the morning with makeup on my face, my hair
combed neatly, a clean shirt and Levis, and for the crown-
ing touch, a dash of Yardley's Bond Street to boost my

morale and remind me of what I hoped was still an essentially feminine nature. By midafternoon I always looked like that poor wounded Indian in the painting called "End of the Trail" that hung sorrowfully in my grandfather's library.

When we were married, Cooney had presented me with a young Palomino gelding from Texas, named of all things, "Silver." Every time I rode beside Sam Roanhorse, I felt as if I should put on my black mask and cry, "Hi ho, Silver, awaaaaaaaay!" But he never seemed to feel like Tonto, which deterred me.

Cooney claims I have petted and spoiled Silver out of the notion of acting the way a cow pony should. We understand each other, Silver and I. We have an unspoken agreement that neither of us does anything foolhardy unless it is absolutely necessary. A feminine Romantic writer of the last century once said that her idea of a glorious death would be to break her neck on a fine horse running at a full gallop. I suppose if one must break one's neck, that is as good a way as any, but Silver and I found it difficult to share her sentiments, being more of a mind with Falstaff's opinion that the better part of valor is discretion.

When we are alone with a job to be done, Silver works cattle as well as any horse we have. Silver, Bess, and I were alone at Porter windmill one day with the cattle we had brought in, waiting for the others to come in from their drives. About a hundred cows and calves were at the windmill and, having already watered, were trying to trot off in every direction. The ground was sloping and rocky, and we had to run around the windmill in circles to head off the cows. When Silver heard the other horses coming, he stopped, pricked up his ears, then gave a deep sigh and kept right on running around in circles until we had the cattle held up again. The minute, the very second, that Cooney topped the hill, Silver came to an abrupt halt, groaned, shifted his weight to one hip, and dropped his head.

Silver is a big, gentle horse, but surprisingly light on his feet. The suggestion is constantly being presented that I need spurs to ride him. I ignore such ungallant remarks. I appreciate the fact that he moves slowly and easily and is not given to fits of temperament. I'll be the first to admit that I am not a particularly fine horsewoman, as horsewomen go. I would never make the Olympics and I seriously doubt if the Bengal Lancers would ask me to perform with them, but I can usually stay on a horse, providing he doesn't throw me off or turn out from under me while trying to head a calf.

Silver has a tendency to go to sleep driving cattle, but that's nothing—so do I. We get along famously and I resent the remarks people make about how good he would look in front of a plow. Actually, he is the best-built quarter horse on the ranch. If anything is wrong with his construction it is that he tends to be musclebound. There is, indeed, a certain amount of superfluous girth beneath his saddle, but his appetite and eating habits only enhance his personality. For one thing, he is fond of Hershey bars and bananas.

Whenever I get down to rest, Silver coyly pulls off my hat and begins nibbling at the brim. About eleven o'clock, we both start rumbling. First there is a low, premonitory growl from within the dark and mysterious cavity of my stomach. This is followed by a yet nobler sound—like the roll of legions of faraway drummers, issuing from the dim recesses of Silver's great belly. There is an echo! At last, the two merge in a grand chorus of protestation against the emptiness of their respective insides.

It wasn't long before I learned that the simple precaution of filling my pockets with jerky, dried fruit, or cookies before I left the camp would prevent at least half of the rumbling on these occasions. Cooney would never pack a lunch because, like a small boy, he starts sampling and eventually consumes the whole lunch before he gets out of sight of the corrals. I was very miserly with my few bites. I would wait until we separated from Sam and the other men so that I wouldn't have to share with them.

One day when we had ridden way to the back of the pasture, I felt as if I might expire from hunger unless I ate the three oatmeal cookies I had in my pocket. Silver had already begun his part of the chorus of growls. I got down off him, my stomach a little weak from emptiness, took the cookies out of my jacket pocket and unwrapped them, while I looked around the country to see if anyone else was in sight. Before I knew what had happened, Silver reached over my shoulder and snapped them out of my hand. I was left with a few crumbs while he stood there munching contentedly, his eyes closed and his stomach rumbling.

At the West Camp, there was a sandy wash above which we had to drive cattle over a barbwire fence which had fallen down. I had never ridden Silver over wire and I wasn't sure if he would throw me off or get his feet tangled in it and cut his legs. Skeeter had bucked with Sam when he tried crossing it. Redman jumped over it and shied a little. Silver stopped and refused to budge an inch. I wasn't too keen about going over it myself, so we just stood there and kept looking down at that wire while cattle scattered everywhere.

Cooney was after some cattle that broke out into the cedars and he yelled back at me, tenderly, "Kick hell out of him!" I closed my eyes, gathered my courage to the sticking point, anchored my feet in the stirrups, grabbed the saddle horn just in case, and kicked hell out of him. Silver went *"Oof"* and proceeded carefully over the wire, one foot at a time, until he had cleared it completely, then took out after the rest of the cattle in a lope.

On those first long drives, I began to have a vague comprehension of some of the many things a good cattleman must know. Most important, he must know his cows and know them well in order to remember what he has sold the previous year, what needs to be sold in the fall, and where a particular old cow has been running. He must keep track of all his bulls and see that they remain well scattered out over the ranch. If he does not see a poor cow or bull for a few months, he looks for it until he has located it.

He must know exactly how much water he has, where it is, and how long it will last. He knows all about the edible vegetation and how long a certain area will sustain a cow; where there are patches of weeds which may be dangerous at different times of the year, like loco weed or rosea.

He can tell the difference between a cow that is thin and wiry ("thrifty" he calls her) and one that is "poor" and almost "on the lift." He can tell nearly to the day by looking at a cow when she will calve, if she has a small or big calf, or if she has lost a calf. He knows which cows produce a calf every year and which ones are barren.

He can estimate, by looking at tracks, how many cattle, horses, sheep, antelope, or other animals were in a place, how long they remained there, which direction they went, if they were running or walking and how long a time had passed since they were there. He can easily distinguish a coyote track from a dog track, a lynx from a lion, an antelope from a sheep, although they are remarkably similar.

He must know all of his ranching country better than most men know their own blocks in orders to gauge exactly the condition it is in and manage his operations aooordingly. If he does not know all of these things and many more, he stands an excellent chance of losing everything he has, because ranching is one enormous gamble at best.

At first the big country had overwhelmed me. Riding west from our home camp, we could see San Francisco Peaks a hundred miles away, blue and snow-capped, rising to fourteen thousand feet above the Colorado Plateau like some great bishop's miter. Across the north, stretched the long horizontal lines of the Navajo reservation, serene, eternal, fading out into violet, purple, and magenta mesas in the farthest reaches. Looking like the mercury in a thermometer, the steel rails of the Santa Fe Railroad paralleled Highway 66 running east and west. We could see the red or green or silver cars of an occasional train gliding along and hear its low roar in the distance. Just past Joseph City is a billow of white smoke pouring out of the Cholla Power Plant, the adjoining lake gleaming in the sun. Ten miles farther east is the green patch of civilization that is Holbrook. In the east, Woodruff Butte, a volcanic stem, rises like a lump of coal from the surrounding plains. Southwest of Holbrook, the A.T. and T.'s microwave tower stands tall and straight and sober as a guardsman. Far, far to the south, eighty or more miles distant, are the jagged blue peaks of the White Mountains, protruding like the edge of a saw from the horizon. Back of us, just under the hill, now out of sight, is our windmill and home.

Cooney worried continually about my getting lost, although he hesitated to say as much. For a long time, he would not turn me loose by myself on a drive. My only concern was how hungry Silver and I might get before we were discovered. I wasn't really afraid of being lost, because I knew my horse had enough sense, if I did not, to find his way back to the corral and feed trough.

The only time I can remember having been lost was at the West Camp. We were gathering cattle to brand and had a rather long drive to make over unfamiliar country. Cooney reluctantly left me with a small bunch of cattle we had found on a cedar-covered ridge. On the west side of the ranch, most of the country consists of rocky hills studded with juniper and piñon and cut with many irregular canyons, often three or four hundred feet deep. It is rough country. Not only is it difficult to find cattle, it is difficult to drive them, even on a well-marked trail. I started the cows and calves down the slope and assured Cooney that I knew where I was.

"Which way is the West Camp?" he asked.

"Oh, back there," I said, gesturing vaguely.

"Point to it."

I made a wild guess and pointed.

"O.K.," he said. "I thought you might have lost your directions."

He headed me the right way and told me to meet them all at Lost Tank, which is just as remote as its name implies. Before long, I spotted some more cattle off to my right and pushed them into the bunch. Then

I saw a few cows and calves under some trees, to the left, so I got them. They began to scatter the way some of those old cows do when they have been around for a long time and know the country and think they can put something over on you. By the time I got them all together again, I hadn't the foggiest idea where I was going with them.

I tried whistling, thinking that Cooney might be over on the next ridge and answer me. The whistles only magnified the silence as they faded out into the trees. I cocked my head and listened for an answer. Silver turned around and gave me a look which meant, "You damned fool, don't you know we have work to do?" Silly as I felt about the whole thing, I left the cattle, which had gotten onto a trail going someplace or other downhill, and rode up on top of the ridge where I could look off for several miles over a broad, treeless flat surrounded by more ridges exactly like the one I was on. For a long time I stood and looked and listened. Then I saw a tiny dot in back of some other tiny dots and I knew it was Sam opposite me, coming in from his drive. A half mile or so from Sam I could make out his son crashing through the trees after some wild cattle. I went back to my little herd and turned them toward where Sam was coming in from his drive. Then, all of a sudden, we topped another hill and there was Lost Tank, a series of five water holes in the bottom of a narrow, rocky canyon.

On drives, when our cattle had settled down, Cooney and I would find the shade of a tree if the weather was hot, or build a fire in a windbreak, if it was cold, and sit there resting, making idle marks in the dirt with a broken twig. As soon as everyone was in from his drive and the cattle had watered out, we would start the herd back toward the ranch.

When we came to a fence line or, better yet, the corner of a fence line, we stopped and worked the herd. Cooney would turn back all the cows with very small calves and the calves which were already branded. That usually took about an hour and a half and it seemed like at least ten hours. Driving cattle isn't bad. At least you are getting somewhere. But standing in the hot sun, holding up the herd while someone else cuts them, turning back the same old unruly cow over and over and being yelled at by your husband is not very much of a lark.

When we would start out in the morning, I would say to Cooney, "Sweetheart, if I go with you today, don't be afraid to tell me when I do something wrong. It's the only way I'll learn. Just treat me as if I were one of the men." The trouble was, he believed me. By two or three o'clock, he would be yelling at me because I let a cow go by me or failed to see a calf under a tree or brought a calf without its mother. I would usually be tired or mad or both and burst into tears until remembering what I had said that morning made me laugh.

Working cattle at two in the afternoon when everyone is sweaty and thirsty and hungry and aching is where I learned to curse. When we were first married, I spent a great deal of energy cringing at various colorful epithets aimed at unco-operative cows. I wasn't long standing in the dust and hot sun before I found similar expressions issuing from my own parched lips. A number of hardened, brown, weathered, bewhiskered male faces would turn to stare when I burst out with, "You damned old sow, get back there where you belong!" or "Can't you stay with your mama, you little son-of-a-bitch?"

Cooney would ride through the herd, giving them one last long look. When he had all the unwanted cattle cut back, we would start toward the camp. There were always some cattle trying to turn back and two or three that would gradually edge over to the right or left, looking back at you out of the corners of their eyes, to see if you were still watching them. There were usually a couple of cows with small calves who resented being driven by a dog and who kept turning back, snorting and bawling, trying to hook Bess or at least chase her away. In the drags, there were usually one or two poor cows with scrawny little dogie-looking calves. In spite of the dust, I never minded working the drags, especially with Silver. We'd just poke along behind, half-asleep. Every so often Silver would reach down and give a little calf a nudge with his nose to keep him stumbling along. Bess would work the sides, bringing back any calf that stopped under a tree or cow that veered off the trail. Cooney took the lead, riding in front to hold up the wild cattle that would otherwise trot all the way back to camp or break loose from the bunch and run away. Sam and whoever else was working with us would scout around to the left or right to see if we had missed any cattle.

Coming home was slow. Sometimes we would be working them in a place where someone could get to us with dinner. If we hadn't eaten, it was slower still. If the drive had not been very long, or if there were no convenient place to work the cattle along the way, we would come in with all of them and work them in the runaround at home.

Those cowboys you see in movies and on television whooping and hollering and chasing cattle hell-bent for home are no more real than the color of a Las Vegas

chorus girl's hair. No self-respecting cattleman would
ever let anyone work cattle or drive them any faster than
is absolutely necessary. The weight of an animal is his
profit and any loss of weight constitutes his loss. Particularly in the spring and summer, when the range is dry
and the cattle are poor, they must be handled as slowly
and easily as possible.

There are times when cattle are run to bring them back
into the herd. There are also times when it is necessary
to rope them and drag them into a corral or whip them
with the double of a rope until they decide to come in.
This is dangerous work, not fun. The cowboy always
runs the risk of being hooked himself or having his horse
gored. The possibility always exists that his horse may
stumble and fall on him, or that he may be trampled
in the herd of cattle. Those are some of the risks of being
a cowboy.

A good horse is important to a cowboy for many reasons. He must be sure-footed enough to retain his footing in rough country. If a horse has been raised in a pasture or in stalls near town and is suddenly turned loose in the wilderness, he stumbles, gets cut by barbwire, turns his ankles on rocks, gets scratched by brush and cactus. If he has lived long in sandy country, his feet spread unless he is shod often. His hooves become chipped and broken when he runs over rocks. A range-bred horse will be on the lookout for rattlesnakes, gopher holes, porcupines, and other dangers. He will also hear or scent cattle before you do.

A good cow pony must have sufficient cow sense to watch cattle all the time. The cutting horse is never off guard. He tries to sense what the cattle are going to do next. He works in a crouch, like some huge cat, his ears held back, his eyes shining. He would rather work cattle than eat.

Often when we were branding at the chutes, Cooney would turn Redman loose, his bridle reins around his neck, in the corral with the calves. He would cut the calves or pen them up in a corner, just for fun. A good cow pony must be able to outrun a cow and turn her as quickly as possible. Fat yearlings die easily from overheating when a horse runs them too far. A cutting horse should have quick, smooth movements that turn cattle without frightening them. I have seen some horses that naturally keep a herd stirred up all the time. A horse should hold his head down and work easily, the way a good sheep dog works. There must be a sixth sense between horse and rider so that they work as one. A cattleman and his horse are as much a unit as the mythological centaur.

When we did not have to work the herd, when there were not any trotty, hard-to-handle cows in the bunch or locoed cows or poor cows with dogie calves in the drags, we usually got back to the ranch about noon. When we got in, we would pen the cattle and let them water out at the drinking tubs while we cooked dinner or ate what someone else had cooked. If I had no one to help me, as was usually the case, I cooked dinner the night before or got up early in the morning to have everything ready to warm up when we got in. After dinner, I would clean up the dishes and the men would go out and start working the herd. If we were shorthanded, which we usually were, I climbed back on my horse and went out to help them.

The cows with unbranded calves were separated from the drys, branded calves, yearlings, and any bulls that happened to be with them. When we got the calves with their own mothers, we drove them into the branding corral. One of the most difficult problems working cattle is to make sure that each calf is with its own mother. They cannot heal easily if they are separated from the warmth, protection, and reassurance of the mother cow or if they have to miss their evening milk. At last, the calves are cut off from their mothers and put into an alley, ready for branding.

The men start the Butane burner, oil the chutes, pour the bone oil and linseed oil into small cans with brushes in them, set out the disinfectant, ear tick treatment, knives, irons, and other paraphernalia. I take the vaccine out of the refrigerator and fill my syringes. Each calf must be vaccinated against blackleg and malignant edema. My job is vaccinating, which consists of getting the proper dosage just under the hide and making sure it does not come back out when the needle is withdrawn.

Almost any scratch or small cut is potentially dangerous when a person is working around livestock. Even the vaccine can cause ugly swelling and infection. The best policy is to wear gloves as much as possible and scrub well after branding.

We brand our calves in a tilting chute, a device in which the calf is held fast and tilted on its side in order to be more easily branded. This method is faster, cleaner, and requires fewer men than the old-fashioned practice of roping calves from a horse, flanking them, and branding them on the ground. In Mexico, where labor is still plentiful, the fastest method is the old way, but in the States few ranchers work over two or three men at branding time. We have some friends in California who use two Australian shepherd dogs to put the calves down the chute while one man does the branding. Martin Jeffers, Cooney's brother in Chihuahua, brands about four or five thousand calves every year. He has about twenty-five men working for him. With that size crew and several fires going at once, the whole procedure goes almost as fast as ours for four or five hundred calves.

Branding is the one job I shall never really reconcile myself to. That first year, I often felt sick from the odor of burning hair and dizzy from the heat and smoke. At that, it was better to be at the chutes helping than sitting inside the house smelling the singed hair and listening to the calves bawling, the dogs barking, and the men shouting. When you are working, you don't have time to think about what you are doing, and before you know it the work is finished.

Branding is cruel. It would be extremely insensitive to

say "it doesn't really hurt them." It does really hurt them.
To a stranger watching branding for the first time, it must
seem like something out of Dante's *Inferno*.

Sam usually works the chute, catching the calves as they
run through, then tilting them over on their sides. If the
calf is a bull, his hind legs are secured with a leg spreader.
The irons are heating to a red glow in the gas burner.
While I vaccinate, Sam brands, putting a "P" on the
left shoulder, an "X" on the left hip, and a slash across
the nose. Yellowish smoke rises from the seared hair, burning your eyes. The calves bawl and kick. Their eyes are
wild and frightened. I spray their ears to rid them of ear
ticks and paint the fresh brands with raw linseed oil to
promote healing and make the brands peel evenly without
cracking or breaking the skin. Wherever the skin is broken
there is a chance that they will become infected with
screwworms, so every open wound is painted with a strong
disinfectant and worm repellent.

Herefords, unless they are polled, must be dehorned or
the cattle buyer docks the rancher a few cents a pound
when he buys them. Polled cattle ("mulies" or hornless
cattle which have been inbred to make them hornless)
have the disadvantage of weighing less because their bone
structure is lighter. Dehorned cattle are shipped by truck
or rail with fewer injuries. They do not hurt themselves
as easily on the range when they fight or when they are
crowded together in feed lots.

I always hate to see the horns come off, even though it
means greater safety for the cowboy who handles them, as
well as for other cattle. It seems to me cattle look naked
and timid deprived of their natural means of self-defense.
The old cows, with their long, curling horns, have a brave,
defiant look about them when they toss up their heads

and start off in a run. Occasionally, cows' horns begin to curl back toward their heads and would grow into their eyes if we didn't catch them in time and saw them off. This happens often with bulls, whose horns are only tipped, not cut completely off.

Dehorning is the most painful ordeal the cattle must undergo. Horns are removed with special equipment. Most ranchers brand at one time and dehorn later. We get the whole process over at once, because it is as hard on cattle to drive them long distances and work them when it is hot and dry and feed is scarce as it is to brand, castrate, and dehorn them once and for all. We sear the horns with hot irons to prevent excess bleeding. I think it must help, because we have only had two or three cases of screwworms on the ranch that I can remember, although many of our neighbors have had huge numbers of cattle infected. An antiseptic paste like bone oil or smear is then put on the horn wounds.

Last of all, a knife is used to underslope the left ear. On the large ranges of the West, cattle must be earmarked. When you are gathering cattle for branding, it is impossible to see brands from a long distance. Earmarking is the only way you can tell whether a calf is branded or unbranded, without riding miles out of the way. Earmarks are important for identification, too. Within a radius of, say, forty miles, most ranchers know each others' earmarks. When you are gathering cattle, you can spot a stray and bring it back with the herd to be claimed by the owner.

Perhaps some day someone will invent a painless but satisfactory way of marking cattle that will replace branding. Unfortunately, chemicals burn just as much as hot irons and the action lasts longer. Ordinary dyes or tattoos can be changed too easily by cattle thieves. There is still considerable cattle stealing in this country where ranches are measured in sections instead of acres and it takes two or three weeks to cover all the places cattle are found. Cattle inspectors are on the alert for signs of theft, but because of lack of evidence, the law has not always prosecuted offenders.

Maybe, too, some day people will be eating bull meat instead of steer meat, eliminating the necessity for castration. There was some talk of it at one time. The meat of a young fat bull is good, although it is not marbled with fat the way a steer's meat is. Now consumers are paying for the fat that is first put on the beef in the feedlots, then cut off the choice cuts by the butcher to please the housewife, who no longer wants fat meat. Without fat, meat has far less flavor. With it, people eat more cholesterol.

Dehorning seems to be a necessary evil, like pulling teeth. It is not as hard on very small calves with rudimentary horns as it is on larger calves with fully developed horns. Small calves do not bleed as much, are less sensitive to pain, and recover from the whole operation much more rapidly. When they have some milk inside them and have had a good night's sleep next to their mamas, they seem to feel normal again.

After branding, the calves are turned in to the cows to "mother up" and then they are all turned out on the open range again. Cooney cleans his knives, emasculators, and dehorners. Sam puts his irons and medicine away. The dogs are weary from all the excitement and full of the "mountain oysters" they have consumed. I plod back to the house, clean the needles, put the vaccine back into the refrigerator (next to the pickles), and shed my manure-spattered, bloodstained, dusty, medicinal-smelling clothes. All that's left to do is wash the eggs, put them away, feed the cats and dogs, cook supper for everybody, wash the dishes, take a hot bath, and pass out.

Branding is the time for accidents. Most of our injuries have happened during branding, and it is not difficult to see why. Once at the West Camp, Sam got a deep laceration behind his arm from a sharp place on the branding chute. I drove him into the clinic in Holbrook, nineteen miles away, while the others finished branding. Cooney has acquired several bad infections from cutting himself while castrating calves. These are often highly dangerous infections which heal slowly. There are inevitable cuts, bruises, skinned shins, and hurt feelings, all in the course of a day's work.

The worst I have ever been hurt at the ranch was during branding at the West Camp. There was something funny about that, too. First of all, let me explain that I have a lot of trouble about Pride. Every so often I begin thinking that I am a rather interesting, intelligent, even charming sort of person. As if that weren't bad enough, at this particular time I had been doing a number of what I considered Good Deeds for various people and began thinking that, besides being good-natured, I was also Generous and Kind. Deciding to examine the state of my immortal soul before it was too late, I had, the night before, composed a prayer which went like this: "Oh Lord, keep me from selfishness and vainglory (whatever *that* is). Strike down the Pride from me."

The next day, when we started to brand, I stepped up to vaccinate a big heifer which was in the large squeeze chute. Cooney had not yet fastened the nose clamp securely. She jumped up in the chute, kicking with all her might. The bolt broke loose, the whole side of the chute flew back, hitting me on the temple, just missing my right eye. The force knocked me about six feet from where I had been standing. Cooney ran over to pick me up. "Are you hurt?" he asked.

"No, I'm all right I think," I answered. To tell you the truth, I was knocked silly and all I could think about was "Pride goeth before a fall" and I really felt as if my pride had been dealt with rather severely, if you want to know. I was almost laughing when I looked down and saw blood dripping from my face. So I staggered to the camp and put some ice on the cut and sat around until Cooney and the men had finished branding. It seemed to me they took their sweet time about it, too. Then they drove me in to the doctor and he sewed up my face. I was half loco for weeks afterward and, in fact, found it was one of the best excuses I have ever had for my habitual absentmindedness.

That first summer we were married, there were times when I doubted if I would make it through the branding. I remember one particularly hot day in which we had made a long drive. When we finished in the evening I was so exhausted I just lay down on the cool flagstones of the porch and went to sleep with one arm crooked under my head. Sam and Cooney cooked supper, then woke me, but I was too tired to eat or take a bath and I just fell into bed in my disgraceful state.

About daylight Cooney woke me with a cup of coffee in his hand and it seemed as if I had just gone to bed. The smell of bacon drifted in from the kitchen. The red-orange sun was just breaking away from the horizon and the air had the stillness of expectancy in it. I groaned and said my back hurt. Cooney made me dress and eat in my semiconscious state because he knew that I would be hurt even more if he went on without me.

"My knees ache," I said.

"So do mine. The only thing to do is get up and get back on that horse. After a while your aches and pains will go away. If you stay in bed today, your muscles will be stiffer than ever."

He was right. After the bacon and eggs and hot biscuits and several cups of coffee, I felt very nearly human again. The men saddled up and Silver and I started off in that easy jog I can take all day. Before long, the hurt went away and I became accustomed to the saddle and forgot all about being tired because there was so much beauty and wonder in the fresh morning world around me.

The wide mauve sky was cloudless. The air smelled as clean as if it had just been created. Larks skimmed lightly over the clumps of bunch grass, searching for insects. A coyote crouched, stared at us suspiciously, then slinked away through the broomweed. The horses were fresh and stepped out bravely. Sam's horse, Skeeter, bucked a little because he felt good. After we had ridden a quarter of a mile or so from the camp, Silver stopped, looked back longingly toward the barn, nickered, then settled down in the trail for the long day's drive ahead of him. I looked around me, shivered a little and wanted to cry out, "This is the day the Lord hath made; Rejoice! and be glad in it."

5

Navajo

It was August. Our first year of marriage had been buried under a mountain of hard work, and once again the
tanks were dry and the grass had turned yellow. We had
been pumping water for the cattle from the 425-foot well
at the house. Sam Roanhorse had, ten or twelve days before, gone into Holbrook for a haircut and had not yet
come back. Cooney and I had been left with all the
chores to do, which included feeding the livestock, checking on five windmills at least every other day, running
the gasoline engine day and night when the wind was
not blowing for the cattle which had been drifting in
from all over the ranch as the dirt tanks had dried up.
Cooney was in his shop hammering away profanely at a
broken part for the pump jack.

"Here comes Sam! Old Sam Roanhorse!" I shouted. A
red pickup with a stock rack was all but obscured by a

cloud of ocher dust as it turned off the Heber Road onto our ranch road. Now Sam was back after his unexplained leave of absence. No matter how put out Cooney had been, and in spite of his usual resolution to let Sam go and do the work himself, it was always with a deep sigh of relief that we welcomed him home.

Sam was our own private perpetuation of the Prodigal Son story. Only he was more like a prodigal uncle. Uncle Sam Roanhorse. Cooney kept on hammering and ignored Sam's approach. Sam walked slowly over to Cooney's work table, his hat cocked to one side, his dark glasses hiding his slightly bloodshot eyes. Sam leaned on the fence and stood there for a long time.

"Well, Cooney," he said, "I'm come back."

"I see," said Cooney.

"You gonna fire me?"

Cooney looked up. "Dammit, I should. That must have been some haircut. You've been gone twelve days."

Sam grinned, showing the two front teeth that were conspicuous by their absence. The teeth that had been displaced during a disagreement in a saloon several years before.

"Sure got good haircut," said Sam. And he had. It was a crew cut about half an inch long which made him look like one of those Japanese wrestlers.

"Where've you been? In jail?"

"Sure," said Sam. "I get pretty drunk down there, Cooney."

"Damned if I don't believe you're still drunk. Well, go couple up the windmill. It looks like the wind might blow after all."

"O.K. Say, Cooney, you got job for Matthew? He want to help us until after roundup."

"I guess so," Cooney said. "We'll be branding soon and I can use an extra man."

Sam walked over to the pickup and spoke to Matthew. Helen, Sam's wife, and Irene, his sister, got out and came over to shake hands with me.

"*Yahteh*," they said. In turn, they took my hand and shook it once, limply.

"*Yahteh*. Have you had any rain at home?" I asked.

"No."

"How are the sheep?"

"They're O.K.," Helen said, with an intonation which meant that they were at least still alive. Her hair hung in braids down the back of her purple velvet blouse. She looked down, shyly. Her scuffed brown oxfords and red socks showed just below the full green satin skirt. They were her best clothes and a row of dimes was sewed around the neck of the blouse. Her face was sweet and softly worn. Fate had somehow outstripped the hope in her life and left her with an expression of bewilderment. There were soft maternal curves to her body and she moved with grace.

Irene was as tall as a man, straight and broad-shouldered. Around her neck were several strands of ancient turquoise and coral beads—turquoise, sacred to the people of the Southwest for so many centuries; tiny beads of coral, like those traded with the coastal Indians far back into prehistory, drilled with finely made bone or rock awls; and white shell beads, holy, symbol of Yolkai-estsan, White Shell Woman, mythological goddess. Her long, slender, strong fingers were covered with silver and turquoise rings. Below the cuffs of her wine-red blouse she wore bracelets with inlaid turquoise stones. She was a wealthy woman.

Her face was calm and pleasant without the trace of
anxiety always present in Helen's. Irene had the patience,
self-assurance, and maturity born of a life of day-to-day
hardships resolved by endurance, caution, good sense,
and humor. She had given birth to one daughter, but had
raised many of her clan's children. Her grandchildren
were home tending sheep during their summer vacation.
She had a flock of good Navajo sheep, plenty of inherited jewelry to pawn for the winter months, and control
of the family business affairs. Her husband, short, jovial,
stout John Cattron, was manageable and seldom drank
wine.

"Where's Genevieve?" I asked Helen. That was her
eldest daughter.

"He's O.K. He's have another baby."

"You want some coffee?" I asked.

They looked at one another in agreement. "Yes," said Helen.

"O.K.," said Irene, using her entire English vocabulary.

John Cattron had walked over to shake hands vigorously with Cooney. Now they were talking, John in Navajo, Cooney in Texan, both of them gesturing and nodding in accord. The fact that neither understood the other's language was irrelevant. Matthew was putting his small bundle of clothes in the bunkroom and Sam was out coupling up the windmill.

Irene and Helen had followed me into the kitchen. I put the coffeepot on. They sat down at the table, serene, patient, stately.

"How have you been, Helen?" I asked.

"O.K.," she said, looking down. We sat without speaking for a while. "I go to hospital in Keam's Canyon last week."

"Are you sick?" I asked, even though I knew it was a breach of Navajo etiquette.

"Yes," she said. Her mouth closed tightly.

Irene spoke quickly and naturally to me, patting her own stomach and explaining what was wrong, in Navajo.

"Gall bladder," said Helen.

"Oh," I said. "Will you go back to the hospital?"

"Yes," said Helen. "Maybe operation."

"Do you take medicine?"

"Yes."

We sat in silence again. It was good to sit there, quietly, with those Navajo women. Some of their calm came into me. And I thought how strange it was that I always felt at ease with them and so uncomfortably alien at a bridge or cocktail party. It came to me that the great blessing of being able to know Navajo people was that it helped me retain my sense of values.

The coffee came to a boil. I turned it off and poured cold water on it to settle the grounds. "I'll see if those men want some coffee," I said.

Helen looked anxiously out the window. Then she said, "Jo, can Sam have some money? Doctor say I eat fruit, can good. No meat, no fried bread. He say no grease. Got no money for can good."

"I'll ask Cooney," I said. Having at last relieved herself of the burden of having to ask for something, she sighed and settled back in the chair, sitting the way only a Navajo can sit, as if she were patiently awaiting the end of the world.

John Cattron, Sam, and Cooney came in. We talked quietly, sipping the strong black coffee that Navajos and cowboys cherish. John and Irene laughed lightly at their private jokes.

"John she want to buy some bull," said Sam.

"Show him that turn-out bull in the buck pasture," said Cooney.

"I already did. She say how much it cost him?"

The turn-out bull was one out of our own herd which had not been cut as a calf and would have looked too staggy to sell if we had cut him as a yearling. There are one or two every year and they must be sold before they are old enough to breed back into the herd.

"He can have it for fifty dollars," said Cooney.

"O," said John, nodding. "O."

"John she come back nex' month to get her bull," said Sam.

Irene and Helen picked up the coffee cups, took them

to the kitchen sink, rolled up the sleeves of their velvet blouses, and began washing the dishes. John Cattron, having decided to leave Sam with at least a month's supply of good advice befitting a brother-in-law, took Sam's arm and began scolding him for his recent absence, explaining that Cooney was a good boss to take him back and that he should show his gratitude by staying on the job this time. At that point, Irene left the sink, came over to interpolate, using her soapy hands for emphasis. Soon they were all three talking at the same time, Sam protesting his innocence and pledging future obeisance, John reminding him that Helen and the kids, to say nothing of the rest of his clan, needed the money, Irene lecturing on the pitfalls of Tokay wine. Once Sam looked up at me, shook his head and grinned, then turned sober again when Irene said something.

Cooney started to go and Helen looked up at me furtively as she put the cups away in the cupboard.

I had just started to speak when Sam said, "Say, Cooney, my folks need some money."

"So do I," said Cooney.

"Helen has gall bladder trouble," I said. "She's on a strict diet."

"How much do you need?" said Cooney.

"Can you give me fifty? Helen she got to get some medicine and grocery . . . can good, something like that."

"Jo, fix Sam a check for fifty," said Cooney.

"Is O.K. if I go to town with my folks to cash check?" Sam asked.

"No, by god, you endorse it and give it to them. You don't need to go back to town."

"Well, whatever you say, Cooney, you the boss."

"Sometimes I wonder," said Cooney.

We walked outside. John tipped his hat to Cooney and shook hands once more. Irene and Helen took my hand, saying "*Yahteh, yahteh.*" No polite "thank you"; no "goodbye." No "How nice to see you again," or "Give my regards to your family" or "You must come and see us some time." Just "*Yahteh.*" Good. It is good. Life is hard but it is good anyway. You help us and we trust you. *Yahteh.* We are friends, I think. No "Yes, sir," or "No, ma'am." We are the same as you. We are freer than you and that is what counts. It is good to be free. The earth is good sometimes and life is good sometimes. *Yahteh.*

Not until the next day did we become aware of somebody else in the bunkroom with Sam and Matthew. Once or twice during the day a small, slim, slightly stooped boy of seventeen or eighteen appeared. His shiny black hair was long above his ears. His color was city-Navajo, pale and unhealthy. The few times he came outside, he was combing his hair. When he grinned, his teeth were even and surprisingly white.

"Who is that boy?" I asked Sam.

"He was Matthew's roommate at school in Oklahoma."

"Is he Navajo?" I asked. He was so delicately featured and light-skinned, I was not sure.

"Sure. I think he's from Fort Defiance . . . someplace up there."

"What's his name?"

"She's name is Raymond."

Raymond never offered to help Sam and Matthew with their chores around the ranch. For several days he stayed close to the room, spending his time combing his hair, reading, or sleeping, except at mealtimes, when he ate with us. At last Matthew asked Cooney, "Say, Cooney, you need another man?"

"Not right now."

"Raymond he want to work here. He say this is a good place."

"I guess he does. He's had free room and board for the last three days. Has he ever worked on a ranch before?"

"No, but he say he want to learn."

Cooney looked at his slender build, fine hands, and city clothes. "O.K.," he sighed. "We'll try him for a few days. I want to get some corrals and fences built this fall and if he works out all right he can stay."

Cooney wandered into the kitchen for some midmorning coffee with me. "I don't think that button will be worth a hoot, but he sure looks hungry."

"He looks intelligent," I said.

"He's a good-looking boy all right."

"I don't know. He's almost too pretty—like a girl."

"Well, we'll see."

The next few weeks produced a metamorphosis in Raymond. He worked. All day he followed Cooney and watched and listened and worked until when night came he was almost too exhausted to eat. He grew brown and hard and developed into a man. Cooney would call, "Oh, Little Boy . . . come here!" and Raymond would grin with his white teeth and run over to help with the well or the pump or the jeep engine. His eyes were Navajo—almond-shaped, black to the depths of them, and shining with an animal alertness.

Raymond and Matthew could smell cookies baking from the same distance an antelope can scent danger. On the days when I baked bread, the fresh yeasty smell would drift out into the corrals and Cooney and the boys would come in the kitchen sniffing like bears after honey. Then we would cut open a hot loaf and tear off pieces of bread and watch the chunks of yellow butter melt on the warm white bread. It always spoiled our supper but it was better than the supper.

It seemed good to me to have youth and appetite and laughter always near. I washed and mended and cooked for them and got mad when they tracked in mud.

Cooney had known all of Sam's boys since they were small. He had taught them what they knew about mechanics and wells and handling cattle. The rest of it—the instinctive awareness of Nature and response to its changing moods—was inborn. They were good cowboys, Sam's sons, but they left whenever they wanted to. I suppose that is the underlying reason so many people in the Southwest say they do not like Navajos. Their values are almost diametrically opposed to ours. We extoll hard work, self-reliance, ambition, the amassing of material things, promptness, and cling to the great myth of the self-made man. The man who struck out alone against Nature and conquered it for himself "won" the West. The Navajo lives with the centuries, not the years or hours. Time in itself means nothing. Time is only the continuation of life processes—the eternal, unending harmony of the universe, the balance of Nature, the changing of the seasons. To the Navajo, until very recent years, material possessions meant enough food to eat, wood for a fire, a pair of boots, a saddle, a strong wife, a good horse, a warm hogan, some sheep, and the family turquoise.

He does not fight Nature because he is a part of it. And because of that, we never "won" the West or anyplace else from him. We may have titles to pieces of land, spend our whole lives working and fighting and loving the land, but it will never really belong to us. It is the domain of the Navajo and Apache—of the antelope, badger, coyote, bobcat, cougar, bear, deer, fox, hawk, and eagle. Of the rain and sun. Of the changing, restless wind. It belongs to God. That is what the Navajo knows and what we do not want to believe.

And the Navajo is free. He will not respect us because we have education or large houses or credit at the bank. He will not be treated as anything other than an absolute equal. If he grew up secure in the affection and interdependence of his own clan, he really feels, in his heart, that he is among the chosen people—the Dineh—he is a Navajo. He will not be "put in his place" or ordered about or handed charity in exchange for humility. Possession of great wealth arouses an emotion more like amusement than envy in him. He sees no other reason to respect a man than that he is truly a man.

Matthew, Sam's son, was my friend. He was quiet to the point of moodiness. He was stocky and sat well on a horse. He thought deeply about things in his quiet way. My friendship with Matthew was based on the uncomplex circumstance that he liked to eat and I liked to cook. After dinner he would push his chair back, carry his dishes out, and pay me the supreme Navajo compliment. "Sure good, Jo," he would say. We didn't talk much, but Matthew always helped me when I needed help and thanked me when I needed thanks.

All day Raymond belonged to Cooney. They became very close and seemed to enjoy working together. His respect for Cooney and Cooney's affection for him grew into a warm and trusting relationship. I liked to watch them work together . . . Cooney's wisdom and strength

and ability coupled with Raymond's youth and eagerness
and quick insight.

Raymond was my friend, too. He talked to me more
than Matthew, because his English was better. At night,
after supper, we would do the dishes and talk. That was
how I found out Raymond was a dogie.

"Where does your family live?" I asked.

"My sister lives in Albuquerque. She's just about same
age as you."

"Your mother and father?"

"Dead. My mother die a long time ago. I never know
my father. All I have is my sister. She raise me."

Once, on a warm night, after supper, Raymond and
Matthew started shouting to us to come outside. All
across the northern sky was a shimmering white glow.

"What the devil is that?" said Cooney.

"It looks like the northern lights I remember seeing in
Minnesota when I was little," I said.

"It's too far south for northern lights," Cooney said.
"Somebody must have dropped an atomic bomb."

We just stood there by the yard fence watching the
lights flare up and dim again.

"Maybe the world's come to an end," said Matthew,
laughing, only he was serious and so were we, but we
were full of dinner and tired and it didn't seem to matter so very much.

Cooney yawned. "We'll know by morning."

"I have to go to town to do the laundry tomorrow.
Maybe somebody in Holbrook will know what caused
that light."

Raymond slowly shook his head. "No," he said. "They
won't know. They don't see nothing. You know, people

in town never look up." He was right. We never did know what had caused the phenomenon.

Matthew was slow and deliberate. He was a country boy—a good cowboy who could handle horses and work cattle easily when he wanted to. Raymond was fast, thorough, good with wells, equipment, carpenter work, or welding. He had to work off his nervous energy. Often he would stay up till past midnight fixing a saddle or bridle. He liked to read. As soon as our new magazines would come in, he grabbed them voraciously and took them to his room.

They were close, Raymond and Matthew. Close to the point of jealousy. I watched Matthew smolder when Cooney would praise Raymond for something he had done. Matthew's English was not as good as Raymond's and he did not always understand what Cooney wanted. And then, like me, Matthew had to turn things over in his mind a long time before he acted upon them.

While Matthew was jealous of Cooney's attention to Raymond, Sam was jealous of both the younger boys. Old Ceph resented me and disliked Raymond because Cooney liked him. Cooney was, perhaps, jealous of the way the men confided in me and used me as a go-between when they were hesitant to ask him something.

That fall during roundup Ceph almost got into a fist fight with Raymond "for getting smart" with him. And then, one morning before breakfast, Matthew came in the door, his eyes dark and cloudy. "Jo, you got some Band-Aid?"

"What's the matter . . . cut yourself on some wire?" I asked.

Matthew's voice was choked with anger. "Raymond bite me," he said.

"Raymond what?"

"He bite me. We have a fight doing the chores this morning. I tell him to leave me alone because he's smaller than me. When I lean over to get that feed bucket he bite me. See?"

Cooney came in. We looked at the red welts in back of Matthew's shoulder. I had to bite my own lip to keep a straight face while I put Merthiolate on the tooth marks.

"Do you suppose Raymond has rabies?" Cooney said.

Matthew grinned, though there were tears in his eyes.

"That little punk. If I'd been you, I'd have knocked those big white teeth of his plumb out." After that, everyone got along a lot better. It seemed to have cleared the tension.

At first, Raymond was impossible as a cowboy. In fact, we doubted that he had ever been on a horse before. When he rode, he bounced up and down, veered to one side, then the other, like a drunk Navajo going down First Street in Gallup on a Saturday night. But he was not afraid. Not of anything or anyone. He had been a dogie too long for that, kicked around and left to fight or outsmart or charm his way through one place after another.

Everything was a challenge to him and he wanted to do whatever he tackled better than anyone else. He was small and light—no bigger than I—but he handled his weight to the best advantage, like a featherweight boxer, and could tilt the biggest calves we could put into the branding chute and dehorn them by throwing all of his body into it. Once, when we were listening to a fight, he asked Cooney why Indians never became boxers.

Sometimes, on Saturday nights, he and Matthew

would take their showers, put on clean white shirts, their black hair shining and their white teeth gleaming. They would come in to get their paychecks, which were usually a week in advance, and say, "Cooney, we wanna go to town." Saturday night movies bothered Raymond, especially the Westerns. "Cooney," he asked one day, "I see lots of shows and they all the same. Why do those white men always win?"

"Because they usually did, I guess," said Cooney.

"Sometime I like to see a movie where the Indians win," he said, shaking his head.

"You know," I said, "once when I was living down at Fort Apache, some movie company came in and hired about two hundred Apaches for a movie they were making in Oak Creek Canyon. They even hired the chairman of the tribal council. I think he got to die in the picture. He told everybody how he fell off his horse and rolled down into an arroyo and got all skinned up. When those Apaches came home and got off the buses, they were limping and groaning and complaining. They said they had to ride broncs. One of them told us, 'The worst part was they make us ride without pants. Over there is cold. Our legs sure get skin up.' I thought those Apaches were supposed to be so tough."

"They should have use Navajo," said Raymond.

When we were not too busy around the ranch, Raymond would play Indian. He would let his hair get loose and wild and go around wearing nothing but a pair of faded Levis. That was when he really learned to ride. We had a gentle sorrel with a light mane and tail. Raymond would jump on him bareback and lope him around the horse pasture, uttering wild parts of Navajo songs he had heard as a boy and all but forgotten. He was Navajo

then. One of The People. His obsidian eyes shone with
ancient meanings and saw the earth symbols as his ancestors had seen them. His crow-black hair flew in the
wind and his brown chest was bared to the sun. He
learned how it was to feel a good horse moving strong
and fast beneath him. In the wind he rode. "Ey," said
the old Navajos, "The wind is life. When the wind goes
into you, you live; when it goes out of you, you die. It is
the wind that gives you life. You can see the swirls made
by the wind on the tips of your fingers." Raymond would
lope back to the corral, jump off his horse, and they
would both stand there breathing hard and sweating.

By the time we were ready to gather cattle that fall,
Raymond could ride. We started our drives at the West
Camp. I went on the shorter drives, but stayed at the
camp catching steers as they came in to water when the
men made the longest ones. When I wasn't sneaking up
to close the gate on a steer, I was in the kitchen pack-
ing juniper branches into the wood cookstove. One day
the men were late. I had used up almost all the wood in
the process of warming over the dinner. At last I could
see a trace of dust coming across the ridge and could
hear the far-off bawling of cattle. Then the lead cattle began coming out of the cedar trees and I heard the men
whistling and shouting behind the herd. When they were
all penned, the men came in, one after another, tired and
dusty, to wash in the white enamel pan on the wooden
stool under the broken mirror. The last man had cleaned
out the gray ring around the washpan when I called
them to eat. "Where's Raymond?" I asked.

"I'll be damned if I know," said Cooney. "We lost him
somewhere."

"I hope his horse didn't throw him."

"I don't think so. If he did, Cottontail would be back here by now. Matthew and he split up over against the fence and Raymond was supposed to meet him at Dutch Tank."

"I wait for a long time," said Matthew, "but I had that big three-year-ol' steer in the bunch. Couldn't hold him up, so I come on."

"Well," I said, "we might as well eat. I never thought I'd see the day a Navajo got lost."

Matthew grinned. "He sure must have get lost somewhere."

"If he's not back when we get through working the cattle, we can go back and try to pick up his tracks," said Cooney.

"It'll be dark by then," I said.

"I think he's O.K.," said Matthew.

When the cattle had watered out, the men turned them out of the water lot, pushed them into the big runaround, and began working the herd. I had washed up the pots and was lying down on Ceph's cot, listening to the cattle bawl and the chickens cackling in the next room. I was almost asleep when Silver, who was tied to the corral fence, began to nicker. His ears were erect and he was straining at his reins trying to look back toward the south. In about ten minutes, Raymond rode out of the cedars, looking limp and foolish.

"What happened?" I asked him.

"I was running some cow over there. Guess I get lost," he said. "I lose those cow too."

"Come in and get something to eat. I kept your dinner warm."

"No. I go down and help Cooney," he said.

That was the first and last time I have ever seen a lost

Navajo. Raymond had been away from The People too
long. He did not know where he was going. He had lost
his innate sense of direction—the instinct combined with
intelligence that had guided them through the wide expanses of Arizona and New Mexico for centuries; that,
thousands of years before, had brought them across Asia,
over the Bering Strait, through Alaska, Canada, and
down into the mountains and deserts of the West to settle precariously in the high, dry, plateau of the Southwest, in their own chosen land, surrounded by the seven
sacred mountains and blessed by the gods.

A Navajo, or any good cowboy, could be led blind-
folded into the bottom of the most isolated canyon on
the ranch and when the blindfold was removed, he could
point as true as any compass to the camp, a remote water
hole, the corner of a fence line, or to the neighbor's
house thirty miles away. But Raymond was lost. Lost to
The People and their life. Even more lost in the dark,
scuddling, jostling, homocentric chaos of our centers of
civilization.

Still, he could play Indian and play it well. It was a
fierce and reckless playing. The next day, when we were
driving cattle, there were four bulls in the drags. We
would yell at them, charge them, hit them with ropes,
and throw sticks at them to break them up, but nothing
kept them from fighting. They would stop, lower their
heads, paw up dust, snort, and charge each other with
their rival fury. Cooney was in the lead, Matthew and
Sam on the sides, Ceph and I in the drags, and Raymond
was all over the place.

Bulls are usually gentle creatures, more placid than
cows. But when they fight with each other they are nothing to trifle with. They may be blind with rage and

charge a man on horseback if he interferes. One of the
bulls had turned on Bess, who was barking to separate
them.

Raymond loped over to us, his shirt open to the waist.
He rode up alongside the biggest bull, leaned over in the
saddle, grabbed the bull by the tail, and twisted it.
Taken by surprise, the bull gave a loud squeal and thun-
dered off to the front of the herd, kicking his heels all the
way.

Sam looked at me and raised his eyebrows. Ceph
turned his face and spat tobacco juice. I swallowed
hard. Raymond looked at Matthew with a white grin on
his dark face.

I went around to cover Matthew's side as the two of
them rode away from the drive to scout for more cattle.
They were as fresh as two colts, with the sureness of
youth, feeling that the world must have been created especially for them. Their battered hats were pulled down
low on their foreheads as they jogged over the ridge.
They looked at each other and laughed with the secret
laugh of boys.

6

The Dogies

We were in the middle of our fall roundup when we had
the Indian trouble. On Saturday night, Sam Roanhorse,
Matthew, and Raymond came in after supper, scrubbed
and shined and polished and slicked down. "We want go
to town," said Raymond in that slow, wickedly smiling
way the Navajos have of saying it, as if all the illicit joys
of the world awaited them. With misgivings, Cooney
warned them, cussed them, wrote them out their checks,
and let them go. He could not refuse because Raymond
had made a down payment on a used black-and-white
Chevy, which provided them with their own transportation.

"We have a hell of a long drive ahead of us tomorrow,"
said Cooney. "If we miss one day gathering cattle, it
throws the whole drive off. The cattle have time to scatter out and we might as well start all over again from the

beginning. So get back here by midnight or you'll be too
deadheaded to work."

"O.K., Cooney," said Sam. "You're the boss."

"We'll be back early," said Raymond. He smiled,
folded his check, put it in his shirt pocket, and left. We
could hear the roar of the car pulling out of the yard.
Raymond always said, "It sounds like some old Indian
car."

Our muscles ached and we were so tired that night
our sleep was fitful and restless. Just before sunup,
Cooney bolted out of bed and ran to the window.

"What's wrong?" I mumbled.

"Those little copper-bellied . . ."

"Cooney!"

"I knew it. I knew they wouldn't get back. They all got
drunk last night and they're probably all in jail this morning. Now I don't know what I'm going to do. Wouldn't
that cork your . . ."

"Cooney!" I said. "Calm down. It isn't daylight yet.
Maybe they'll show up. Wait just a little while longer before you blow a fuse."

"I ought to kill every one of them."

"Oh, good grief," I said. "There's no reason to get that
upset."

"You'd think so if you had to run this damned outfit.
You don't have any responsibility and it's easy for you to
say that."

"Oh, no, I don't have any responsibility. None at all."

"Well, you don't."

"You needn't be cussing the men all the time. You can't
expect a man to work for wages the way you do when
you own the place. They don't feel the same way about
it we do."

"If I were working for wages, I'd do what I was told to do."

"I can't imagine you ever working for someone else."

"Well I did—for my dad—all the time I was growing up. I had to live in a little old shack and do work I was ashamed to do . . ."

"What kind of work would anyone be ashamed to do?"

"Plenty of it. I had to stay home and do all the chores and those other ranchers' sons never did anything but give orders to someone else. Now, by god, I have something and they don't, but I sure as hell had to work for it."

"I don't know very many people who haven't had to work . . ."

"There were plenty of times when I didn't have enough money to buy cigarette papers."

"Oh!" I got up, threw my robe on, and went in the kitchen to put on the coffee. "I don't mind arguing at night, but I can't stand it first thing in the morning!" I slammed the lid on the coffeepot and banged the skillet down on the stove. I've always been more of a slammer and banger than a fighter.

He followed me out in the kitchen. "I'm not arguing, hon. I'm just saying that I'm going to fire all the sonsof-bitches. I can run this outfit myself if I have to. They just get me in a tight spot and take advantage of it. They think they can put anything over on me when we're gathering cattle. I trusted that Raymond too."

"Oh, Cooney, I don't think they're trying to put something over on you. It's just that they've been working hard for two weeks and they wanted to go to town. Anybody works better if they get some time off once in a while."

"They were just in town last week. I never have any time off. I've had to sit over some damn ranch all my life."

"Oh, come off it. You and I go to town all the time."

"I wish I liked Indians as well as you do."

By that time I had started to cry. I always cry when I get mad. "They're human beings, just the same as we are."

"Do you think I'd go off and leave somebody I was working for when he needed me?"

"You've gone off and left me plenty of times when I needed you."

"But I'm not working for you."

I couldn't help laughing then, in spite of myself.

We heard the chain on the corral gate clinking. Cooney looked out the window. "It's Raymond," he said. "But I don't see anybody with him. He must have wrecked his car and walked in. Well, they can just kiss my butt. I can get along without them."

"Here, sit down and drink your coffee."

We started to eat breakfast when Raymond walked in.

"Where's Sam and Matthew?" Cooney asked.

"Over there," said Raymond, motioning with his head toward town.

"In jail?"

"No. I try to get them home las' night, but they drinking lots of wine and won't go. They're still sleep in my car, I guess."

"Where is it? Did you wreck it?" Cooney asked, hopefully.

"No. Sam and Matthew want to go back to town when we get halfway home. They start fight with me so I jus' pull off the road, like I'm drunk. I pretend I can't start it again. Then they go to sleep and I walk home."

"Well come on and eat some breakfast, then you can go get the horses in the jeep if they haven't come in yet. Jo can help us today."

I had time to wash the breakfast dishes and dress before Cooney called me to say the horses were coming. When I got outside, Cooney was standing against the corral fence, squinting toward the east, his hands shading his eyes from the red sun on the horizon. "What in the devil is that out there?" he said. "Can you see it?"

"It's two of something—across the arroyo. Coyotes, maybe?"

"No, I don't think so."

We watched for a while. Whatever it was disappeared into the arroyo. Then they reappeared and were coming very slowly toward the ranch.

"It . . . looks like . . . it is! Sam and Matthew. Only they don't seem to be walking."

"Hell, no. They're too drunk to walk. They're crawling."

They would get up and stagger a little while, then fall back down on their hands and knees. At last, Sam, weaving back and forth, steadied himself and began to walk upright. We watched as Matthew struggled a few steps, stumbled on a clump of sacaton, fell down, and rolled over on his back like a playful dog. He lay there a minute. Then he lifted himself on his elbow, took a bottle out of his pocket, and with his head held back, poured every drop into his gaping mouth, shaking the bottle several times. And you know those old movies about the Foreign Legion with a man crawling across the Sahara and draining the last drop of water out of his canteen? I thought

about them and started to laugh. I sobered up in a hurry,
though, when I saw the look on Cooney's face. His eyes
were narrow and red with anger. He was gritting his
teeth so hard I could hear them. I was afraid. He threw
open the gate and jumped into the jeep.

"Where are you going?" I asked. I had never seen him
so angry.

"Out to get those bastards."

"You won't hurt them?"

"I *feel* like killing them."

"Wait. Don't go without me."

The look on Cooney's face made my hands turn icy.
He seemed like a stranger then. He drove recklessly over
the ditches until we came to Sam.

"Get in this jeep," said Cooney. "If you can get in."
Sam lurched over to the jeep, shrugged his shoulders,
mumbled, "Sure," and swung himself into the cab.

Cooney's jaws were still clenched tightly when we
drove up to Matthew, who was making a commendable
effort to stand. Cooney jumped out, grabbed him by the
shoulders, and shook him as if he were trying to shake
the dust out of an old carpet. Matthew was limp, still in
a drunken haze. His tongue rolled around trying to form
words. Cooney picked him up under the arms and
dragged him roughly into the back of the pickup, letting
his feet hang over the edge. He was too filled with sup-
pressed rage to talk. When we drove into the yard, he
slammed on the brakes, got out, went around, and
pitched Matthew out of the jeep like a sack of feed. Matthew landed in the dirt and stayed there, motionless.

"He's hurt," I said. I started to bend down and look at
him.

"Go back in the house," said Cooney. "He's too drunk to get hurt."

I went in and heated the leftover coffee. For the first time I realized that it was I, not Sam or Matthew or Raymond, who had kindled the real anger in Cooney. He was out in the bunkroom, now, reading it off to Sam, telling him to pack up his things and go.

Matthew dragged himself slowly to his feet, brushed the dirt and manure of the yard off his Levis, and shook his head a few times to clear it. He shuffled over to the kitchen door. His eyes had a dark, blank, lost look. "I'm gonna back to town," he said.

"You're not in any shape to go anyplace," I said.

"Well, I'm go now anyway." He turned away. I put my hand on his shoulder and shoved him back into the kitchen. "Sam!" I called, "Come have some coffee."

They sat at the table in silence except for the noise they made sipping coffee. They reeked of wine. I fried two eggs apiece for them and made some toast in the oven. Sam sat at the table, holding up his head with his left arm, concentrating on the fried eggs. Bess came over to him, yawned, and put her head on his lap. "Besh," said Sam, "want some egg, Besh?" Slowly, slowly, the light returned to Matthew's eyes and he was almost a man again. They wiped their mouths, carried their dishes to the sink, and started out the door. Matthew turned to me. "Well, thanks for everything, Jo," he said. "I'm go now."

"Don't go back to town until you sleep it off," I said. "The cops will pick you up as soon as you get there."

Cooney, Raymond, and I made the drive that morning. It was a long one, way back against Gibson's fence. We had to cover the canyon and several tanks. We met at

White Tower, an old well which had turned salty and had to be abandoned. We still used the corrals there and the small holding pasture when we were gathering cattle.

It was noon. Cooney's mother had driven out with our dinner. When we rode in, she was making coffee in an old coffee can over a fire she had built. It smelled strong and good. We tied our horses, got down around the small fire, and filled our plates with roast beef, beans, carrot and cabbage salad, and corn bread.

"I'm afraid we missed some cattle over around Coyote," said Cooney. "I saw some over there yesterday. Dammit, you just can't make a clean drive with three men."

"What's all that dust over there?" I said, looking up.

"Where?"

"Coming from White Tank."

He climbed up on the fence to look. "Well I'll be . . ."

"What is it?"

"It's a whole bunch of cattle coming this way."

I got up on the fence to look. There they were, strung out for two hundred yards or more, coming over the hill. In back of them we could just make out the figures of two men, on horseback. They rode with their heads down, limp in the saddle, swaying from one side to another.

"Do you know what?" said Cooney. A wide grin broke across his face. "Those bastards got their horses and made a drive right behind us."

I jumped off the fence. "Good old Sam," I said. "Good old Uncle Sam Roanhorse!"

"My god—look at those cattle . . . there must be fifty head of cows that we missed."

We sat there drinking the black coffee and lit our cigarettes on the red-hot end of a stick from the campfire, watching them come in with their cattle. More cattle than Raymond, Cooney, and I had found all day. They were weaving back and forth behind the cattle. Their faces were sweaty and sober as death, but there was a look of defiance in their eyes. I felt that the least somebody could do would be to hum the "Triumphal March" from *Aïda,* so I did.

"Come over here, Matthew, and get you a plate," called Cooney's mother. Matthew turned white and swallowed a few times. "No thanks," he said. "I'm not hungry."

"What's wrong, boy, are you sick?" asked Mother Jeffers.

Matthew smiled weakly. "Got some cold water?" he asked.

"You bet we've got water," said Mother Jeffers. She poured him two cups full of ice water out of the glass jar. Matthew drank until the water trickled down his chin and left streaks in the dust. Then he wiped his mouth with the sleeve of his jacket and sat down heavily in the shade of the old steel storage tank.

Sam ate all he could stack up on his plate. "Sure hot today," he said.

"That's good for you," said Cooney. "That sun will bake all the wine out of you."

Sam laughed and shook his head. "Matthew sure get sick," he said.

Sam and Matthew stayed on until the roundup was over and the last steer had been loaded onto the Santa Fe. It is not very easy to fire a Navajo when he does not want to be fired or to hold him on the job when he decides to go someplace. And I suppose that is another reason so many ranchers lose patience with them.

The Navajo is free. Except for the limitations of his body and the bonds of Nature, he is free. When he wants to go to a Yeibechai ceremony for some sick relative, he goes, not because he has no sense of responsibility, but because he has the deepest sense of responsibility to his clan, his family, his friends, and to himself. Instead of spending a large part of his life trying to run from himself, he is free to be himself.

Except from the burden of fear, he is free. Not fear of physical dangers or hardships—they are part of his everyday life—but fear of the creatures of the night, of lightning, evil, sickness; of witches, owls, werewolves; of the new schoolteacher, the shot of penicillin, the unfamiliar plumbing, the bed that stands up off the floor; at last, of death. Facing death is not so bad. Death itself, the thing devoid of life, movement, beauty, warmth, is repugnant beyond measure. These are things which mar the Beauty Way, which disrupt the harmony of a good life.

Cooney did not fire Sam and Matthew. They just left because there was not enough work for three men during the winter months. Sam went home to Jeddito to stay with Helen and help her take care of the sheep and get wood for the winter. He would stay at home for a while and then he would go to Gallup with somebody and maybe get drunk and maybe find another job someplace.

It was a long time that Sam and Helen had been married. Maybe thirty years, maybe more. They had had a wedding in the Catholic Church. There was never any more money after that, just more children. First they had Genevieve, who was my age, then Matthew, Curtis, Jeffrey, LeRoy, Pauline, and Helene. No one knows how many they had lost. Helen was a good mother to all her children. There was seldom enough to eat; even more seldom fresh water to drink, but there was affection, discipline, hard work, and patience. Although the kids were small, they were healthy—even Pauline, who had congenital heart trouble, and Jeffrey, who never grew much after he had been crippled by a car in California. They were close to one another in that family, giving and taking what little money there was among them. And they had the security of the clan.

Not Raymond. He had not known a father. He was a small, sensitive boy when his mother had died. He remembered her a little with vague warmth and longing. His sister had taken care of him, but for a long time now, she had had a family of her own to raise. There had been no aunt, whom Navajo children call "Mother," or cousins, whom they call "Brother" or "Sister." No kind, old-fashioned grandmother. No friends or clansmen who would take him to raise as one of their own. Just a sister, a little older than himself. Since he was a little boy he had been in the government boarding schools, but somehow he always seemed to cause trouble. Partly because he was clever; partly because he was a very good-looking boy. And so he had left before graduating from high school.

There was the time, that fall, that he had the hubcaps stolen off his car in Holbrook. He had seen some teen-age boys stealing them and had gone up to a gang of them and tried to get them back. He was afraid to get into a fight because there were so many of them and they were white boys. One night when he was drying the dishes for me I asked him why he didn't report them to the police if he knew who they were.

"Because they never believe an Indian, those guys," he said.

"Maybe they would. Some of them would."

"Those boys always want to get me when I come to town."

"Why?"

His face flushed and he looked down intently at the dish towel. "You know that girl she's cashier at the show?"

"A Navajo girl?"

"No, she's white girl."

"No. I never go to shows. What's she got to do with it?"

"She always talk to me. She's a nice girl. She want me to go out with her after the show."

"Why don't you go?"

He looked up, surprised. "Those boys don't like when she talk to me. That's why they want to get me."

I threw the silverware down in the drawer. "Oh, stupid . . . what's *wrong* with people . . ."

"Anyway," said Raymond, "I don't want to go with her. I don't like her much. I just talk to her sometimes, because she wants."

It was Thanksgiving Day when he got into the real trouble. For some time a law had been in effect legalizing the sale of liquor to Indians. Before that, the bootleggers had made a killing. Navajos would pay as much as ten dollars a pint for whiskey. Afraid of being caught and jailed, they would down it in an alley as fast as they could and stagger blindly down the railroad tracks or pass out in some gutter. And I have heard the good Christian White People say, "Indians shouldn't have liquor. They just seem to go crazy."

Thanksgiving weekend, my relatives from California had come to visit us. We had a big dinner with turkey, dressing, sweet potatoes, cramberries, peas, celery, and carrots, pumpkin pie and whipped cream. Raymond had sat at the table beaming like some Mongolian Tiny Tim. After grace, he said that we were just like the Pilgrims, having Thanksgiving dinner with the Indians. That afternoon, he went to Holbrook.

Raymond hadn't come back in the night. Cooney had gotten up to do the chores in the frosty morning air. I thought about the gang of boys who had stolen his hubcaps. "I'm afraid Raymond is in some kind of trouble," I said.

"He's probably in jail. Of all times, when we have company and I wanted to visit some . . ."

"It isn't like Raymond. He hasn't been drinking, as far as I know. Maybe his car broke down."

"This is the first time he's ever pulled anything like this. Do you reckon we'd better go in and see about him?"

"Oh, please. You need him back to do the chores, anyway."

"Let's wait. If he isn't back tonight, I'll go in the morning and try to find him."

Late that afternoon, my mother drove out to the ranch to tell us that the city judge, an old cattleman and a friend of Cooney's, had called her. Raymond had been thrown into jail for drunk and reckless driving, which carried a stiff fine. He would be up before the judge in the morning. "George said for you to see him, Cooney," Mother said. "He seems to think something is wrong. He said that Raymond's eyes were clear and he couldn't smell liquor on him. He doesn't think he had been drinking at all."

Cooney talked to the judge and then to Raymond. Raymond had picked up two older Navajos he knew in town.

They were driving around and the two other men were drinking beer. It was very dark and Raymond had run a stop sign—the same one I always forget—on a quiet, residential street. A police car just happened to be parked there. When Raymond had failed to stop at the intersection, the policeman stopped him. They had tried to hide the beer cans under the seat, but the car was searched. The two older men were released, but Raymond was held because he had been driving. He swore to Cooney that he had not been drunk and the judge believed him. He was fined for not stopping at the stop sign and released into our custody.

Raymond was at home with us. The first home he had ever had. He would sit quietly after dinner and read magazines or talk to Cooney, while I washed the dishes. He helped cut and decorate our Christmas tree and went to Holy Eucharist with us at midnight on Christmas Eve. Cooney gave him a watch that Christmas and he was very proud of it.

That fall we had not been able to sell the cows and calves as pairs and when their mothers were sold, we were left with fifty small dogie calves to hold over the winter. They had stood in the corral bawling for their mothers for four days and nights. After that they had given up and started eating grain and hay. Raymond had taken it upon himself to feed the dogies that winter. Every morning and every evening he fed them, calling the littlest one Peanuts. He would squat down against the barn door, in the pale rays of the winter sun, watching them crowd around the feed troughs. Eventually, their hollow sides filled out and their coarse hair grew soft and thick.

That was the winter we had felt prosperous enough to build onto our three-room house after two and a half

years of marriage. During the month of January, Sam and
Matthew returned to help with the new addition. I know
no better way for a married couple to start hair bristling
and sparks flying than to build a house. Cooney thought
that the living room should be small and cozy. I wanted
it large and roomy. The final dimensions were eighteen
by twenty. Cooney suggested we might charge admission
and hold public dances.

We almost came to blows over the fireplace. I would
rather have had a fireplace without a house than a house
without a fireplace. Cooney failed to see anything aes-
thetic about a method of heating that required wood-
cutting, hauling, chopping, stacking, and ash-carrying. I
wept and vowed to do all the work connected with it.
"You'll burn up in front and freeze behind," he said.

"Well, we'll install a gas heater on the other side of the
room," I said.

"Then why do we have to have a fireplace?"

Being a woman of devious methods of persuasion, I won
out. We hired a local stonemason, a kindly, shuffling man
with pale eyes. I wanted to use the buff-colored flagstone
from our ranch for the entire fireplace. The mason did
his best to convince us that we should let him get rock
from Utah, Colorado, Canada, and Mexico to mix with
the native sandstone and let him create a masterpiece,
using forty colors. It wasn't easy, but we compromised
and settled for the local red, buff, and white flagstones.

I often baked cookies and took coffee to the carpenters
and other workmen in the morning. The first time I offered
cookies to the rockmason he said, "No thank you. They
always give me heartburn." Raymond and Matthew nearly
died at that and called him "Heartburn" from then on.
He had lived on the reservation and spoke Navajo to

them. At the carpenter's request, the boys helped Heartburn because he was about two weeks behind with his
fireplace. One thing about him, he was thorough. They
would mix cement for him and carry buckets and keep
up with his trowels which he was always losing. The fireplace was nearly completed when Heartburn mysteriously
disappeared for five days, holding up completion of the
house. He explained that he had been to a basketball
tournament.

The contractor was an old friend of Cooney's. Once,
when he had owned a garage, he pulled one of Cooney's
cows out of a steel water tank with his wrecker. I had
some detailed blueprints made by the time he called on
us. He took one look and tore them up. "Hey, what are
you doing?" I asked.

"Hell, those guys can't read blueprints," he said. He
took a cocktail napkin out of his pocket. On one side was
his estimate. "Here," he said, handing me his ballpoint
pen, "just show me what you want on here." I drew one
oblong room, a small bedroom, bath, and closet. "Now
when those boys start work, you put that knitting away.
They work so fast you won't have time to knit if you
tell them what to do."

Next day the carpenters came. They were from up-
country somewhere. The straw boss was a witty, cynical
character who worked like heat lightning and never had
to measure anything twice. Another man did the nailing.
His face was covered with a perpetual two days' growth
of black whiskers and I couldn't figure out when it was
he shaved. He pounded nails all day long. Occasionally
he would hit his thumb and yell, "That cockeyed nail
was bent!"

Our biggest problem was the cesspool. We have about

eight to twelve inches of topsoil resting on solid rock. Many of the ranches nearby were without plumbing because of the rock. Sam insisted on going to the reservation after some "blue mud" with which to dynamite a hole in the ground. "Blue mud's sure good," he told Cooney. "It make hole go down, not up."

Cooney refused Sam's generous offer. He and the contractor had decided to blast their own cesspool. It was to be at the end of the new addition, near—of all things—the Butane tank. Next day, they placed three sticks of dynamite in the ground, without the benefit of Sam's blue mud. I kissed Cooney goodbye, took one last fond look around, got Bess, and drove to town before they could light the fuse. To my astonishment, the house was still standing when I returned. The three sticks of dynamite had scarcely dented the ground. In the end, Raymond and Matthew had to dig a cesspool with a crowbar. It took about a week.

When the roofing men came, Bess took an immediate dislike to them and was determined to get them off of the roof of her new house, where they had no business being. She barked and got in their way and followed them, snarling, all day. In fact, she did everything short of biting to remove them from the premises. While it is difficult to carry buckets of hot tar with a dog clutching one pants leg, the roofers were a brave lot and somehow completed the job. It wasn't their fault that we chose a pebble roof and half of it blew off the first windy day in spring.

We did most of the finishing ourselves. Raymond and Matthew plastered the outside and I painted the inside. Our old furniture looked skimpy in the new rooms and I began resurrecting antiques. One of them was an old maple bureau that had been brought from Germany over a hundred years ago by my grandmother's family. Mother had it in her pantry. The scarred, varnished surface hid some beautifully grained and colored maple. It had been in a bedroom in our cottage by the Minnesota River. When I opened the drawers to refinish it, a familiar, damp, mousy smell lingered in the wood and childhood memories flooded my mind.

For some reason, I suddenly thought of the time I had lain in bed at the cottage under an ocean of quilts, and heard the terrible snap of the mousetrap in the stillness and blackness of the night. I was only three or four. I had risen, tiptoed across the cold floor, stood on a chair, and lifted the mousetrap off the mantel of the fireplace. When Mother found me I was sitting on the floor, stroking the soft brown and white fur of the dead field mouse and sobbing as if my heart would break. "Oh! Don't touch that, dear," she had said. "It's dirty!"

When our house was finished, Sam and Matthew left again. It was spring. On Easter Sunday, Cooney and I took Raymond to the White Mountains. We all went to church in McNary, a lumbering town. My friend Anne was still teaching at Fort Apache. She got a date for Raymond with a pretty Apache girl. We all had lunch together in the forest and Raymond and that Apache girl didn't speak to each other the whole time. Partly because they were shy and partly because Navajos and Apaches are naturally suspicious of each other.

By May the dogies were ready for branding, but no one wanted to brand them. So we put it off. We had many late calves, too, from the year before, that had been too small to brand in September. Finally, the bull calves got so big Cooney knew they would look staggy if we didn't cut them soon.

That spring, Cooney, Raymond, and I branded over five hundred calves. It wasn't easy. We had to spread out far and wide on the drives. When we branded, Raymond pushed them down the chute and Cooney caught them. Then Raymond jumped over the fence and came round to help Cooney dehorn, castrate, and brand.

One day at White Tower the wind came up, strong and hard, beating against us. We could not see twenty-five feet away. I had to brace myself against the chute to stand. We had driven the calves a long way and couldn't turn them back out, so we carried on with sand in our eyes, noses, ears, and mouths until we had branded forty of them.

Somehow we made it. All but the dogies. Every evening we'd look at the gentle little dogies and think of some excuse to postpono branding them. And then one day Cooney was in a black mood. He swore and complained and growled to himself. "I'm going in to wash clothes tomorrow," I said.

He looked up. "I thought I'd brand those dogies in the morning. You don't have to help us if you don't want to. We'll get them."

"No. I'll help. Do we have enough vaccine?"

"There's seventy-five doses in my clothes closet."

The next morning we were all three in low spirits. We snapped at each other over breakfast. Raymond saddled up the horses and we rounded up the dogies in the horse pasture in morose silence. The dogies were hard to drive because they were so gentle they would not get out of the way. We put them in the corral and into the crowding pen. Cooney lit the burner and sharpened his knives to a keen edge. I filled my syringes slowly. Raymond stood in the crowding pen, staring sullenly at the young animals. The irons began to glow red in the roar of the blue flame.

"O.K.," said Cooney. "I'm ready."

"Oopah!" shouted Raymond, grabbing a calf, whipping it, and shoving it roughly down the chute. The neckpiece banged shut. The calf was tilted over with a thud. It just lay there, motionless, its eyes wide and wondering. There was no fierce kicking and struggling; no wild, frightened eyes; no loud bawls and squeals—only a low moan, when the hot iron seared the flesh. We were yelling at each other to counteract the silence, handling the dogies rough and hard and fast. "Crunch," went the dehorners. The long winter hair sizzled and smoked under the hot irons. The calf twitched and groaned and its eyes filled with water when its head was seared. Then it was over. The chute was tilted upright and the neckpiece released. Instead of breaking free with its hind legs kicking in defiance and bellowing for its mother, the dogie walked out, dizzily and slowly, not knowing what had happened or why it had to happen to him. It shook its head a few times and wandered over to the feed trough, because it had no mother to run to.

And we went on, shouting and swearing and working as fast as we could, because we were not sure what was happening or why it had to happen, either.

7

Cats and Dogs

Not long ago I was reading a book called *The Farmer's Dog, Border Collie Training—Theory and Practise,** by a British trainer of working sheep dogs named John Holmes. Speaking of choosing a pup, he said:

> Many shepherds I know, when they go to select a pup, simply pick up the one which reaches them first. That method is not nearly so much of a lucky dip as it sounds. The bright puppy is nearly always first off the mark and the bold one will go straight to anyone, so by adopting this method you are likely to pick the brightest, boldest pup, which is just what you want. . . . Even if you cannot be sure that the bold pup will remain bold, you can at least avoid the shy one which has every chance of remaining shy. . . . If a litter comes running out and one, on seeing a stranger, bolts back to its kennel or sits in the corner looking coy . . . *leave it there.*

* Popular Dogs Publishing Co., Ltd., 178–202 Great Portland St., London W.1 (1960).

If I had read Mr. Holmes's book and followed its honest and good advice ten years ago, I would never have had my Bess.

That April day, the sun shone bright on the squirming litter of pups in the owner's backyard. No sooner had I walked up to them than one, independent and aloof from its brothers and sisters, eyed me suspiciously, waddled over to a parked car, and hid ungraciously behind a wheel. Every now and then, as I was examining the friendly puppies who rolled around my feet, the fuzzy white pup would peer out of the darkness and stare with cold indifference.

"Here's a lively little fellow," said Johnny Lee, the owner. For a long time I hesitated, looking back at the puppy in the shadows under the car. "If it's all right with you," I said, "I'd like that one."

"Well, you picked the Queen," he said. "She rules the roost around here, but she's not real friendly." He walked over to the car. The snow-white pup cocked her ear, but did not try to run. He picked her up carefully. There was something about her, even then, which demanded attention, but discouraged roughness or playfulness.

I held her soft body in my arms. She tolerated her position, but made it entirely clear that she was being subjected to something of an indignity. With an attitude of resignation, she at last lay her head in my lap in the car.

Her mother had been a heavy-set pure white bitch, long-haired and rather bad-tempered. Her father was a hen-pecked, simple, strong dog, white with bluish-gray markings. Both were registered Australian Shepherds, a hardy breed used extensively for working cattle and sheep throughout the rugged expanses of the western United States.

When I got her home, I put her down in the middle of the kitchen floor, poured out a saucer of warm milk, and set it in front of her, coaxing her to drink. She just sat there, looking down at the milk. She sniffed it once, then walked over to a corner, lay down, and stared at me with her ice-blue eyes, trying to make up her mind about the strange surroundings. She sensed that she would no longer rule the litter of pups, but must reconcile herself to a new companion who fed her in this bizarre manner.

During the night the pup whimpered a little on her blanket next to my bed. I rolled over and looked down at her. She was sitting very still, staring at me as if to say, "You took me away from my mother, the least you can do is sloop with me." I lifted her up on the bed, not because of her complaints, but because I felt obligated to her. Her coat, silky, luxurious, soft, and clean, had a sweet milky smell to it and invited petting. To this day, I have never seen a child who did not feel compelled to stroke her back and bury his head in her warm fur.

About daylight, in that half-waking, half-dreaming stage I felt somehow restless and uneasy. When I slowly opened my eyes, I was startled to see another pair of eyes, blue as Wedgwood, looking back at me. The pup had been sitting beside my shoulder, staring intently, piercingly, at my own closed eyes. She had wanted to wake me, but was afraid to disturb me.

I had wanted to call her Peg, but thought it might provoke the displeasure of my mother's Scottish friend, Peggy Bush. One day when Peggy and mother were gossiping and knitting over tea, I asked, "Peggy, what are

some common names of sheep dogs in Scotland? I want
to give my pup a good, sensible, Scottish name." She
thought a bit, took a sip of tea, peered up over her knitting, and said, "'Ow aboot Bess? A good many farmers
name their dogs Bess. It's a good name, that."

So Bess it was. Anyway, Johnny Lee had said it, that
she was a queen. And since Elizabeth I had been my
favorite queen in all history, well, that's what I would
call her. I suppose it shall be the everlasting lot of European aristocracy to have all manner of dogs, cats, and
horses named after them.

Not long after I acquired Bess, a young patrician An-
gora cat of my mother's acquaintance produced, quite
suddenly and without explanation, a sizable litter of kittens. As you can imagine, the blessed event was somewhat awkward for her family. Because of her tender
age and heretofore unblemished reputation, the whole affair was hushed up and the kittens disposed of as dis-
creetly as possible. Out of respect for the family, we
agreed to adopt one of the foundlings, and with a somewhat sacrificial attitude, took a female.

She, like Bess, had long, fine, white hair (which had a
peculiar magnetism to the clothing of visitors), a few gray
spots, and large yellow eyes. When she and Bess slept
together, one could not be sure where dog ended and cat
began. We called her "Mehitabel" after Don Marquis'
saucy wanton in *archy and mehitabel*.

Those early days of kittenhood and puppyhood were
passed carelessly, save for the mild but necessary disci-
plinary measures occasioned by the theft and entangle-
ment of a skein of yarn or the chewing to bits of a tan-
talizing house shoe. Punishment generally took the form
of a severe lecture. Bess would droop her head and tuck

her tail between her legs, promising to mend her ways. When supper was ready, my mother would call, "Here, kitty, kitty," and Bess would dash around the corner of the house, reappearing shortly with her teeth firmly clamped over Mehitabel's head, the rest of the kitten dangling limply and helplessly from her mouth. This caused me much concern and anxiety, lest I would wake some morning to find a headless cat on the floor. Mehitabel, however, seemed to take it in her stride and, at times, positively enjoy it.

When I left home to seek my fortune in California, I had been forced to abandon Bess and Mehitabel to a foster home—namely that very ranch where I would, a year or so later, be making my own home. Bess, a pampered young female, soon learned what it meant to be a dog. She took instinctively to working cattle, with little or no tutelage. Mehitabel, stranded ten miles from town with a new litter of babies to feed and care for, was less than satisfied with her bucolic surroundings. Disliking the strange atmosphere of the country, she immediately scurried, with her little ones following, to a stack of old railroad ties and set up temporary housekeeping back in the dark recesses of the pile. No amount of coaxing or wheedling could convince her that the camp was her home. Sam Roanhorse patiently walked a couple of hundred paces from the bunkhouse every evening to leave her food where she could get it. Only after dark would she creep out of her den to hunt field mice for her growing offspring.

And then one day, after surveying the litter and assuring herself that they were capable of self-preservation, she left. O Mehitabel! All softness, femininity, capriciousness, and affection on the surface; all courage, stamina, stealth, and perseverance within. Who knows what dangers, hardships, hunger, and loneliness you suffered in your hazardous attempt to return to the warmth and familiarity of your old home? Hiding in culverts, abandoned fox holes, taking cover under rocks in the daytime, she traveled at night, now running desperately from a coyote or lynx, now dodging the airborne attacks of owls. By her wits and hunting skill, she managed to survive, stopping to rest now and then near a water hole or dirt tank.

Poor Mehitabel! Did her heart not bleed those lonely star-filled nights for the young ones she left behind? No, it did not. To be honest (and that is our sincere endeavor), we must inform you that that most admirable of all instincts—the maternal—was, through some oversight of Nature, sadly but undoubtedly lacking. Do not (heaven forbid!) let me imply that she was not a good mother. She was an excellent provider, but more from a cattish sense of duty than from adoration of her darlings.

Mehitabel has always been one of those devastating female creatures who possesses beauty, cunning, affection, courage, and boldness, who is both formidable and charming; who is one moment rubbing persuasively against your ankles, and the next, digging her claws painfully into your knees. She is her own master, forsaking her social responsibilities for her own pleasures and, when she is so inclined, throwing caution to the fickle wind. In short, she has always regarded her kittens as more of a burden than a blessing and, without question, an impediment to her amorous and adventurous spirit.

One day, about six weeks after Mehitabel's departure into the great unknown, my mother chanced to see a stray cat in her yard and began throwing rocks at it and pronouncing "Scat!" "Shoo!" among other epithets generally reserved for dismissing unwanted felines. The scrawny, mangy, grayish, disreputable-looking cat was strangely persistent. When a flying missile narrowly missed her ear, she only ducked and mewed pathetically. After repeated bombardments she ran into the shed and hid. Not until that evening, when Mother looked out the window and saw the battered alley cat perched on top of a high clothesline pole in the yard, calmly surveying the neighborhood, did she recognize her old friend. She called, "Kitty, kitty." Mehitabel leaped grandly off her pole and ran to the back door, purring, mewing, and rubbing against her. At last she entered the house to begin her long convalescence.

Bess had, by this time, firmly established her position at the ranch, which was that of undisputed mistress of all she surveyed. Bess was born to the purple and carried herself like a queen wherever she went. Sam Roanhorse had been good to her, getting up two or three times during the night to let her outdoors if she felt pressed to bark at a passing coyote. He treated her royally—to some extent because of an old Navajo belief that white animals are associated with good luck and have power to dispel evil, but largely because Bess naturally demanded royal treatment.

When Cooney drove anyplace in his jeep, Bess was with him, sitting straight as a ramrod in the cab beside him, eyes forward, carrying herself with the dignity, sobriety, and demeanor imputable to her position with Jeffers Cattle Company. The populace would turn to stare and smile as the green and white cab-over jeep bounced down the streets of Holbrook—Cooney wearing his battered work hat, a cigar clamped firmly between his white teeth; Bess riding calmly beside her chauffeur, like some old deposed queen peering out at the common people above an enormous white fur collar. So self-possessed and decorous is she that it is as difficult now to imagine Bess as a puppy as it is to imagine Queen Victoria as a baby.

Although Bess is, by virtue of her good manners, courteous to everyone, there is no secret about who are her special friends. When a man comes to the house, Bess is polite after she has dutifully barked at the car. If he is wearing boots and smells like manure she is more friendly than usual. But at the arrival of a woman, especially one of her old friends, she is beside herself with joy, twisting from side to side, making gurgling noises deep down in her throat, carrying on a dog-like conversation as if she were fairly bursting with the news of what has happened since last they met. At the quiet announcement, "Bess, Mary's coming" or "Jesse" or "Mother," she pricks up her ears, bounds to the the door, and runs out the gate, looking hopefully down the road.

Although she rather dislikes and distrusts small active boys between three and eight years old, Bess has always been fond of baby things. Like some doting maiden aunt, she seems to feel that she is far more capable of caring for newborn things than their mothers are. If some friend brings a baby to the house, Bess watches it nervously, running from it to me if it should cry. Upon hearing the news, "We have a newborn baby calf, Bess," she dashes out the door and runs straightaway to the back corral, poking her nose in the sheds and pens until she finds it. Once a tiny chick nearly drowned in the drinking tub. She sat uneasy and still, licking it now and then until it peeped and walked off.

Bess is my dog around the house. When there is any work to be done, she is Cooney's. Bess, like myself, is not by nature an early riser. During our hardest work—branding or roundup—we often have to wake her in the morning lest she sleep until eight o'clock or later. When she does wake up, she blinks, yawns, stretches leisurely, and wobbles out to the kitchen looking like some tousled woman-about-town the morning after a wild party. She stands, bleary-eyed, looking down distastefully at the meat or egg on her plate. She belches, swallows hard, smacks her mouth as if a stale taste lingered there, and shuffles back to the fireplace, flopping down for a few minutes of meditation. Only after she is thoroughly awake can she eat her breakfast. By then, she is ready for action and begs Cooney to go to work by putting her head on his knee and whining.

Bess's eyes are unlike the eyes of any animal I have ever seen. Blue and clear as willowware china, they can plead, condemn, adore, or tease with equal facility. One moment they are begging for a morsel at the dinner table; the next, they narrow with jealousy at the petting of a cat. Her eyebrows raise and lower in response to emotions of anger, fear, resentment, curiosity, affection, playfulness, concern, or disapproval.

The only people I have ever heard argue that animals are stupid are people who have not lived around animals. A working dog's value to a person depends upon his instincts, temperament, intelligence, and desire to please his master. These elements of personality vary as much as they do in humans. For those who live in the country and have the opportunity to study animals at close range, they are almost as fascinating as the study of human nature.

Bess is something of a displaced but effective aristocrat. As John Holmes expresses very well in his book on Border Collies:

There are, of course different types of intelligence in dogs
as in humans. There is the super intelligent "highbrow";
sensitive, often touchy but, in the right hand, quite brilliant. Then there is the level-headed "lowbrow"; not so
brilliant but with much more common sense. I hardly
need emphasize that conditions on the general farm are
rarely congenial to highbrows on two legs or four.

Even highbrows, providing they have sufficient amount of
gumption, can live and work efficiently in the country.

There have been, among naturalists, psychologists, zo-
ologists, farmers, and sheep herders, many arguments concerning the ability of animals to think as opposed to obey-
ing only natural instincts. Again, most observing people
who have lived every day among animals are usually on
the positive side of the argument.

The first time I was really convinced of Bess's ability
to reason was the day Cooney and I went into Holbrook
for some lumber. We had bought several one-by-eight
boards of knotty pine which rested at an angle, braced
against the front seat and protruding out the open rear
window of the station wagon. On the rough country road,
the boards rattled and bounced, producing an unnerving
amount of noise. Nothing was more distressing to Bess's
sensitive ears than loud, irritating noises. She turned
her head to stare grimly at the boards next to her, looking at us from time to time with great displeasure. Putting her head on Cooney's shoulder she began to whine.

Cooney is accustomed to talking to her when they are
driving—about everything from the condition of the cattle
to world politics. More for her comfort than her elucida-
tion, he said, "Well, Bess, if that noise bothers you, why
don't you sit on those boards until we get home?" We
drove on, idly talking, when suddenly we realized that

the banging and clattering had stopped. Simultaneously, we turned our heads to see what had happened to them. Bess had crawled, not without difficulty, upon the lumber which lay at almost a forty-five-degree angle. She was sitting triumphantly but precariously on the middle board, her front legs resting on the two outside boards. She rode them all the way back to the ranch, a distance of five or six miles, her jaw set in profound determination, the corners of her mouth turned down grimly.

As all women who are great ladies seem to have a touch of bitchiness in them in order to survive the particular society in which they happen to exist, all great bitches seem to have a dash of the lady in them, which distinguishes them from other dogs. Whatever the quality, it demands respect. Every cowboy who has ever worked for us has, without prompting, said, "Excuse me, Bess," whenever he passed her, stepped over her or, of necessity, dislodged her from a reclining place. People who know her seem to think of her as somehow transcending dogdom. When we stop at the post office in town and greet friends, they often ask, "And how's Bess?" with genuine concern usually reserved for children, mothers, or rich uncles.

Bess is inordinately fond of riding in the jeep. She will listen, slyly, in the morning, and at the least hint that Cooney or I are going somewhere, will ask to go outside and stand guard by the jeep or car until we are ready to leave. If there is some obstacle, like poison baits set for wild dogs at the tanks, Cooney makes Bess stay at home. All he need say is "You can't go, Bess. You must stay home." She hangs her head, drags her feet back to the yard, and slumps down on the ground, sulking and pouting until he is out of sight.

If we are planning a vacation—perhaps two or three days away from the ranch—we cautiously refrain from mentioning it in Bess's presence. How she knows, I can't imagine, but if we let one word slip about going away, she grows touchy and anxious at our every move, reluctant to let us out of her sight. When at last we take our suitcases down from the shelf, she knows her worst suspicions have been confirmed. She hates staying home when we are gone and often refuses to eat. If we tell her that we will be gone a few days and will be back on a certain night, she is content to sleep with Sam until the night we are to return. Then, suddenly restless, she will lie down outside the yard fence, watching the road far into the night until our car lights appear and she runs down the road to meet us.

Cooney complains that Bess cannot or will not open gates for him, but I think that he should open the gates and let her drive, since she is renowned for the exercise of caution. She watches the road like a driving instructor with a new pupil. Sometimes, to tease her, Cooney will leave the jeep in low gear longer than is necessary. Bess looks down at the gear shift, frowns, cocks her head, and then looks up at Cooney as if to say, "What's wrong with you, you blockhead?"

At first I had difficulty navigating our ranch roads and would often pass up a turnoff when I was taking lunch to the men. On these occasions, if Bess went with me, I would say, "Bess, you *know* I can't remember where the road to White Tower is. Tell me when it's time to turn." We would bump along, Bess dozing in the seat beside me, until we arrived at a distance of a quarter of a mile or so from the road, at which point Bess would jump up, look out of the window, sniff the air, them look back at me.

One summer day a car appeared, roaring down the Heber Road at abnormal speed, churning up a cloud of dust. The perpetrator of this atmospheric disturbance was none other than my mother. Breathlessly, she related a tale of scandal and woe. Mehitabel had, in spite of solemn advice, stern lectures on Chastity, discourses on the Sinfulness of bringing Unwanted Children into the world, repeated attempts to confine her to her quarters for the duration of her madness, produced at regular intervals over the years, litter after litter of fine, strapping kittens, apparently without a tear of contrition or regret unless it were for a certain loss of freedom which accompanied her maternal condition. Never able to tear all the little ones away from Mehitabel's fond bosom (although Mehitabel, if the truth were told, would not have protested more than was necessary for the sake of propriety) and reluctant to give them up to families she harbored the least doubt about, Mother had kept at least one kitten from each litter.

Somehow the situation had gone out of control. The supply of kittens exceeded, by an embarrassing margin, the demand. Perhaps no one in the past century has afforded more positive proof of the theories of that eminent economist, T. R. Malthus, that the population tends to multiply faster than its means of subsistence, although there is some skepticism about whether or not the proving of Malthusian theories was foremost in Mehitabel's mind when they were enacted.

My father, being a well-read man, foresaw the consequences of prolonged behavior of this sort. Although my parents had not yet disposed of the family jewels and silver to buy cat food, the time was drawing perilously near. Already thirteen of Mehitabel's hardy descendants were being fed and sheltered in the laundry shed. My father, who was a practical man and, I am loath to say, something of a hater-of-cats as well, sat down one day at his desk and began some computations. After a time, he arose, thrust several pages of pertinent figures before Mother's eyes, and announced that, at the present rate of production, Mehitabel and her female descendants would, in three years' space, have a total of 10,050 kittens. Faced with this terrifying prospective, he set down an ultimatum to Mother which, very briefly, was: "Either the cats go or I go." It must have been a difficult decision, but Mother at last consented to a sort of mass felinicide after Father had assured her that the process would be as fast and painless as possible.

Remembering all of Mehitabel's hardships, wanderings, and tribulations; her fierce and courageous stand against the neighborhood dogs who now trembled at her approach, her civic-minded attitude toward the problems of rodent eradication, her loyalty to her little ones, one could not help overlooking her numerous indiscretions and, to be perfectly honest, eying her blithe and reckless *affaires du coeur* with some envy.

Mother and I embarked immediately upon our desperate mission to save Mehitabel. "Hurry, Bess," I shouted. "We've got to go rescue Mehitabel from the jaws of death!" At the word "Mehitabel," Bess leaped into the car. As we sped into Holbrook, Bess held her head out the window, ears flying in the wind, eyes alert for whatever dangers we might encounter.

Our errand of mercy was a success. With immense relief we found Mehitabel not only surviving this atrocious

plot against her life but apparently enjoying a quiet nap
on her favorite pillow near my father, who was reading
in his armchair with a deceptive look of innocence on his
face, the other cats being nowhere in sight.

There was, perhaps, a glimmer of regret in her yellow
eyes as she looked out the rear window of the car toward
her old trysting places, the backyard fences, the high pole
from which she scanned the block for stray dogs to do
battle with. But this time Mehitabel was content to stay
at the ranch with her childhood friend, Bess, and myself.
Oh, there were moments when she longed wistfully for
her old days of youthful abandon, but middle age had
quieted her rebellious high spirits and she spent her hours
dozing peacefully in a bright spot of sunshine on the rug
or curled up in an Apache basket on the coffee table before the fire. When she felt the need for solitude, she
would jump up on the top shelf of my closet, hide in the

folds of a sweater and, like T. S. Eliot's famous cats, would meditate on her "ineffable, effable, effanineffable, deep and inscrutable, singular name."

When the old fighting spirit welled up once more within her breast, she would lurk in the shadows and pounce upon one of the ranch cats, all of whom had been at one time her own dear kittens. Now she held nothing but contempt for them and desired only that they leave her alone. Woe to the unsuspecting cat who chanced to pass her way when a black mood was upon her. She would leap halfway across the room, landing on her prey, howling, squalling, and hissing like a hundred banshees. With fur flying in all directions, she clawed and scratched and bit until she got it all out of her system or until, by some stroke of good fortune, they escaped her clutches.

Mehitabel had not been at the ranch long when a rather macabre incident occurred. We had been, for a time, in possession of a sinister-looking pitch-black cat named Schwarz, a slinky, cold-blooded cat of somber disposition. It was his custom to nap in one of the dark nests in the chicken house, a habit I never seemed to remember when I was gathering eggs. To my continual horror, I would grope around for eggs and come suddenly face to face with two slanting yellow eyes peering at me through the darkness. One day Schwarz sickened with some mysterious feline ailment and, by nightfall, was quite stiff and dead. We buried him down in the arroyo, with some evil presentiments on my part.

About a week later, Cooney, Bess, and I were returning home late in the evening from a drive around the ranch. As we came in the gate, I caught a glimpse of a coal-black cat with yellow eyes looking out the window. It disappeared in an instant. For a moment I thought I had seen a grisly inhabitant of the spirit world. Hesitantly, I opened the door, "Cooney! What's that black cat doing in our house?" I said. "How would I know?" said Cooney. The ghostly cat ran out the door with Bess in hot pursuit. When they reached the loading chute, the cat stopped, boxed Bess's ears, and ran back to the house mewing plaintively. She came to me and I stroked her back, there being something familiar in her voice. My hand, when I withdrew it, was covered with soot. "It's Mehitabel!" I cried. From the tip of her plume-like tail to her formerly pink nose, she was black. Black as the ace of spades. She had been cavorting in the fireplace after a bird who had flown into the chimney and was thus transformed to her present sorry state. "Oh, well, what can you expect?" said Cooney. "All the women these days are dyeing their hair."

We must pause, now, for a brief introduction to another cat, who may or may not intrude his presence later on in the book. A son of Mehitabel's first litter was Charlie, gray, short-haired, and unexceptional in appearance. But, as with humans, appearances are sometimes deceptive. When Charlie was young and virile he enjoyed nothing as much as gazing at his reflection in our bedroom mirror. For a quarter of an hour or more he would sit on the bureau, preening and admiring himself—now looking coyly over his shoulder; now staring himself boldly in the eye. But vanity retreated as age advanced. After he became a battle-scarred veteran, he forsook his innocent pleasures and acquired a more menacing one.

O how it pains me to relate this, but, since the terrible truth must some day come to light, I may as well admit it now: Charlie is a peecat. We were not aware of his affliction (for like the alcoholic or dope addict, he is more to be pitied than censured) until the surprise visit of an old friend. The gentleman, whom we shall call Kenneth Kalb—we shall call him that because that is his name—was, as usual, faultlessly attired in a new pair of dark brown trousers. He entered the living room, sat down in a comfortable chair, crossed his legs, and began a conversation with us, not once, if my memory serves me correctly, making so much as an equivocal remark concerning cats. Charlie listened politely, then sauntered across the room, backed up to Kenneth's pants leg, raised his tail, and let loose a stream which trickled from the knee to the cuff of Kenneth's new trousers. Enough cannot be said for the poise and *savoir-faire* with which Kenneth met this distressing situation. Not only does he still speak to us, but it is to his everlasting credit that he visits us occasionally and in a most magnanimous manner inquires after the health and well-being of our notorious peecat. Unfortunately, that was only the beginning of Charlie's feats as a peecat, which are marvelous not only for their slyness, but for the frequency of their recurrence.

Charlie is sturdy, masculine, and tough, walking with the swagger of a military policeman. When he is out prowling around for excitement, he emits low guttural "meows" and squints his eyes with unfaltering male egotism. If I am out walking with the dogs, he trots along behind, preferring their company to that of his fellow cats, whom he considers his inferiors. He was unquestionably ruler of the ranch cats until Mehitabel's appearance. Fearless, he will not back down from anything less than the feminine harangues of Mehitabel. When she feels affectionate, she calls him, wheedles, mews, and rubs against his broad shoulders. If she feels capricious, she teases him. But when one of her black moods is upon her, poor Charlie is helpless against this petite but formidable adversary. She sits up and boxes his ears mercilessly, while he merely humps his back, ducks his head, and takes it.

Whatever else you may say about Charlie Cat, you cannot accuse him of being niggardly. If his luck in hunting is good, he will proudly drag and carry a large jackrabbit all the way home and deposit it on the front porch as a feast for the other ranch cats, proving not only his generosity, but his prowess in hunting.

The cats and dogs, like married couples, somehow resolve their differences and forget the quarrels of the day when the darkness and silence and isolation of night draw over the country. In the warmth of the kitchen, amidst the comforting smells of meat frying and potatoes cooking, they all eat together on a piece of doubled newspaper spread on the kitchen floor. And I hope, while the tea kettle comes to a boil, that none of the ladies I know with sanitary houses done in French Provincial or Danish Modern will happen to drop in at that particular moment. Just before Christmas, Cooney and I had coffee with a woman who was baking cookies. Her daughter found a cat hair on one of the cookies and the mother hastily threw it into the garbage can with a shudder. If I threw away all the food that had cat hairs on it, we'd starve. In fact, I may invent a new casserole some day—"*Chile colorado enchiladas con queso e pelo del gato.*" (Red chili enchiladas with cheese and hair of the cat.)

The newest member of our ménage is Annie, a young blue-and-white Australian Shepherd. A hearty sheepman who is always embroiled in a friendly rivalry with Cooney gave her to us. For the first few weeks, the squirming, whining, tumbling, shoe-demolishing pup almost caused Bess to have a nervous breakdown. Bess hoped desperately that she was just visiting and that her real owners would soon come to claim her. Eventually she resigned herself to Annie's status as a permanent resident with the same degree of enthusiasm Catherine of Aragon must have shown for Anne Boleyn.

To Bess's amazement and relief, the slim-bodied, long-legged, awkward pup continued to grow until she reached proportions equal to Bess's, which marked something of a turning point in their relations. While Bess still takes bones and playthings away from Annie when nobody is watching and snarls at her more flagrant breaches of etiquette, she has acquiesced to sleep beside her at night and ride next to her in the jeep, crowding as much as she dares without reprisals from us.

Annie shows promise of being as good a worker as Bess. She is so eager to learn we can hardly restrain her. When she was only five months old, she went with us on short drives and helped instinctively with the cattle. When the ewes finish lambing, Annie may be able to start working with them and earning her room and board. Sheep or no sheep, she is here to stay. The intelligence and honesty with which she meets your eyes, her bold and gay manner of walking, the alertness of her ears, and her affectionate nature have endeared her to me. Now Bess condescends to play with her when they are outside together. On the mornings when Cooney leaves them home, they trot down the fence line, taking inventory of all the bones they have buried and sniffing to make certain no stray dog or coyote has made off with them.

Annie is a good dog who minds cheerfully when she clearly understands what is expected of her. But there are moments when she, like all of us, gives in to temptation, risking punishment for the pleasure of the moment.

Such a mood came upon her not long ago. In the chill of the hours before daylight, she awoke, looked longingly at Cooney and myself sleeping soundly in the warm depths of our feather bed, and felt lonesome. Surreptitiously, she got up, listened to make sure we were asleep, jumped softly onto the bed and wedged herself, by degrees, between us, where she promptly fell asleep herself.

When I woke up that morning, I thought Cooney had pushed me close to the edge of the bed. Half-awake, I pulled on the blankets which barely covered me. I could feel Cooney's warm breath on my neck. He began to make a peculiar sucking noise so irritating that I decided to wake him up. When a jab with my elbow did no apparent good, I turned my head and stared into the blissfully sleeping face of gentle Annie, her head resting on the pillow, her whiskers twitching from a dream and one of her paws affectionately resting on my shoulder.

Annie continues to grow on fresh warm milk, scraps from the table, and cat food. In fact, she will eat anything except dog food, an eccentricity that we gladly overlook. If we are having a drink before dinner, Annie asks for an ice cube, so that she can participate in the social hour. If, because of her tender age, she forgets her manners, becoming rude and wild, we say, "Bess, make Annie behave herself." Bess walks over, curls her upper lip, and stands menacingly by until Annie settles down.

On cattle drives, Bess always watched Cooney constantly, trying to anticipate his next move. When we separated on a drive, Bess went with me, not because she looked to me for commands, but because she knew I needed her. While she obeyed Cooney, she preferred to use her own judgment with me, treating me with respectful solicitude, looking up at me now and then as if to say,

"Don't worry, I know more about these cattle than you do."

I use the past tense because Bess has, of her own free will, retired from the hazardous, strenuous, and thankless work expected of a cow dog. When she was about nine years old, her legs and feet began to feel the strain of having run hundreds of miles in intense heat and cold, blinding snow, rain, or windstorms, over sharp rocks and through deep sand. After a grueling day, helping me roust cows out of the brush and then working back and forth for three or four hours in the drags on a cattle drive, her legs ached and her feet were raw and swollen. Last spring, after helping us on some of the shorter drives, her good sense presided over her inbred passion for working cattle and one day she quit—gracefully but positively.

While we were saddling the horses, she came out to the corral to watch, as usual. She trotted out through the corrals with us and then she sat down in the middle of the gate, watched us wistfully until we were far down the fence line and with her head held down, turned and walked slowly back toward the house and yard. I kept looking back to see if she would change her mind, but she never appeared and I had to wipe away the stream of tears that trickled down my cheek at the pang of losing my old companion and protector.

I have read many stories about faithful Australian or British sheep dogs who preferred to work until they could no longer drag themselves around, or until they dropped dead in the execution of their duty. Bess simply thought it best to quit while she was ahead. No amount of coaxing or calling has ever induced her to follow us horseback since the day she made up her mind to retire. Often, if we were going for a short ride, I would try my best to entice her to follow, just for exercise, but she would give me a sort of look which meant, "You may go if you like, but as far as those cross-country marathons are concerned, I've had it!"

Sometimes, if I begin walking out to bring in the sheep or pen a cow we want in the corral, Bess is delighted to follow along and help me drive them in, but at last, she is always pleased to return to the house, flump down in her own corner by the fire, and have another short snooze before dinner.

Bess is ten years old now, a bit arthritic, deaf, with a sudden portliness brought on by her retirement which results in a double chin and snoring at night. She is at times rather grouchy and impatient with young Annie, but is still vain about her appearance, doing her best to stay snow-white and beautiful. She moves about the house with queenly authority, greeting guests when they come and bidding them goodnight when they leave.

Every Christmas for the past seven years we have given her a package of English walnuts, gift-wrapped and tied with ribbon. On last Christmas Eve, when we returned from Midnight Mass, she wiggled her tail impatiently and stood with her double chins resting on the edge of the coffee table, begging. Cooney sat on the hearth, warming himself. "All right, Bess, if you want your present now, you can go get it," he said. She waddled over to the stack of packages, sniffed a few times, picked hers out of the middle of the pile, and dragged it onto the floor.

"It's all right. Open it," I said. She tore off the ribbon, opened the paper and lay contentedly on the Navajo rug, cracking walnuts and picking out the meat, Annie watching with large round eyes until she learned how to eat them, too. When we went to bed, Bess stretched, plodded into the bedroom, and plunked down heavily on her quilt beside our bed. I reached down to hug her furry neck once more before we went to sleep. My heart, filled with old, fond sentiments, beat strong and I thought to myself, "Oh, dog, dog! You are mine and I love you."

8

Winter

On some November morning every year since we have been married, I wake up, throw my wool robe around me, hurry outside for an armload of kindling to start the fire, and shiver at the fresh chill and smell of wetness coming off the wind. A hundred miles to the northwest stand San Francisco Peaks, three crowned, like a Holy Trinity of Nature, covered with a white mantle of new snow—snow which will remain there until May. Winter in northern Arizona has come.

The long-tailed housebirds who build their stringy nests along the terrace roof beams have gone now. So have the bullbats who swoop low and cry out on summer nights. The water-loving kildeers are silent, if not departed. Winter belongs to the sparrows—the homely little sparrow families, chattering and quarrelsome, who fight to defend their claim to a warm space under the eaves. Flocks of dark snow-birds descend on the ground picking up bits of grain and hay that the cattle and horses could not get. At some alarm signal telling of the imminent approach of Charlie or Mehitabel, they rise in a fluttering, frightened mass, seemingly suspended in air, until their erratic flight takes them to the other side of the barn.

The winter after we were married, flocks of blue birds swarmed into northern Arizona and stayed for several months until they had consumed most of the juniper berries which were very thick that year. Every day we would find dozens of dead birds who had drowned in the drinking tubs and storage tanks. Just trying to keep our water fit to drink was a serious problem that winter.

One year a stray female mallard lighted on the duck pond for a free night's board and lodging. Not unlike other travelers in Arizona, she found the climate and food to her liking and decided to stay the winter. When Cooney noticed her, she was quite at home with the ten tame mallards who had taken her to their hearts, no doubt enthralled by her tales of exotic adventures. She was, for all her travels, a plain, timid creature, smaller and darker brown than our ducks. When the flock waddled from the duck pond to the yard for their evening feeding, she would take great care to stay in the middle of the bunch. Like an uninvited guest at some exclusive social event, the moment she felt curious eyes on her, she would duck her head and squat down low in order to be as inconspicuous as possible.

For a month or so one winter there was a flamingo living down at Woodruff Well. We would drive up on him while he stood, meditating on one leg, like a Yoga, surrounded by the tules and tamarisks. His great yellow eyes would stare in annoyance at our intrusion, then he would snap out of his trance and fly off in a huff. His great wings lifted him slowly up from the water and held him aloft, where he circled until we left him in peace once more.

By mid-November, the cattle and horses have grown shaggy coats as a protection against the bitter cold of our windy, mile-high plateau. The drakes are in their bright feathers, sporting turquoise rings around their necks. Jack the noisy gander wears pearl gray and white plumage; the down on his breast has grown soft and thick. Bess and Mehitabel shed in ever-increasing quantities, providing employment and profit for Tom Burns the dry cleaner.

The winter air is crystalline. Often you can see gray smoke rising from the lumber mill at Flagstaff, ninety miles away. At night, beneath clouds of stars, you shiver in the still, penetrating cold and breathe the sweet pungence of cedar wood burning in the fireplace.

The dishes are washed. The smell of supper half-lingers in the living room. For a little while peace fills the house, drawing dogs, cats, and humans to her quiet breast. We sit before the fire, reading, until our limbs grow too heavy and our eyes too drowsy to bear wakefulness longer. With great effort, we climb into bed, pull up the quilts, and drop off into heavy sleep.

Round about Thanksgiving time, a snowstorm usually drifts in. If we are lucky, it brings a heavy, wet snow which melts in the noonday sun, depositing moisture deep in the ground. Or it may bring a howling, blinding, wind-driven dry snow which is shifted and piled up into high drifts by fierce gales out of the north. Then, if the temperature drops below freezing and remains there, the top layer hardens to an icy crust and the cattle must survive on whatever brush protrudes through the snow. Some years the tumbleweeds which have matured break away from their moorings and roll in armies across the desert, piling up against a barbwire fence until they push the fence over with their combined weight. Tumbleweeds, when they are wet with snow, become soft and make good feed for cattle. In the old days ranchers sometimes stacked, salted, and pressed them down to feed, like hay.

If the summer rains have been scanty and feed is scarce, we must start feeding cattle by the first of December. Feeding was always a problem on the immense ranches of the West. A favorite feed with many ranchers is salt mixed with cottonseed meal. Salt is added to feed to control its consumption and prevent cattle from being poisoned by eating too much protein. But salt and the finely ground meal blow out of the troughs almost as soon as they are poured into them in this country. In recent years, blocks have been developed by most feed companies as a supplemental feed for range cattle. They weigh about thirty-three pounds and are easily hauled and scattered so that all of the cattle have a chance to lick them. If feed is poured out into troughs, the strongest cattle often get all the feed and the weak ones grow weaker. One winter when we were without any help, Cooney averaged driving about one hundred miles a day in the jeep, putting out feed at all the watering places.

Another winter chore is breaking ice at the dirt tanks and drinking tubs. There are three tubs around the house. When the temperature drops below zero, the ice is often three or four inches thick. If it is not cut every day and thrown off the tubs, the water freezes down to the bottom. While the winter nights are cold, the days are usually

sunny and bright so that there are often no more than
two or three weeks out of the year that we must cut ice.

We had two very bad winters when, for almost a month,
an icy, thick, white, miserable fog clung to the Little
Colorado River Valley and enveloped the country for four
or five miles on both sides. The temperature hovered near
zero for two weeks. Every morning the horses and cattle
would come in for water like hoary ghosts, their hair stiff
and white with frost, their breath steaming out of their
nostrils. The trees and fences were frost-covered and the
weight of the ice broke telephone lines and snapped wire
fences.

Almost everything that goes wrong chooses January to do it in. One winter when Cooney had gone after some horses his brother was driving up from Casas Grandes to the Mexican border, everything began happening at once. The day Cooney left, Sam felt a sudden urge to go to town, leaving me with all the chores to do. As if that weren't enough, the water lines to the house and drinking tubs froze and the big steel storage tank cracked and began to leak. I drove to town that night in a mild fury, and with reluctance called Cooney in Columbus, New Mexico.

"Honey," I said sweetly.

"What's happened now?" said Cooney.

"Sam's in town. The water lines are all frozen and the steel storage tank burst."

There was a long silence before he spoke. "Jo," he said, "call King Pearce and ask him to get Sam and take him home. Tomorrow morning tell him to dig up the water lines and build fires over them. Never mind the storage tank. If it's not leaking too fast, it will last until I get home. We may have to pour a new concrete bottom in it."

Sam built fires until the whole ranch was engulfed in black smoke. He would come in the kitchen from time to time looking as if he'd been working in the pits all day. We had decided to shovel some dirt into the storage tank to stem the leaking as much as possible. I was up on a ladder dumping in bucketsful of dirt that Sam handed me when I noticed the saddle horses were all huddled up together with their heads down right beside the yard fence. Then I heard a shrill "Waaaaa" and ran over as fast as I could. A ewe had lambed next to the fence and all eleven saddle horses were standing directly over the tiny, wet, wobbling creature. One misstep and the lamb

would have been no more. Holding my breath, I shooed
the horses off and grabbed up the lamb, holding it in front
of its mother to coax her into the yard where she would
be safe. With all the other trouble, lambing had begun.

When the ewes began lambing out, it was down to six-
teen below zero at night. Sam watched them closely and
as soon as a ewe began to make bag, he kept her close to
home. Often he would stay up all night looking after a
lamb that was weak or had chilled down, or get up
several times at night to feed a weak lamb with con-
densed milk and water or to warm it by the fire. He would
go out in the corral with his flashlight during the night
to check and see if anything had been born. When lambs
are newborn they can stand very little cold and die almost immediately if exposed to harsh weather conditions.
As soon as they are dry and have some warm milk in
them, they can stand freezing temperatures.

My sheep herd came into existence a few years after
we were married. Several large sheep outfits move their
bands from the Salt River Valley up across the Mogollon
Rim and into northern Arizona every year to their summer ranges. They cross parts of our ranch, going back and
forth. Occasionally a few head of sheep stray from the
bunch. One fall, two ewes and a yearling wether wandered into the ranch. Their owners were, by this time,
too far away to come back after them, so we kept them,
intending to fatten them for the deep freeze. As Cooney
and I drove in one evening, he said, "Well, this is as good
a time as any to butcher those sheep, I guess."

I was horrified. "No, we can't eat them now," I said.
"Let's just keep them for pets."

Gunnar Thude, the big Danish sheepherder whose summer range borders our ranch, sent his foreman, King

Pearce, over with a buck that summer. His Paradise Sheep Company bought good bucks, usually registered ones that cost from two hundred to five hundred dollars. They kept them until they were three or four years old then sold them or cut their throats. My first buck was a broad, surly Rambouillet with curling horns. He caught Bess off guard one day and tossed her against the barn with his horns. This incident destroyed any enthusiasm for sheep which might have been bred into Bess. She helps drive them sometimes but with an obvious lack of pleasure. Cooney's aversion to live sheep was exceeded only by his aversion to cooked ones. He has nothing personal against them, only his ingrained cattleman's dislike of the ancient rivals for grazing land. We carried on, under the same roof, a sort of miniature range war. The longer I had sheep, the better I liked them. I like the strong acid smell of sheep and the feel of their wool. There is probably nothing in the whole world as pretty and soft as a baby lamb. Finally, in spite of himself, Cooney became attached to them.

It seems nobody bothered to tell the ewes that they were no longer in the Valley of the Sun, and they went on blithely having their lambs in below-zero weather. We had lambs everywhere—in the bunkrooms, and in the chicken house, with the emergency cases bedded down in my kitchen. When a lamb is chilled down, I fill the bathroom lavatory with warm water and soak him until he is warm, then I dry him off with a warm towel and put him in front of the fire. We had a dogie lamb once who was not only half-frozen, but premature. I held it in my arms and rubbed it for about an hour until it stopped shaking. Then I put it by the kitchen heater, got up every two hours in the night, and fed it by bottle. It never looked like much, but I called it "Daisy" and it

came in and out of the house whenever I called it. When
it was half-grown I sold it to a man who wanted a pet
for his little girl. That fall, at the County Fair, I noticed
that a fat Rambouillet ewe had won a blue ribbon. There
were a lot of children standing around petting it. When
I looked at the name of the owner I realized that the
prize ewe was none other than the scrawny dogie called
"Daisy."

When we kept a lamb in the house, Bess was frantic.
She would run to the lamb and back to me whenever it
cried. Lambs sound almost exactly like babies when they
bleat. In January and February, the whole ranch echoes
with as many cries as a maternity ward.

We have a big black-nosed ewe who, last year, grew
to frightening proportions. Her sides bulged, her bag almost dragged the ground, and for the last ten days of
the waiting period, we had to help her up off the bed-
ground every morning. Then one day, without aid or as-
sistance, she produced three strapping babies. Her bag
was the size of old Holstein's and her teats were so swollen the lambs couldn't suck. I gathered my courage and
asked Cooney if he would mind milking out the sheep.
He gritted his teeth, hunkered down on the ground, and
in a spirit of dire humiliation began milking the ewe with
his thumb and forefinger. I held the lambs while he
milked into their mouths until they began eagerly tugging
at their mother's dugs, their tails twitching with each swal-
low of warm milk.

We were very fortunate, that bad winter of 1962–63,
to have saved all the lambs. Not so with the cattle. We
had a series of dry years, the range was in poor condition,
and we had to begin feeding in December. Between the
lack of feed, the severe cold, and attacks by packs of

wild dogs, we came out with about a 50 percent calf crop, which was just about enough to make ends meet.

On frosty winter nights, when we are tucked away in the feather bed, scarcely conscious of the yellow flicker cast by the fire on the wood-paneled walls, the silence is broken suddenly by the roar of a diesel engine, and the headlights of an approaching vehicle flash in the window. Though it be well past midnight, the big truck pulls up to the Butane tank, a corpulent man shuffles around in the sub-zero night, opening gauges, and begins pumping gas. It is Mr. Carter, the indomitable Bu-gas man, working eighteen or twenty hours a day to deliver propane to hundreds of people over the hundreds of square miles he serves.

I lie there in my warm bed feeling guilty, wondering if he has had his supper. Ranchers come and ranchers go, but the Bu-gas man goes on forever, braving ice, fog, mud, sand, barking dogs, stingy customers, amorous widows, roving livestock, leaky valves, and all manner of impediments to progress. And if there is a Heaven for Bu-gas Men, surely Mr. Carter will go there one day and be privileged to fly around with a pump nozzle in one hand and a statement in the other, nodding politely to all the ladies as he wafts past, smiling.

Since all of our appliances are gas, as well as our light plant, we consume vast quantities of the smelly stuff. Our 350-gallon tank needs refilling about once a month in the winter. There appears to be a physical law governing all Bu-gas tanks, and it may be stated thus: "Whenever the Bu-gas man goes past the ranch on his appointed rounds, the tank is full, but whenever he is two hundred miles away in the farthest reaches of the Navajo reservation, with the added provision that we are expecting company that very day, the tank is empty." I discovered this particular law one morning when I was preparing for the arrival of about forty cowbelles (cattlemen's wives), this being my first time as hostess. In a frenzy, I dashed into Holbrook, reported the tank was down below the red mark, and dashed back, hoping everyone liked their meat rare. Somehow the gas lasted through the coffee-making and dessert. No sooner had the last of the ladies departed and the last flame petered out than Mr. Carter drove up in a cloud of dust, his face very red from exertion and exasperation.

Even then, I imagined this event to be an isolated incidence and tossed it off as mere carelessness on my part. That was before the law once more took effect. Cooney was host for a Bishop's Committee meeting one evening at the church, which meant that I had to help cook dinner for thirteen men. Right in the middle of the roast beef, the gas began to sputter and pouf. I had to take the roast and rolls into Holbrook to finish cooking them.

This characteristic of our Bu-gas tank remained dormant for a year or so before venting its full fury on us. We had been to a cattlemen's meeting in Reno with Hack and Betsy Wiseman, who had bought our cattle that year. A blizzard struck and we drove back nearly all the way on solid ice. Our nerves were edgy and we were tired and hungry when we drove into the ranch. Instead of the refuge we expected from the coldest weather we had ever had, we were greeted with a cold house, no gas, no lights, no stove, no furnace, no hot water and, by morning, no water at all, as the pipes had frozen during the night. Betsy and I at once displayed an amazing skill at cooking in the fireplace. We slept in front of the fire, getting up every three hours to pile on more logs. Just be-

fore daylight, when the chill began to penetrate the
bottom quilt, we called on Bess and Mehitabel, who
obligingly came to the rescue by curling up on the bed
beside us. While the Bu-gas company takes the somewhat prejudiced view that I do not check the gauge often
enough, I am sure that these events are merely the result
of uncontrollable natural forces.

Throughout all these adversities, Mr. Carter has not
only retained his sanity but, more creditable still, his
good humor. When he delivers gas in the daytime, he
usually stops long enough for coffee, cookies, and a good
talk. I considered him, for a while, something of a private possession until I learned the truth: he stops for coffee and cookies with all his customers. I was ordering gas
one day at A. & B. Schuster's general mercantile store
from Mr. Lizitsky, the manager. "Please tell Bob Carter
that I'm out of gas and just baked a chocolate cake," I
said, by means of enticement. Mr. Lizitsky raised his eyebrows. "So I'd like to know what's going on here," he said.
"I get the *strangest* phone calls about Carter—from
women—all the time."

"You mean there are *other* women?" I asked.

"Everyone in Navajo County, I think. There was a
message on the bulletin board today from a woman in
Heber who said to tell Bob she needs some gas and left
a coconut cake in the refrigerator."

In spite of the rigorous competition, I still receive a
visitation every once in a while. Sometimes Walt Troxler
comes with Bob Carter. One winter day, when I was
going in to do the laundry, I left word with Sam for the
Bu-gas men to come in and help themselves. I had made
a *kügelhopf,* which is a special kind of German coffee
cake my grandmother used to make, with raisins and al-

monds, baked in a ring mold. They delivered the gas just about time for an afternoon coffee break, came in according to Sam's instructions, heated up the coffee, and sat down at the table for a thin slice of *kügelhopf*. It seems that Walt's family was Swiss and his grandmother had made *kügelhopf*, too, and it had been a long time between *kügelhopfs*, so to speak. Bob had another slice to go with the coffee that was left in his cup. When the coffee cup was empty there was more *kügelhopf*, and so it went, on and on. They fell to talking about various unrelated subjects and, as Walt reached for one last piece, his face turned red. "Carter," he said, "do you know what we did?"

"Mmpf," said Bob.

"We ate up all the coffee cake."

"Oh my gosh. Jo sure will be mad at us. You'll have to deliver gas next time. I'm scared to."

"Not me," says Walt.

Duty prevailed over nicety, however, and Mr. Carter greeted me about a month later with a sheepish grin on his kind face. "I was afraid to face you after we ate up all of your coffee cake that day," he said.

"I'm glad that you liked it well enough to eat it all," I said.

Mr. Carter shook his head and looked down. "Gosh. We were just like a couple of little kids. I guess we got carried away."

For many years he worked at a salary with no payment for overtime or for the repair and maintenance jobs he did on appliances, valves, and pipes. We would sit at the sunny kitchen table drinking coffee and I would ask him, "Why don't you take a vacation or at least slow down a little, Bob?"

"Look who's talking," he'd say. "You look tired. There's no use killing yourself, is there?"

"You're the one who has diabetes," I said. "I'm not sick."

"Well, you don't look good."

"Thanks a lot, that makes me feel fine," I said.

"Oh, as Troxler says, 'You don't have to be crazy to drive a Bu-gas truck, but it helps.'"

"I think you just like to visit with people."

"No, it's not that. You know, when it's cold I just feel sorry for all those people with little kids and some of them are so poor. I usually fill up their tank whether they can pay for it then or not."

"Have some more coffee."

"Say, do you ever hear from your old neighbor, Marie Moore?"

"The last time we heard they were going to buy another ranch in Nevada."

"I used to get a kick out of her. One night I drove in at two in the morning to fill their tank. She yelled out the window and said, 'Bob, I don't mind making coffee for you before midnight. I don't mind getting up at four in the morning to cook breakfast for you, but I'll be darned if I'll get up at 2 A.M. for any man."

"These ranchers' wives give you a bad time, don't they?"

"Yeah, but that's not all that gives me a bad time. Did I ever tell you what happened to me over at a ranch near Winslow?"

"No. You'd better not eat any more cookies. You're supposed to be on a diet."

He gave me a dirty look. "Well, I pulled up at the gate after dark and started to get out to open it. I could see a lump of something under my feet when I opened the cab door. They always used to have a big pile of manure there against the fence and I thought that's what it was. So I stepped down on this pile, only it turned out to be a big black bull asleep beside the gate. When I touched his back, I jumped about four feet in the air, climbed back in the cab, and slammed the door. The old bull jumped up, bellowed at the top of his voice, and took off as fast as he could run. Well, you know, that bull was so scared he never did come back to the ranch house. He stayed out all winter, spring, and summer. They were gathering some cattle the other day and found him way back in the hills. He was kind of poor so they brought him in with the bunch. It just so happened that that very day I was delivering gas again. The old bull was standing in the water lot when I drove up. He lifted his head, listened to the engine, took one look at the truck and began snorting, pawing up dirt, bellowing, and came charging over to the truck, still mad. I couldn't get out of the cab until they ran the bull off."

"What did your dog Mugs think about all that?" I asked.

"Mugs? Oh, he just sat up in the cab and barked."

"Do you have plenty of fresh water for him in the truck?"

"Sure. I always carry his water and lunch with mine."

"He must be a lot of company. You've had him a long time."

"He's been riding that Bu-gas truck for ten years. I guess he'd be just as lost without it as I would. Did you ever see Mugs's sunglasses?"

"Sunglasses? For a dog?"

"Yeah. You know in the summer that sun is so bright

coming in the windshield I was afraid it would blind him, so I got him some little sunglasses and fitted them for his head. He sure looks cute. You should see the way people look at us when we drive down the road. Old Mugs sits up and looks out the window with those dark glasses on just like another person. Well, I've got to go to Heber and Joe City before I turn in tonight. Better be on my way."

"Why don't you and your wife and daughter and Walt come out some night? I'll make spaghetti. Walt says he likes Italian spaghetti but everybody around here loads it with too much chili."

"I'd sure like to but I'll have to ask Gussie and Baby . . . now that they both teach school, we never know which night we can all get away. When do you want us?"

"How about next Tuesday?"

"O.K. We'll be there if nothing comes up."

"Tell Mugs to take care of himself."

"Thanks for the coffee. Here's the statement. You can air out the house now that the gas man's gone."

The following Tuesday gray clouds began rolling in from the west. I put on the spaghetti and sauce and kept my fingers crossed. By six o'clock the wind was howling and snow was beating against the windows. Cooney and I were home alone with a big fire, enough spaghetti to feed a regiment, and no possibility of anyone getting through in the storm. I looked at Cooney, then at Mehitabel and the three other cats who were all sitting around the floor sniffing the tomato sauce. "Do you suppose cats like spaghetti?" I asked. "Hell, I don't know. Let's try it and see," said Cooney.

We sat down at the table, lit the candles, and dished up. I pulled a noodle about two feet long off my plate and dangled it in front of Mehitabel. She followed it with her yellow eyes while it swung back and forth, like a pendulum. Then she pounced on it and began swallowing and swallowing. She sat up and begged for more. Bess, curious by this time, came over and took ahold of the other end of a noodle Mehitabel was consuming. Not only were they surprised when they met in the middle, but somewhat confused. Before long, the cats were sneaking up on spaghetti, then jumping on it and eating it all over the kitchen floor. They went absolutely wild. When Bess discovered she was being laughed at she started putting on an act. She would beg for a noodle, gobble it halfway down, then begin jumping around the room, shaking it and at last lie down clutching it between her forepaws until she slurped up the last inch. If anybody wants to know what people who live on remote ranches in Arizona do when they are snowed in without a telephone or television, I can tell them: we manage to amuse ourselves.

That winter we had acquired another dogie. Her name was Grace. She was a slim, pretty Navajo girl who lived at the dormitory in Holbrook. In all the peripheral towns bordering the Navajo reservation the government has established modern, comfortable dormitories where Navajo boys and girls from all over the reservation live while they are attending public schools. The girl's adviser was a good friend of mine—a Cherokee woman from North Carolina. I had asked her one day about a girl to help me clean once a week. She suggested Grace, who had been raised at the Episcopal Good Shepherd Mission at Fort Defiance. Like Raymond, Grace had no mother or father, only brothers and an old grandmother with whom she had lived during the summers. I would pick her up Saturday mornings and we would spend the day talking, laughing, scrubbing, and polishing. When we finished, she would sometimes go for a horseback ride with Curtis, one of Sam Roanhorse's sons who worked for us then. He was very shy around Grace. She seemed so worldly and self-possessed to a boy who had been raised in an old-fashioned Navajo family. He was surprised when he discovered that she still spoke Navajo, even though she had been raised at the Mission. Grace used to laugh at Curtis' shyness. She told me one day, "You know, that boy is a real Navajo."

She loved Bess and the cats and went about her work talking to them and petting them fondly even when they were in the way. One day when I was baking bread, she watched me a long time then said, "You know, my grandmother was always making bread. You remind me of my grandmother sometimes." She laughed. "I don't mean your age, just the way you do things. When my grandmother went blind I had to cook for my brothers. I used to get so mad at those boys. All they ever wanted to eat was mutton and fried bread. I'd make a salad or something like that and they never ate it. In the summer we took our horses up into the mountains . . . around Lukachukai. There are lots of bears up there. The old people say those mountains are sacred. It is good up there. Those women who weave go to Lukachukai to get roots and berries and bark to make colors for those rugs."

She was lovely and graceful, but with an air of quiet, strange power about her, such as few women possess. When I looked at her shining black hair and calm eyes I thought of Estsanátlehi, Woman Who Can Change Herself, goddess of turquoise, hard objects, the earth. Grace looked, in all respects, like a modern teen-age girl, but when we sat on the fence in the evening, watching the horses run, hearing the drumlike thunder of their hooves, her hair would blow in the wind and I thought, "*Dzinih!* How beautiful! Beneath this disguise of hers is an eternal Navajo woman."

We were both very nearsighted. We would sit there together on the fence, drinking in the air, the feel of the wind, the low animal sounds around us, until I would say, "Grace, is that Curtis coming on horseback?" She would squint and I would squint and then we would start laughing about who was to go back to the house after glasses. English was her best subject and she made excellent grades in composition, considering her linguistic background. She talked to me about her schoolwork and grade average. I was a little disappointed, somehow, when she decided to go to Beauty School instead of the University and reflected about how difficult it was to be a poetic woman, or even just a woman at times. But she would be doing something creative, would be making a good living, and, I hoped, would be happy doing it.

She had lived for one summer with the Episcopal priest and his family, helping them to care for their new baby when it was born. The people in the church were all fond of her, and the adviser at the dormitory treated her like a daughter. Yet there was always a distance between Grace and other people. A distance which seemed to consist not of culture but of centuries.

We asked her to have Christmas with us that year and she seemed happy about it. She helped me polish the silver plate, dust off the china, and iron the linen. We went up in the forest and cut juniper and piñon branches to decorate the house. Curtis was staying with us over Christmas that year, partly because there was a lot of ice to chop and partly because I had told him Grace was coming.

That was the year of the Great Plum Pudding Disaster. It had been decided by the powers which decide such things that Christmas dinner would be held at the ranch. Besides my mother and father and Cooney's mother there would be a wide assortment of friends from near and far. Dr. Kalb and his wife, two of their nephews and wives from Flagstaff (including Kenneth Kalb, the peecat's one-time adversary), a maiden lady from Phoenix, Curtis Roanhorse, and Grace.

Feeling ambitious as well as festive, a week or so before Christmas, I went up to get Nancy Jeffers' grandmother's famous old English plum pudding recipe. In copying it off, I failed to take notice of the number of people it would serve. At the time I remember thinking the quantities sounded more than ample, but reflected that I was feeding fourteen people. I started one morning with the flour, sugar, bread crumbs, suet, and baking powder. By the time I had gotten to the cherries, almonds, and fruit peel I had to switch to my largest mixing bowl. After the currants, raisins, and eggs, I was running over again, so I put the whole mess into my biggest roaster. The batter was so heavy I couldn't stir it. After adding more beer to the batter and drinking some myself as a sort of strengthening tonic, I found I could stir fairly well if I used the full force of both arms. Then began the frantic search for bowls. I got down my five large bowls. Hardly a dent was made in the batter. I searched cupboards and ransacked closets until I had resurrected all the bowls anybody had ever given me and filled them with batter. Even then, I had to pour some out for the chickens. A young pullet ran over cackling eagerly, stepped in the sticky dough, and promptly got both feet stuck.

I washed my hands, wiped up the spilled batter from the floor, breathed a sigh of relief, sat down, and continued reading the directions on the next page. At the very next line I gasped with horror. It said, "Steam or boil for ten hours." It was then about three in the afternoon. I sat there a while with my head in my hands, drank all the beer that was left over from the batter, and murmured to myself with the desperation of Lady Macbeth, "What's done cannot be undone."

When Cooney came in, the kitchen resembled a Finnish sauna. I was hovering over the seething pots upon the stove, cackling and singing to myself, "Double, double, toil and trouble; Fire burn and cauldron bubble." Long past the witching hour I sat sewing, reading, and tending to my unholy brew. At last, when the cock crowed, I turned off the stove, removed the cloths, and poured brandy over the steaming puddings. Lady Macbeth was still with me, saying, "Wash your hands, put on your nightgown; look not so pale . . . to bed! To bed!"

The next day I began immediately after breakfast to steam the second batch of plum puddings. The dark business proceeded all day until the sun sank in the west, the chickens went to roost, and Cooney, once more, came in from doing the chores. "What the hell are you doing?" he said.

"Making plum puddings, of course," I said. "What else do I do?"

"Oh, for . . . why don't you throw the whole mess away?"

"Do you have any idea how much those things cost?" I asked.

"But what are you going to *do* with all those plum
puddings?"

I stood there, wiped the perspiration from my forehead, and intoned icily, "Stuff them down people's
throats."

By Christmas Eve we had recovered our sense of proportion about plum puddings and life in general. After
Mass, we went with all of the friends and relatives to Joe
and Ida Romo's house for *posole, chile con carne,* and
tamales. Beautiful Ida stood like a queen in the middle
of her kitchen, surrounded by hungry children and
grandchildren, friends, relatives, and dirty dishes, smiling
graciously as she dipped spoonfuls of *posole* and *chile* out
of enormous kettles. It made me feel a little ridiculous.

After we had cut the ice on the drinking tubs, I started
Christmas dinner. By two o'clock everyone had arrived
in varying states of sobriety. We had a few more festive
rounds of wassail, then sat down at the tables. There sat
the maiden aunt blushing becomingly as Curtis Roanhorse passed the wine to her. Grace, still glowing from
the surprise of a new wool coat, sat beside Cooney.
Cooney and Hazel were arguing about politics with great
gusto. Kenneth had made his peace with Charlie Cat and
sat serenely, even trustingly, with the infamous peecat at
his feet. John was feeding Mehitabel under the table, his
face wrapt in an expression of boyish delight. Father was
reading aloud from the *Decameron* to anybody who
cared to listen, which turned out to be himself. Mrs. Kalb
was wondering where I got the Nottingham lace table-
cloths. Ruth and Mother were being as efficient in the
kitchen as anyone could be at Christmastime with three
Tom and Jerrys under their belts. Dr. Kalb was wishing
very much that we could get dinner over with as soon as

possible so that he might steal away to the back room for
a quiet nap. In front of the snapping fire, Bess lay on the
Navajo rug cracking English walnuts to her heart's content. Warm with the joy and contentment of Christmas,
the heat from the fire and the red table wine, we ate the
turkey and roast beef before us. At last, we sat quietly
talking of the unimportant things that are so important.

I got up from the table, and with as much enthusiasm
and vigor as I could possibly muster, asked, "Is everyone
ready for his plum pudding?"

A sudden hush came over the room. Then, one by one,
in politely muted voices, the Christmas guests announced
that they were either too full or too sleepy or had had
too much to drink for dessert thank you anyway and
could they please have another cup of coffee instead.

Shortly after Christmas we had a fresh snowfall at the
ranch. I couldn't wait to get on my horse and have a look
at the clean new world outside. Cooney was going to
look for a bull, so I put on as many clothes as I could
without rendering myself immobile and prepared to go
with him.

It was a day I'll always remember for no other reason
than the sheer beauty of it. Our horses stepped out
proudly, exhilarated by the sharp, clear air. The white
vapor of their breath came out of their nostrils in regular
puffs. Jogging across the soft new snow was like riding
across clouds. A gray-winged hawk circled around, then
swooped low over our heads to have a closer look at us.
The only sounds were the squeak of leather, the occasional snorts of the horses, and the swish of their tails.
The acrid good smell of the horses' sweat came out strong
in the clean air. Across the trail ran the zigzag tracks of a
cottontail. Behind us, the whiteness was broken only by

our hoofprints. Smoke from our chimney rose high into the thin blue air. In silence and peace we rode. Into my head came a translation I had once read of a song from the Navajo Night Chant:

> I am walking on the tops of mountains.
> The Gods are before me.
> The Gods are behind me.
> I am walking in the midst of the Gods.*

* *The Pollen Path*, by Margaret Schevill Link, Stanford, Calif.: Stanford University Press (1956).

9

Spring

In March the winds come. Out of the west they come, pushing before them great, billowing clouds of ocher dirt which reach hundreds of feet into the air. If there has been snow that winter, the range begins to green up as soon as the frost leaves the ground. But when the winds begin, the short, tender grass shrivels, curls, and turns brown under a layer of dust. Where there has been no snow, the fierce, driving wind pulls at the topsoil, rips last year's tumbleweeds, from the ground and whips them in dizzy spirals across the open country.

Day after day the wind blows. Fine sand sifts in the windows and around the doors, filling the house with reddish dust. The windmill creaks and bangs violently with each turn. I grow so accustomed to the noise that I am strangely upset if it should stop for a while.

The Navajos say that the wind is life. In spring, the

moving, restless wind stirs the emotions of people to a high pitch, battering down the calm façade of day-to-day life until, in torment, I must block the doors and windows with damp towels, pull the drapes, darken the room in an attempt to shut out its unbridled violence and unrestrained power, or put on a windbreaker, tie a scarf over my head and nose, and go out to fight it.

My Grandmother Scofield used to say, "The wind makes me wild." It is the same with me. In a truly violent storm, I cannot bear to stay inside and watch the house fill up with dirt. I always find myself in the middle of it, being buffeted around, shouting and stumbling and swearing at it while my nose and eyes fill with sand. When it is over, I am somewhat pleased with myself for having outlived it.

One spring we sold our calves instead of waiting until fall because the range was so dry they could not have made it until the August and September rains. The day we gathered cattle out of the holding pasture, the dirt was blowing so hard we couldn't see fifty feet away. Bess was with me that year, working back and forth, rousting cattle out from under the trees where they had lain for protection. All morning we worked in the storm. Our faces were caked with dirt and sweat. When we got in with the cattle, Bess's eyes were swollen nearly shut from the stinging sand. That was the last drive she made before she quit of her own accord.

The best spring we ever had we lost about eighteen yearlings. The late fall rains had been heavy. Toward the end of February, the weeds and filaree began to come up in the warm places under the trees. We had a bull in the corral who couldn't eat or drink unless we forced it down him. His tongue was thick and stiff with a disease called "wooden tongue" from eating wild mustard. Wild flowers which had lain dormant for years suddenly grew and bloomed. At the West Camp, whole sections bloomed golden with buttercups or sparkled white with wild poppies. In all this beauty there was death. Some of the weeds were so poisonous that a yearling, having eaten them, would start in to water and drop dead in the trail without so much as a struggle.

Spring in most parts of the world means hope, new growth, birth. It means robins, crocuses, violets, and Wordsworth's "host of golden daffodils." Here, in the bleak beauty of this endless plateau, the green spears of irises push up through the damp earth of the yard, grow and even bloom, only to have the west wind, one day, bend them to the ground, ripping their fragrant purple blossoms from their slender stalks and beating the strongest of them against the wooden fence until they are shredded, bare, and withered. Still, the bulbs go on multiplying beneath the earth to come up stronger and thicker next year.

In Shelley's "Ode to the West Wind," he cries:

> Wild spirit, which art moving everywhere;
> Destroyer and preserver; hear, oh, hear!

Nowhere could the wind more truly be both destroyer and preserver. The wind evaporates the water which was deposited in the dirt tanks the previous fall. It also turns the windmills so necessary to pump water for the cattle. Without wind, we must run gasoline engines day and night to pump water. With too much wind, the tanks dry up quickly. Spring is the eternal struggle for the survival of vegetation. It is a battle between the sun's warmth,

which brings new growth, and the wind, which destroys
it.

Along about May, the tanks begin to go dry. If the cattle have not already drifted away to other watering
places, we take a couple of horses and drive them to the
next tank and then to the windmills. If the tank does not
have a sandy or rocky bottom, if a great deal of sediment
has been deposited by a heavy runoff, the tanks often get
so muddy that cows, especially when they are poor, bog
down in them. They can stand perhaps a day and a night
in mud up to their bellies, but their strength soon ebbs,
their legs grow cold and stiff, and they die.

Raymond, the young Navajo who had become a real
cowboy under Cooney's direction, found a cow bogged in
the mud at Five Mile Wash one spring. He had gone off
to fix some fence line. When he didn't return home for
supper, Cooney went out looking for him. He had dug a
hole around the cow almost big enough to bury a car, but
she was too weak to move. The nights were so cold
Cooney knew she would die if they left her until morning,
so they built a fire and kept working with her until they
got all of her legs free. Then they fastened ropes around
her and pulled her as far out as they could. They came
home after fresh water and hay. When she had some
nourishment and the next morning's sun had warmed her
a little, they managed to load her into the jeep and haul
her home.

On horseback one day, Cooney and I came upon an
old poor cow bogged down at the edge of the water of
one of our dirt tanks. Her face was nearly in the water;
her hind legs uphill. After looking the situation over,
Cooney decided that the only way to get her out was to
try to push her toward the tank and get all of her legs

in the water in an attempt to get the circulation back in
them. We stripped down to our underwear and hats and
began digging in the mud around her legs until we had
them partway out. Cooney pulled on her horns and I
pushed from behind until, with one last heave, she was
in the tank.

Her eyes opened wide with surprise to find herself free.
Instead of being grateful for all our efforts, she decided
we were somehow responsible for her predicament and
balked out there in the waist-high water. We maneuvered
her around until, at last, in desperation, she had to swim
or go under. While she was paddling along, her head
held high, snorting water from her nose in disdain, I
looked back and saw that the horses we had left on the
tank dump had disappeared.

While Cooney steered the cow, I stumbled out of the
water and ran over the hot rocks and sand in my underwear and hat, hitting an occasional grass burr, wondering
if anybody could see me from the road, and feeling fairly
silly about the whole thing. "Damn you, Silver," I said,
when I found them grazing a few hundred feet away,
"you'd better not go any farther if you know what's good
for you." The horses let me catch the bridle reins and I
led them back to where Cooney was emerging from the
opposite end of the tank with the wet, muddy old cow.
She stood there on her shaky legs, her head down, snorting in displeasure, hooked at Cooney once, gave us both
a look of utter disgust, and walked over to the salt trough.

Toward the end of spring, as soon as the nights begin
to warm up, it is sheep shearing time. Northern Arizona
nights are usually cold until the middle of May. When
the sheep are first shorn, they cannot stand much cold.

An afternoon shower or a bad windstorm is enough to make them sick or kill them.

The first two years I had the sheep, there were so few that Matthew Roanhorse and I sheared them with hand clippers. We turned them into the corral and Matthew roped them. We put them on a tarp in the shade of the barn, because they were so fat that they would have died if they had lain in the sun too long. The tarp kept the wool clean as it came off.

Navajos do not shear sheep the way Australians do. The Navajos usually lay a sheep on its side, being careful not to have its back downhill, and fasten two or three legs with a piggin string. Instead of starting with the belly wool, they usually start with the left front leg, working up around the neck, head, then down the back and belly toward the tail. Matthew had watched his mother and aunts shear sheep but had done very little of it himself. He trimmed their heads exactly the way he would have given somebody a haircut, trimming slowly and carefully around their ears and eyes until the length suited him. Cooney kept wanting us to trim the big pet wether like a French poodle, and every time I thought about how funny he would look, I was tempted to try, but in deference to the wether's dignity, we gave him a crew cut instead.

That first year, I got so upset every time I knicked their skins that I put Merthiolate on the cuts. The sheep's own lanolin helps heal cuts, too. When we finished, we rolled the wool clean side in, tied it with paper twine, and bagged it in a gunny sack. Every year I have sent my wool to Eldorado, Texas, to be made into blankets.

Instead of selling my buck lambs, I traded them to some Navajo women I know for ewe lambs, so that after

three years my sheep herd had increased to twenty
ewes. Sheep shearing by that time had become an important annual event. Sam's sister Irene and her husband,
John, came down from the reservation with Sam's wife,
Helen, and about eight children and grandchildren. You
cannot always be sure just whom Navajo children really
belong to, because they generally live with whomever
wants them most. It is not uncommon for a woman with
many children to feed to give two or three to a female
relation who has none. And that is as it should be.

So they arrived on a Saturday, the pickup bulging with
children. It was understood that Irene and John would do
the shearing and the rest of the family would supervise.
I think these times when the ranch was suddenly overrun
with Navajo people wandering around, looking at the
horses, cattle, corrals, scales, chickens, sheep, and equipment made Cooney very nervous. They gave me, instead,
a feeling of peace. Before we had a kitchen in the new
bunkroom, I used to let them use my kitchen. Maybe ten
or twelve of Sam's family would cook supper and eat
there. I often went off to town and left them alone. When
I came back, the kitchen was invariably cleaner than it
had been before.

Irene was fast with the sheep. Her long, slender fingers
moved quickly and surely. John caught and held the
sheep for her. She knelt on the tarp, her velvet sleeves
rolled up, her fine turquoise and silver bracelets showing
up bright against the smooth brown arms. I always think
Navajo jewelry doesn't look quite right against the skin
of a white woman. The children's laughter came from out
near the duck pond. In the shade by the barn, the shears
clicked endlessly. A ewe bleated once in a while when
she was cut, and Irene would shake her head and say,

"Ey!" Irene worked without talking. Once I brought cold water and we sat drinking it, resting. I folded and tied the wool. Its warm animal smell was good. The lanolin from the wool made my arms and hands soft.

At noon they came in to eat. I had a big kettle of stew, some hot biscuits, fresh celery and tomatoes and canned peaches. When the meal was finished, Irene and John sat back in their chairs, their hands resting quietly on the table. Helen and her girls washed the dishes. By sundown, the shearing was over. Helen had asked me for some old sheets and scraps of material for quilts. Irene's grandson, Edward, told me he wanted to buy some chickens that summer for his 4-H project. He was a straight, handsome, clean, well-mannered boy of twelve or so. I would have been proud of him if he had been my son.

The ewes stood in a corner of the corral, ashamed of their nakedness, but relieved, too, to have the hot wool off their backs. Irene and John shook hands with us, said *"Yahteh"* again, piled into their pickup with the others, and drove back down the road. It was evening, then, and the ranch seemed suddenly very quiet. Bess and I walked out to the windmill, watched the sun go down, and listened to the shrill pipes of the killdeers at the edge of the water.

Winter is merciless on the old cows. If it stays cold for long periods of time, a cow who is poor freezes a little more each night until at last she gives up the ghost. Or, perhaps, in early spring, a cow gets started on loco or some other noxious weed because she is so hungry for something green, and gradually she dies. Sometimes the two-year-old heifers go off and leave their calves. For one reason or another, during the winter, some cows lose their calves and some calves lose their mothers. And in the spring there are always a few dogies wandering aimlessly around the range.

It is not difficult to spot a dogie calf. There are other poor calves to be found with long, shaggy, dull hair, with their bellies swollen from malnutrition, their faces pinched, and their eyes sunken. There is something else about a dogie. His nose is usually dry and cracked from lack of milk, but that is not what you notice first. He has given up trying to find love. He doesn't bawl for his mama, because he knows that it won't do any good. He stands alone with his head down, neither seeking nor expecting love from any source, intent only on foraging or stealing what milk he can to survive.

Last year, at the West Camp, we found a dogie wandering around with two other cows and calves. "He looks like he's sucked," said Cooney. "He looks like a dogie, though," I said. "Let's watch him and see what he does." We drove up toward him in the jeep. He knew we were looking at him and he ran to one of the cows. He reached down to suck her, but she kicked him away. Then he followed another cow that was walking down the trail. She turned and bawled and her own calf ran up to her. Now the dogie was alone. We drove over to him. He ran behind a tree. At last we roped him, put him in the back of the pickup, took him home, and put him on the milk cow where, for the first time in his life, he had his fill of milk.

Cooney has been threatening to sell old Holstein every fall for the last four years, but I've begged him not to. Almost every year she has raised two or three dogies along with her own calf, and the least we can do in appreciation is spare her life as long as possible. Every fall we think she's too old to have another calf, but she shows up one day in February or March with a black calf following her in to water. Holstein bellows like a fog horn for her feed in the morning and evening. She gets mad, throws tantrums, kicks and treats the dogies as if they were undesirable stepchildren, but still she raises them.

The cows who run back in the brushy country and down in the canyons usually winter all right. As soon as it warms up, they begin to shed their winter coats and start licking themselves until they are sleek and shiny. If they have ranged long in a certain area, they know exactly where they are going to give birth to their calves, having already chosen a protected spot. In a day or so, the cows will come in to water, leaving their calves hidden behind a clump of sacaton grass or under a cedar tree. The calves know instinctively to lie still at the approach of a dangerous animal. They have little scent and are not easily found by coyotes or eagles. When the calves are about a week old, they follow their mothers in to water.

Like human mothers, cows baby-sit. When there are four or five cows with their baby calves staying together, all the cows but one will go in to water, leaving the one to watch the calves. One day last spring, I drove up on ten small calves all soundly asleep in the sun, sprawled out on warm, sandy spots near the road. One drowsy-eyed cow lay among them, chewing her cud and watching over the brood.

When calves are very small, they will run to anything they think might be their mother. Bouncing along in the jeep, you are startled to see several calves jump out from under the trees and run toward you, bawling. Cows and little calves are hard to drive on horseback. When the calf gets hungry or wants to lie down, he will wobble over to your horse, get underneath it, and start looking for his dinner. It is virtually impossible to run one off when he once starts following you, unless his mother comes back to him and calls him away. With curiosity, the calves will come up to Bess, smell of her and try to follow her until, in desperation, she barks, sending them bustling off to find their mothers.

In the spring, the milk-pen calves discover their new world with wonder. They make themselves giddy watching butterflies. Exploratively, one will follow a hen with chicks around the corral until he is stopped abruptly by a sharp peck on the end of the nose. Just for excercise, they may run as fast as they can from one end of the alley to the other. When they are tired, they will find their mothers and lie down close to the broad, warm sides of the cows.

Cooney would rather take a beating than milk a cow. Before we had a man who could milk, he gave me to understand that if I wanted fresh milk I would have to do the milking. Never one to back down, I got up early one morning, grabbed the milk bucket, and trudged out to the corral. I would never have been brash enough to start on Holstein, but we had, at the time, a gentle part-Hereford cow who had been raised there. That first morning I milked about a pint. The next day I got nearly a quart. At the very best, I never milked more than a half-gallon. For one thing, she wouldn't give her milk unless the calf was with her. He started on one side and I on the other, but he always seemed to resent my share and we fought over our rights to certain teats. At last, he would run over to my side, push me off balance, and grab all the rest. As the calf got bigger, my success decreased, until I capitulated and let him have it all to himself. But it was good, in the early morning, bent over with my head resting against her warm side, watching the steam rise from the foaming white milk, smelling its grassy sweetness, listening to her munch hay while the greedy calf tugged at her teats, sucking and swallowing noisily.

My refrigerator is always full of milk jars in the spring. I skim off the cream to churn butter in the rotary churn. What milk we can't drink or use in bread or custards or for cooking, we pour out to the chickens. Sometimes I make cottage cheese, letting the milk clabber, then draining it slowly. I even tried to make *queso,* Mexican cheese, one year, without much success. It is made from the curd, seasoned, pressed, and aged. My milk never got sour enough, probably because it was too cold.

If there is one thing prettier than a baby calf, it is a lamb, and lambs are even livelier. With the sheer joy and exuberance of youth, they run and jump high in the air, kicking their legs together in extravagant gyrations. They play a game similar to leap-frog, jumping over one another or their tolerant mothers. In another game they follow the leader over feed troughs, through gates, around the corral, and then stand, butting one another, backing off and running at each other once more.

Although a few calves inevitably come in the middle of the winter when bulls stay with the herd all year, as ours do, most of the calving occurs in March, April, and May. The two-year-old heifers who are calving for the first time must be watched as closely as possible, around and at the watering places, so they can be brought into the corrals if they look as if they might have trouble. Often they don't make as much bag as an older cow and it is harder to predict when their calf will be born.

We seldom lose many heifers calving, but occasionally the mother is killed or badly torn up and broken down in the back from a calf that is too big for her, that is backwards or twisted somehow in the womb. We had a dwarf heifer one time which we had kept up in the corrals intending to sell. Her head and body were normal, but her legs were short. Like most dwarf cattle, her heart was enlarged and she wheezed hard when she breathed. Before we could sell her, she grew heavy with calf. She was nearly as broad as she was long and she grunted and groaned under the weight of the calf.

One morning about two o'clock, Sam got us out of bed to say that she had been trying to calve most of the night. We took a flashlight and Coleman lantern out to the pen. She had depleted nearly all of her strength by that time and couldn't help us much. Cooney rolled up his sleeves to see if he could find the head and forelegs of the calf which are supposed to come out first. Its head seemed to be twisted backwards. When Cooney quit, I tried for a while because my hands and arms were smaller. No matter what we did, we couldn't straighten the calf or pull it. When we started, we felt warmth and movement, but now the calf was dead and its mother's strength was spent. It was very dark and very cold. The men's faces, with their exaggerated shadows in the dim light of the lantern, showed pity and despair. And at last Cooney walked back to the house to get his .22 rifle to relieve the misery, suffering, and pain of the dwarf heifer after her futile attempt to create new life.

Spring in northern Arizona is not a time of rejoicing. Seeds begin sprouting, plants are coming back to life, animals are being born. Then the wind starts and all the sweet hopes are dashed and scattered to the four winds.

One spring day when I was home alone, a young and wild heifer we were keeping up in the corral started to calve. The men were all away working on a well which had quit pumping. I checked on her a time or two. The water had come, but she was still straining to give birth to her calf. An hour or more later she was running back and forth in the corral with wild, frightened eyes. The calf's forelegs had begun to come out, but no matter how hard she pushed and contracted her sides, it would not be born. I was afraid, but I ran to the house, changed to my old clothes, got some dry sacks, and ran back out. By that time she had lain down and was breathing in short, labored grunts. I was shaking from fear of losing the calf.

I sat down in the dust of the corral, braced my feet against the cow's hips, and got a tight hold of the calf's slippery feet. Whenever she strained, I pulled as hard as I could. Inch by inch he began to appear. With one final effort, he emerged, wet and limp. His tongue was blue and protruded from above the small white teeth. His eyes were shut tight and he was not breathing. I could feel his heart beating softly, so I cleaned out all the mucus from his nose and mouth. He gasped once. Not knowing what to do, I took hold of his hind legs, swung him upside down and began to shake him as hard as I could. At last he coughed and breathed.

After I had wiped him dry with the sacks—a chill wind was blowing that day and he was beginning to shiver—I left him with his mother hoping that she would claim him. Some young heifers walk off and leave their calves to die, especially when they are as wild and frightened as this one had been.

In half an hour or so I went back out to look. The cow was standing up now, but the calf hadn't sucked yet. He

lay there, trembling. I rubbed him hard all over to get
the circulation going and at last he could stand alone on
his wobbly legs. And suddenly I wanted to hold him
close to me. I held the helpless small thing in my arms
tightly, put my head against his soft fur, and began to
cry. There in the dirt of the corral I sat, covered with
blood and dirt, holding that calf and sobbing.

When I started to cry, the heifer turned and looked
down at me. Then she took a few steps toward her calf,
lowed softly to it, and began to lick its face. He shut his
eyes, opened his mouth, and bawled, loud and clear.
Slowly, painfully, I let him go to his mother. She nudged
him around with her big rough tongue until, at last, he
found her bag and began to suck hungrily. I wiped the
dirt and tears off my face, got up and walked toward the
house knowing that this, really, was what life was all
about.

10

The Red-Necked Steer

I suppose the reason I always went to sleep over at tho West Camp, the other part of our ranch, was that it was so quiet over there. Cooney and I would spend the morning going around to different tanks in the jeep, checking the water and the condition of the cattle. By noon we would drive up to the West Camp, open the creaky gate, unload the feed or salt we had brought to old Ceph, and walk through the sand to the house.

It wasn't much of a house . . . just a one-room shack made of railroad ties covered with boards, with a tin roof and a door at each end so that the sand that blew in the west door could blow right on through and out the east door. There had been a good three-room bunkhouse there until it blew up one day. Ceph was, fortunately, out in the corrals doing his evening chores when something happened to the Butane refrigerator and the whole house blew sky high. The concrete foundation is still out in front; but for some reason, nobody has ever gotten around to building a new bunkhouse. About a hundred yards from the present edifice, and facing the road, is an outhouse with no door. Cooney's Aunt Zone used to say she'd keep a horse saddled to ride out there if she had to live at West Camp.

There were a couple of windows on hinges which opened back toward the ceiling and fastened with bent nails. On a stool beside the door was a white enamel pan with rings around it which served as a washbasin. The minute we would get in the door, Bess would trot up to Ceph and beg him for a drink of fresh water from the enamel washbasin. She never liked to drink out of the watering tubs at West Camp. Next to the stool was an open cupboard containing a motley assortment of pots, pans, chipped dishes, cups, and unmatched silverware. On this cupboard hung the dishrag and towels. The dish-rag had been, in better days, long-handles. The buttons were left on for the excellent reason that they made good pan-scrapers. I never liked to dry the dishes with those towels because, with all that sand blowing in all the time, you would just get them dirtier than they had been before you washed them.

Beside the cupboard stood the wood cookstove. I loved that stove. My mother had bought it for fifteen dollars at a second-hand dealer, but there wasn't room in my kitchen for it so we hauled it over to the West Camp. It was trimmed with chrome and had iron curlicues all around the edges of it. There was a warming oven above, just right for rising bread, and two round iron plates that dropped down above the stove top to set pots on and keep them warm. The oven only got hot on one side so that if you cooked a roast you had to keep changing it around. The first time I cleaned it out, the ashes of decades filled four buckets.

Hanging on nails driven into the wall were dishpans and a heavy iron skillet. Three water buckets sat on the table. Two were tank water for washing and one was fresh water for drinking. Ceph drew drinking water only when the well was pumping because the tank water at West Camp had a salty taste to it.

In one corner was an ancient oak icebox which was used for the storage of potatoes, onions, canned goods, and tobacco. On top of the icebox was strewn an assortment of toiletries. There was a straight-edged razor and shaving mug, a few bottles of patent medicines, a bottle of Bactine, some veterinary supplies, and a comb. Above the icebox hung a broken mirror and a towel on a nail. Next to that was a calendar with the days carefully penciled out with exes.

When we remodeled our kitchen at the ranch, we brought our Butane stove and refrigerator to the West Camp. Our enamel sink was there, too, but since there was no running water, it served more of a decorative than practical purpose. We ate off another table, covered with blue-checkered oilcloth. The floor was rock and had coffee stains on it from where Ceph started pouring out the coffee before he quite got to the door. Some chrome kitchen chairs with plastic seats were placed around the potbellied stove.

Against the south wall, next to the chicken house, was an iron bedstead. It was covered with four or five quilts and a tarp, so that the dogs and cats didn't get the quilts dirty when they took a nap on the bed. Whenever we came in from a jeep ride, Ceph would make coffee for us.

I would sit, drinking that acid coffee, in one of the chairs by the potbellied stove, and listen to Cooney and Ceph talk about a certain old lineback cow or the bobtail one the coyotes had gotten ahold of, until my eyes grew drowsy. At last I would flop down on that lumpy bed and sleep so soundly they would have to wake me up to eat.

When we were gathering cattle at West Camp, and had gotten within a mile of the camp, I would start thinking about that old lumpy bed. Believe me, that camp looked good to us when we came in from a long drive. I remember once, in the fall, we had just turned the herd into the holding pasture and started back toward the house when a storm broke loose. As Roy Sommers would say, "It was a real toad-choker." The thunder rolled; the lightning cracked around us. We loped all the way back over wet slick rocks, turning our faces sideways against the cold driving rain. Our clothes, saddles, everything, were soaked. The wet horses steamed. Our boots were so filled with water that they sloshed whenever we took a step. Inside the camp, Ceph built a fire in the potbellied stove and when it began to warm up in there, our faces burned and the smell of wet wool clothes and one very wet dog filled the room. As soon as I dried out a little, I curled up and went to sleep under a quilt. I think no dinner in the world ever smelled or tasted as good to me as the one old Ceph cooked that day. When I woke up, we ate thick-sliced fried potatoes, salt pork, cream gravy, canned tomatoes, and sourdough biscuits.

The country around West Camp consists mostly of rocks, sand, and cedar trees. One lone cedar stands in the middle of the water lot and it proved very useful the day an old cow on the prod kept Ceph up in that tree for several hours. Every so often the men clean the foot-deep sand out of the corrals, but by the next summer it has blown back again.

Sometimes when I stayed at camp to cook instead of going on the long drives, I would keep a horse up and catch the steers when they came in to water. I was always being bitten by ants over there. The whole place is full of red ant beds. If you sit down on the ground, they crawl up your boot and bite you. I had a badly inflamed bite one day and my leg had started to get numb. Ceph said, "You may not like this, lady, but it'll durn sure take the swelling down." He took a wad of tobacco out of his mouth, put it on the ant bite, and wrapped a rag around my leg. Sure enough, in a few minutes, the pain left and the swelling went down.

Ceph's grandparents had come West on the Oregon Trail and settled on the Pacific Coast. As that country became civilized and populated, the sons headed South. One, Ceph's father, went back to Texas where he raised good horses and had a successful goat ranch. They had raised a Negro boy with their own children. An uncle settled in the wilderness of Arizona near Camp Verde. Ceph had punched cattle in Mexico, New Mexico, and Texas and had known Jim Jeffers, Cooney's father, years ago over on the Rio Grande. He had worked for the Jefferses in New Mexico before coming, at last, to Arizona to work for Cooney.

Ceph was a real old-time Texas cowpuncher. When he stayed at West Camp, he was in his seventies, tall, slim, broad-shouldered, and bowlegged. The necessities of life to him consisted of a plug of Day's Work tobacco, a pair of Levis, a work shirt, a suit of long-handles, a pair of boots, a felt hat, a saddle, a little salt pork, beans, potatoes, coffee, and, every month or so, some recreation.

This recreation usually took the form of a trip to town, twenty miles away, a stop at the barber shop, and two or three days spent visiting with his friends.

Ceph had stayed, alone, at the West Camp for eight years, his only companions being Brownie, a lively, short-haired dog of indeterminate species, Blue Kitty, some chickens who followed him around pecking at the tobacco he spit out, the cattle, and Lucky, or, as Ceph called him, "That little yaller horse." Once or twice a week Cooney or one of the men would go check on Ceph to see what supplies he needed or, as Ceph put it, "To see if I'd croaked yet." When his hair reached the stage in which Ceph was beginning to look like a mountain man, he'd go to town.

In town, he'd begin telling any and all listeners about the trials and tribulations of his life at the camp, emphasizing each sentence with "Right?" This expression was so well known among the citizens of Holbrook that most of them called him "Mr. Right," and few of them knew his real name. "How's old man Right?" people used to ask us.

After a day or so, when he had his fill of night life, card games, and conversation, he'd send word to Cooney to bring him home. We'd drive in at night, track him down, get him into the jeep, and head for home. We were entertained on these occasions by stories which began, "As the old cowboy used to say . . . ," and a bar or two of some cowboy refrain like "Just a-bummin' around," interspersed with the exclamation "Right?" By this time he would be lonesome for his dog and cat and horse. "Poor little Brownie's lonesome . . . right? She's been minding the coyotes off the chickens. Blue Kitty's hungry . . . right? There's only three things I love in this world . . .

Brownie, Blue Kitty, and Cooney . . . right?" I always felt a little hurt at that statement, but consoled myself that I was, after all, a mere woman and he hadn't known me very long.

"When I go," says Ceph, "Cooney, you take care of Brownie and Blue Kitty. Jo, you can have my chickens . . . right?"

"Right," I said.

"That's right," said Ceph and he spat tobacco juice out the window.

He was probably the best shot in all Arizona—with tobacco. Sometimes, when we branded or drove cattle, you had to be careful to stay on the lee side of him, because, on a windy day, there was always the danger of being hit broadside by a flying missile of tobacco juice.

Ceph cared nothing for material things. His whole life was wrapped up in his cows and his pets. He was the very best of what he was, which is more than I can say for myself or most people. Although his opinion of the human race, in general, left something to be desired, he was open-hearted and generous with anybody in trouble or need. If Sam Roanhorse's wife and children stayed at West Camp for a few days when they had fencing or other work to do, Helen would scrub the camp from top to bottom and wash all of Ceph's things for him. He always gave what money he had to her and the kids when they left. He seldom owed money, and if he did, he just kept working until he had paid back every cent.

On his excursions to town, somebody drifting through would find him, figure him as an easy touch, and ask to borrow some money. Ceph usually gave it to them if he had it, but not completely gratuitously. Over the years he has struck some strange bargains. One time he came

back to the ranch with a tough old black and white tom-
cat he had bought from a couple of sailors for five dollars.
No telling where that cat had been, but he looked as if
he'd seen the world from its back alleys and knew the
facts of life, all right.

Another time he came home without his brown nylon
jacket, but wearing, instead, a purple and white high
school letter sweater with '54 on the pocket. When we saw
him drive up in a pickup he had hired to bring him home,
wearing his black going-to-town pants, boots, his old high-
crowned stetson, and that purple high school sweater,
Cooney asked him if the numbers stood for "1854." Sometimes he'd bring us presents he had taken in on a debt
. . . a billfold for Cooney . . . a ring with an enormous
glass ruby setting for me.

For a while, Ceph was having a lot of trouble with his

eyes. They would get red and water when he was working out in the wind and sun all day. We suggested getting a pair of sunglasses on his next trip to town and he
did. He came back with a pair of pixie sunglasses with
pink frames. He wore those "shades," as he called them,
all the time we were branding over at West Camp. On
his next trip to town, they mysteriously disappeared.

When Ceph first began having stomach trouble, we
thought it was partly from not being able to chew his
food. He had postponed being fitted for dental plates
again and again. On a trip to El Paso one Christmas to
see his family, he went across to Mexico and had a fine
pair made in Juarez for fifty dollars, "guaranteed to fit."
The only trouble was, he was always losing them. He
came back to the ranch one day without his jacket or
teeth. I was going in to town to do the washing, so I
stopped at the saloon we fondly refer to as the "Bucket
of Blood" and inquired about Ceph's jacket. "Say, lady,"
said the bartender, "there's a pair of teeth in the pocket,
so be careful not to break them."

Ceph loved animals. We never had a man working for
us that took greater interest in the ranch, watched the cattle so closely, or took such good care of them. As soon as
he spotted a cow that was poor, he would put her up in
the corral and feed her. Many were the times he stayed
up all night doctoring a sick cow, helping a young heifer
calve, or hand-feeding one that was "on the lift." When
cows get so poor that they can no longer walk, they must
have belts of gunny sack or leather tied under their bellies and be hoisted up on their feet in order to get their
circulation back. Sometimes Ceph would go out a dozen
times a day to turn a sick cow on her other side so she
wouldn't bloat, to tail her up for a while and then care-

fully let her back down when she grew tired. If cows' positions are not changed frequently, they die.

Ceph saved many cows and calves. He liked them all, but his favorite was a freckle-nosed milk cow, part-Jersey, part-Hereford. No one could drive her horseback, but Ceph could do anything he wanted with her on foot. In the spring, she'd always try to hide her calf, but he'd go out and find it, bring it in, and keep them both up in the corral, feeding them hay and milking her out every day. I never felt that Ceph thought much of me until one day at West Camp I heard him calling his milk cow "Jo" and I felt honored to think he had named her after me.

His affection for animals did not extend to snakes. Ceph hated snakes, even harmless ones. There used to be a big bull snake at the camp who discovered, to his delight, that there were mice between the ceiling and roof. Cooney talked Ceph into keeping him there as a mouser, saying that he did a lot of good and no harm at all. Reluctantly, Ceph spared the snake's life because Cooney was the boss. Then one day Ceph met us at the door with a grim look on his face. "How's the old bull snake?" asked Cooney.

"He's gone," said Ceph.

"How come?" asked Cooney.

"Wall, I was fixing to cook supper last night. I reached in the drawer to get a knife and fork and grabbed ahold of that old gentleman instead. I decided right then and there he had to go, so I picked up the butcher knife and murdered him."

Cooney and Ceph argued, whenever we sat down to eat, about two things. One was directions, about which Cooney was always right and Ceph was always wrong. Cooney threatened to get him a compass for Christmas every year. The other thing was the weather. Ceph was naturally optimistic and felt that it had to rain sooner or later. Cooney was entirely pessimistic and seemed to think that it would never rain again. Ceph would stalk back and forth across the rock floor, open the screen door, spit, and look up at the sky. "It's bound to rain this evening," he'd say.

"Hell, no, it's not going to rain," said Cooney. "What makes you think so?"

"Those clouds over in the west look plumb bilious," said Ceph.

"Oh, it's too late in the day. They have to start building up by ten or eleven in the morning to do any good."

Ceph frowned. "Anyway, it's a wet moon," he said.

"What do you call a wet moon?"

"Wall, look right yere, on this calendar, the moon's tipped over thisaway. That's a sign of rain."

It's *been* tipped over and I haven't seen any rain spill out yet."

"It's going to rain all right. Supposed to get rain all this month."

"Well, if you keep predicting it long enough, it's bound to rain."

"Look at them clouds . . . they're turning around and coming back thisaway. It's raining right now over to Winslow."

"Winslow, my foot. You're pointing right straight at Joe City."

Finally Ceph would grin. "Might be I'm pointing to Phoenix, but wherever it is, it's raining."

"That's nothing but a cussed dirt storm."

"Wall, it'll rain sometime. I can't believe the Good Lord would put all them old pore cows on earth and then not take care of them."

When we were on drives, Cooney and Ceph would usually be in the lead, turning the cattle. I'd be in the drags
with Sam or one of the Navajo boys. Ceph had been out
of sorts one day, not talking much, just trotting along on
his little yaller horse, chewing tobacco and letting the cattle stray off to the side. Cooney, out of patience with all
of us, yelled at him to turn the cattle back. He spat and
took off in a long lope after them. All of a sudden smoke
started rising from the seat of his britches. I took out
after Ceph shouting, "You're on fire!" Well, he discovered
the fact himself before I reached him, got down off his
horse, and began beating it out. He'd been carrying a
few kitchen matches in the back pocket of his Levis and
when he started loping, the friction had ignited them.

One year when we were gathering cattle at West Camp,
we ran across a big red-necked steer, coming three-year-
old. Somehow, we had missed him two years in a row
and we knew he must be running way back in the canyons
or the rough country where the cracks are. Covering
maybe a section, these fissures in the rock are long and
narrow, from six inches to four feet across. Horses get
spooked over there and will hardly cross that country.
I don't blame them—I get spooked too. You can throw
a rock down one of the cracks and it just keeps rolling
and rolling until you can't hear it any more. You ride over
beautiful red, buff, and black sandstone covered with li-
chens and moss and then, quite suddenly, come to the
cracks. All kinds of brush and many cedar trees grow out
of the cracks in the rocks. It is difficult to see cattle in
that country, and the ground is so rocky that tracks are
hard to pick up. One day, over in that area, we saw the
big red-necked steer. Matthew Roanhorse took out after
him. Before long, they were out of sight. Late in the eve-

ning, long after we had gotten in from the drive, Matthew
rode in. His horse was sweaty and nearly run down. He'd
been after that steer all day, but it had gotten away from
him.

A few days later we found him again in a different
place. He was as wild as a black-tailed deer. After an
hour so so, Matthew managed to get him with a couple
of gentle cows and calves and drive him into the holding
pasture. Next morning there was a hole in the fence and
the big steer's tracks going back out to the open range of
the West Camp.

Ceph worried about that steer all day. When we came
into camp that night, Ceph told us that he'd catch the
steer on water as soon as Lost Tank dried up. He went
out to the water lot way before daylight and checked until after sundown for months, but he never did see the
red-necked steer. That big steer had been free too long to
run the risk of being caught now, so he came in alone at
night to water out when there were no humans in sight.

Ceph kept thinking about that old steer and wondering
why he hadn't caught him. Whenever we'd come by the
camp, he would ask, "You haven't seen the old red-necked
steer, have you?"

"No," said Cooney, "but we'll get him next year."

"He must have jumped the fence and gone plumb over
into McCauley's pasture."

"I kind of believe he's still in here somewhere."

We never saw the red-necked steer again that year.
Ceph's health was beginning to fail and that steer still
preyed on his mind. At the same time, I had a feeling
that he wanted the big steer to go free and would have
felt bad if we had sold him. Ceph complained a little
now and then about backache and stomach troubles, but

not enough so that we suspected anything was seriously wrong. Then he lost weight and began to look hollow around the eyes. One day we drove up to the camp and he asked us to take him to the doctor right then.

It was terrible, waiting around to learn what the diagnosis would be. At last the X-rays returned and the doctor told him that he would have to go to a specialist in El Paso for an operation immediately. We would have driven him, but he insisted that he would be all right on the bus. "Hell, I'm all right," he said. The doctor had told Cooney the chances were slight that we would ever see him again.

The next morning we took him and his few possessions to the bus depot. He was still chewing tobacco when the bus pulled in. "Take care of Brownie and Blue Kitty," he told us.

"Come back whenever you get well," I said.

He grinned. "I'll greet you in the spring with a smile on my face like a wave on a slop bucket—right?"

"Right," we said. Cooney and I got back in the car, wiped our eyes, blew our noses, and rode home in silence.

While Ceph was gone, we hired another man to stay at the West Camp. Brownie and Blue Kitty disappeared shortly afterwards, picked up by rabbit hunters, we thought. The new man was a great hulking bear of a man, with a long beard and hair down to his shoulders. He kept the camp very clean, took good care of the cattle and fences and wells, but it was never the same after Ceph left. We still cooked on the wood stove when we were working cattle at West Camp, but the food never tasted or smelled as good as when Ceph was there. And I have never gone to sleep on that lumpy bed since he left. The peace and homey disorder have gone and now it is just a place to eat when we are working.

That fall, after Ceph had gone, we found the red-necked steer again. This time two of the men stayed with him until they got him into camp. We kept him up in the corral until we were ready to take the herd across to the other ranch. Everything went well until the day before we shipped. The men day-herded the cattle and, that evening, when they were driving them back to the corrals, four or five big steers gradually worked their way to the edge of the herd and broke out. It was so dark by that time we couldn't begin to find them or track them down. With those steers was old red-neck, free once more. When they told me at supper that night, I felt a strange elation.

For a long time we didn't hear about Ceph. Then we got a letter from his daughter saying that he had had surgery for cancer, was doing as well as could be expected, but would never be able to work again.

The winter passed and the spring winds began to blow. It was a mild spring. King Pearce, a neighbor, had stopped by the house for coffee. "Say, I just saw old Ceph in town," he said. "He says he's had all he can take of city life and he's coming back out here to see you in a day or two."

Sure enough, in a couple of days, Ceph showed up with a new hat, new boots, and a big grin on his face.

"How do you feel, Ceph?" I asked.

"Like I told the doc the first day after that operation . . . he come in to see me, real quiet . . . I guess he was afraid I'd croak . . . he stepped over to the bed, felt my pulse, and said, 'How do you feel, Ceph?' 'Well, doc,' I says, 'I never felt better or had less in my life.' I reckon they tuk durn near all my insides out, so I don't have nothing left to bother me. Them nurses was sure good to me. The first thing I asked for after that operation was a chew and, you know, they got it for me."

No matter how hard we tried to persuade him to stay off horses, he would saddle up once in a while and go down the fence line or check on cattle in the horse pasture. It would have been unthinkable to let him have the West Camp again, because he would be so far off that he couldn't get help if anything happened to him. That was a blow to him, but he seemed to enjoy sitting on a keg in the sun, puttering around, doing the chores, and helping out around the ranch. In the morning, he would come into the house about daylight, put on the coffee, and holler, "Are you awake?" If I hadn't been, I was then.

Everything went along all right until the next fall, when the cold weather started. Ceph began getting aches and pains once more. At last, he decided to go to El Paso for good and live out the rest of his life among his children and grandchildren. Once more, we bade him farewell and told him to come back and visit sometime. Once more, we doubted that we would ever see him again.

We heard that he had had two more operations and that he was a very ill man. Then, last summer, not long after the Fourth of July, a pickup drove up to the ranch and out stepped Ceph. Cooney and I looked at each other and smiled. He walked over and shook hands and there was something about the way he stood there that told me he hadn't come back just to visit. "I can't stand that durned city any more," he told us. "Guess I just get too lonesome for those old cows."

He put his few things in the bunkroom and began walking around the corrals, looking the cattle and horses and sheep over. Then he found his old nail keg, set it in the sun next to the barn, and sat down, at peace with the world.

He still hits town occasionally for a few days' recreation, indulging in mild forms of gambling suitable to his dignity and old age. At the races last year he told us he'd seen the "fastest little horse that ever hit Arizona," but by some streak of misfortune, the horse lost and he came back home.

One midnight, after Christmas, we heard the front door open stealthily and boots tiptoed into the kitchen and back out. The next morning when I went out to start breakfast, I was greeted by an unbelievable sight. There on the dining room table lay a gallon bottle of whiskey, tied up in red ribbon. Ceph had won it in town and presented it to Cooney as a Christmas gift. We invited all our neighbors over the next Saturday night for *tamales, enchiladas, and rofritos,* put a pump on top of the whiskey bottle, and had a party.

Cooney says he thinks we sold the old red-necked steer last fall. I don't think so. I think he's living out his days over at the West Camp, tall and rangy, running wild and free back there in the cedars somewhere. At least, I like to think so. At any rate, Ceph doesn't worry about him any more and neither do we.

11

Summer

Summer is a long, dry waiting for rain. It is watching the range dry up day after day, until the spring's new growth of grass has yellowed and burned and crackles under the cattle's hooves when they walk. It is seeing the tanks dry up and the cattle roam restlessly from one spot to another looking for a few tufts of dry grass. At the last, it is pumping water at the house, the West Camp, Saunders' Well, Porter, and Woodruff, keeping the gasoline engines going constantly if the wind is not turning the windmills hard enough to get water.

Most of the well trouble occurs when we need water desperately. Trouble may take the form of a broken windmill, worn out or disconnected rods, holes in the pipelines, or an engine in need of repair. The alkaline soil in some areas eats the rods until they are so riddled with holes the water leaks back and they must be replaced.

Every day Cooney must check the water to assure a constant supply for all the cattle now watering out at the wells. Sometimes a float valve gets stuck and we can lose a tankful of water in a day by such an accident. Often salamanders, or "water dogs" as we call them, get into the pipelines and valves and have to be pulled out slimy piece by slimy piece.

At the ranch, the spring calves have grown and matured until they are ready to be branded. Our biggest branding usually takes place in July or August. The last few years we have had to wait until late in September, after the rain, because the range was in such poor condition that the cows and calves would suffer too much from "chowsing" around. It is usually a toss-up as to whether we brand when it is dry and the cattle are easy to catch coming in to water, or whether to wait until after it has rained, some grass has appeared and the cattle are full, but must be driven long distances away from all the watering places. Every year Cooney must weigh these things carefully and decide which will be easier on the cattle.

People are always asking us when our "busy" time is on the ranch. I suppose you could say that it is from the first of January up until around the last of December. But our hardest work usually takes place between July and November. It always seems to me as if we scarcely finish branding when it is time to gather cattle for fall roundup.

In spite of, or maybe because of, the hard work in summer, it is a pleasant time. The spring winds begin to diminish in May. June and July are hot, but the nights are so cool you must sleep under a blanket. When I think back on summers, my most pleasant impressions are of evening meals outside, smelling steak broiling or lamb barbecuing, leaning back in a chair after dinner, smoking, and looking up at a whole sky covered with stars. Then, too, I think of the days spent riding horses in the hot sun, the unexpected delight of finding a new ruin, some potsherds, a mano, metate, or stone ax or some arrowheads. Cooney always finds them first. Like an Indian, he knows what to look for and sees many things in one small sign. I never find arrowheads and never see ruins until we are almost on top of them.

Long ago, probably between A.D. 800 and 1200, there were many villages and settlements along the canyons. I think there must have been far more water then than there is now to have supported so many people and the game they must have lived on. There must have been springs with a constant water supply. Every half mile or so along Porter Canyon there are a few scattered rocks and mounds which were once rooms. Some are square, some rectangular, and a few are round, like kivas, present-day Hopi ceremonial buildings.

It always seems strange to me, poking around in those ruins, that at one time this country supported thousands of people and it now supports so few. In direct contrast to the rest of the United States, this arid plateau decreased its population instead of increasing it. Why these pueblo people left, no one knows for certain. The reason may have been a combination of drouth, raids by enemy tribes, and disease, or it may have been one terrifying and calamitous natural disaster, such as the eruption of Sunset Crater, near Flagstaff.

High on the canyon walls, many petroglyphs were carved in the rock—signs and symbols of a thousand years ago. Over at West Camp there is an almost perpendicular sandstone slab marked with petroglyphs. On a flat rock in the bottom of a canyon are carved deeply the imprint of a man's feet and a child's feet. It occurred to me one day that all the signs, over many square miles of country, point directly to San Francisco Peaks, even today the home of the Hopi Katcinas, and to the Navajo, the sacred mountains of the West.

Once in a while you find broken pieces of tiny pots or a miniature metate. I often think, sitting there in the cool shade of a cedar tree above the canyon, that at one time Indian children played there. And now they are gone—men, women, and children. There is nothing left but the sand and rocks, some broken pottery, and the wind in the cedar trees.

When summer comes, I often think of the season Pauline was with us. Pauline is Sam Roanhorse's daughter, the one who had been ill so much and stayed smaller than the rest. They didn't know about her heart trouble when she was little. Not until she went to the government boarding school at Keams Canyon and the teachers noticed that she got tired easily and felt sick often. Then the doctors found out about the valve in her heart and the Navajo Tribe flew her to Salt Lake City for a catheterization. For a while she was better and had begun to grow a little.

Sam's wife, Helen, wanted to go to work in the cucumber fields in Snowflake until the harvest was over that summer, but she had no place to leave Pauline. Sam worked for us then and so she stayed at the ranch. She slept in the bunkroom with her father, but first thing in the morning she would come to the house for me to comb her hair.

Washing and combing hair, with Navajos, is more than an act of good grooming. It is almost a ceremony. At home they use yucca root, which lathers like soap and makes hair clean and shining. When Navajos wash one another's hair, it is an act of intimacy and trust. It is as if one were saying, "You may touch my hair because we are good friends."

I had known Pauline since she was a little girl, and now she was twelve years old. She still looked like a child, with her long, brownish-black braids and her short, stocky figure. Unlike most Navajo girls she was something of a tomboy and had always been close to her father. Sam was affectionate with all his children, but I believe he felt closest to Pauline. When he talked about her there was a special glow on his face.

Pauline liked to wear Levis. When she came, I got her a new pair of tan riders and a Western shirt so she could save her two dresses for good. Cooney bought her a hat and a pair of new boots of which she was exceedingly proud. She went with us on horseback a few times, but got so tired that I was afraid to let her go any more.

After breakfast she would start washing the dishes or drying them for me, using the kitchen ladder to put them away in the cupboards which were too high for her to reach. She always asked if she could run the vacuum cleaner, which fascinated her, or dust the furniture, stopping to look carefully at my grandmother's china cups and saucers. "What is this *for?*" she would ask about some strange object. Sometimes I would say "It just looks pretty," and she would look at it a long time, trying to decide why. She would go on to sweep the porches without being asked; then, if I had nothing special for her to do, she would run outside to see what the men were doing.

Sometimes we would walk out in the stillness of the

evening and bring in the sheep. "I sure like to herd sheep," she said.

"How old were you when you started herding sheep for your mother?"

"Just small. My sister and I herd sheep all summer when we were small like that. My mother buy us a little compass and teach us how to use it so we don't get lost out there."

"Were you afraid to go by yourself?"

"No, I'm not afraid. There are snakes out there, but my mother taught us a song to sing to the snake so he won't bite you."

"Doesn't anybody ever get bitten?" I asked.

"No," she said in her definite, final, conclusive way. "When a snake comes around, you have a feather and drive him away and sing that song to him. It tells him to go away and not bother you any more."

We had a good relationship, Pauline and I. She was very outspoken with me, although never disrespectful. She was not slow to give me mature and solemn advice when she thought it was necessary. One day she looked around, put her hands on her hips, and said, "You got too many things."

I taught Pauline to take showers often, wash and comb her hair, keep her clothes neat, and how to behave herself when people were around who had to be behaved to. Pauline adored my mother. They had fun together and Pauline used to call her "Little Grandmother." Mother was very affectionate with her and would always hug her when she came out to the ranch.

One day Pauline and Little Grandmother and I went all over the country delivering cowbelle beef promotion posters to the grocery stores. We were, all three, in a devil-may-care frame of mind. In fact, we were so devil-may-care that we walked out of the first grocery store with a bag of Fritos and forgot to pay for it. We drove on munching corn chips and had to drive back about ten miles to pay for them.

Pauline would look out the window at a herd of cattle and say, "*Be'goshi a ha yu.* Lots of cows." She said, "You know, there's an old lady at home named Lizzy S'Nez. My father is always calling me that when he tease me sometime." So we started calling her Lizzy S'Nez. Every once in a while she would look up at my mother, her eyes sparkling, and say, "You are funny, Little Grandmother."

"When I herd sheep I always make songs," she told us.

"What about?" I asked, foolishly.

"About herding sheep," she said.

"Sing some of them," I said.

"O.K." she said and began abruptly in a Wagnerian contralto.

"Hey-ya-ya-ya; all day long, the sheep ya-ya-ya . . ." It went on for about six verses, half in Navajo, half in English, with a few noises that sounded like part of the Night Chant thrown in for good measure.

"That's a good song," I said. I really thought it was, too.

"You should hear Matthew when he sing. He's funny. He's always make up funny songs for me when he come home. There's one he sing about an old fat lady. I'll sing it for you. "Ya-ya-ya-ya; old fat lady, ya-ya; sits in the corner, all day long. Ha-ya-ya-ya. She go this way, she go that way, because she drink too much wine . . ."

"See those trees over there?" she said once. "Those are monkey trees."

"What?" I asked.

"We call them monkey trees. Sometimes when Curtis and I were herding sheep we would sit under those trees and eat the seeds. We call them monkey nuts. They're sure good."

After supper one night when we were washing dishes, she said suddenly, "When I am thirteen I'm going to have my coming-of-age ceremony." She communicated this to me as if it were the most precious and beautiful secret in the world.

"That's wonderful," I said. "How do you know?"

"My mother tell me."

I was filled with a sense of pride and happiness for her.

"When I come of age, there will be a ceremony for me out at Jeddito. Everybody comes and brings grocery and they have a big ceremony."

"What do you do at the ceremony?" I asked.

"You get up early in the morning when the sun comes up and have a race. You race with all those boys—a long way. You get tired. Then those old women tell you things you must know to be a woman. Those people say prayers and songs and things like that. Sometimes those boys must have a horse race. They race a long way. Sometimes those horse they die, but they must die, because it is a ceremony. When it is over the people go all away and you are a woman then."

"That is very good," I said.

"I just make up another song," Pauline said. "You wanna hear it?"

"Sure," I said. She opened up in her most splendid manner with a love song, in Navajo. Afterwards we laughed, ate some cookies, and she started out to the bunkroom. "Well, goodnight, Jo," she said. "Sleep tight."

"You, too," I said, "Lizzy S'Nez."

That last week she stayed at the ranch, she began telling me the other side of her life at home. She was carrying the steaming dishes over to the table for our supper one evening. "When we eat at home," she said, "we fry a big pan full of potatoes and make some fried bread and that's our supper."

"Where do you get your water at home?"

"The tribe they put up a windmill over at Jeddito, so we got good water. Before that, we get it out of the wash."

"Doesn't that wash dry up sometimes?"

"Sometimes, in summer. That water get real low. It's dirty and it taste bad. Then all those baby get sick when they drink that water. Everybody get diarrhea."

"Your mother is coming this Saturday, she said in her letter."

"I know," said Pauline. She was very quiet all through supper. Afterwards, when we cleared the table, she said, "I don't get lonesome for the reservation. I like it here."

That was when panic struck me. I wondered if I had gone too far. I remembered the social worker telling me one time, "We never have much luck placing Indian children with white families. It gets them all confused. They start feeling as if they don't belong anywhere."

If I had hurt Pauline, oh, if I had, what then? We changed, that last week, toward one another. Sometimes we were critical of one another's ways, sometimes aloof. Pauline stayed more with her father. I kept more to myself. I think we both knew that to show love would be too painful when Saturday came at last.

I washed her hair for the last time Saturday morning and braided it for her. She wore a dress that day. We gathered her things together in morose silence. Then the pickup drove up to the ranch. Her mother, her sister, two of her brothers, and her cousin got out.

Helen came over and shook my hand, looked at me a long time and said, "Thanks for taking care of my kid, Jo." Pauline looked up at her mother, then at me. "Well, goodbye, now, Jo," she said. "You must write to me at school this year."

"I will," I said. "Goodbye, Lizzy S'Nez."

Helen and all the kids came to get Sam and take him home for Christmas that year. After he drew his paycheck, they drove him to town and came back out to the ranch loaded with presents for us. Helen gave Cooney a box of handkerchiefs and Sam gave him a box of cigars. Pauline had bought me an ashtray with a painting of a horse on it. Helen had made me a big, lavender, tufted cushion and an apron which I wore nearly every day.

The next spring after Pauline's visit, Sam got a letter saying that Pauline was going to have open heart surgery at City of Hope, California, in the summer. The next few months Sam grew more and more quiet and depressed until he hardly spoke at all. One night we were having supper alone. "You are very worried about Pauline, aren't you, Sam?" I said. He had tears in his eyes. Then we talked a long time. I told him that the best doctors in the whole country would be taking care of her and that, when it was over, she would feel better than she ever had in her life. I was talking as much to convince myself as Sam.

Before Pauline and her mother left that summer, they came out to the ranch to tell Sam goodbye and to see me again. I knew that Pauline had had her ceremony that summer and had become a woman. Her hair was short and curled and she wore new black-rimmed glasses. She was very quiet. Her face seemed white and drawn. She and Helen sat on the edge of the sofa, nervously. When they started to go, I asked her, "Are you very scared?" She looked up at me and nodded her head. I hugged her tightly, which I had never done before. "All those doctors and nurses will take good care of you," I said, "and you'll feel good when it is over." She nodded her head again, but didn't say anything.

The tribe had chartered a plane to fly Pauline and her mother to California. It was July. Two days after the operation, I drove Sam into Holbrook and put in a call to the hospital from my mother's house. Sam talked to Helen, in Navajo, for a few minutes and then, suddenly, hung up. "Helen she start to cry," he told me. "I guess she scared. She say Pauline sure sick. Sho got a bad cold. They don't let nobody see her." We sat in silence going home.

All week we waited and hoped and prayed. I had sent Pauline a get-well card saying I hoped she felt better, before we knew how bad she was. Then we called again. This time the news was better. Pauline had gotten over her cold, was out from under oxygen, doing well, and would probably be home in about three weeks.

We stopped by the post office to pick up the mail before going out to the ranch. In the box was a letter addressed to "Jo Cooney" from Pauline Roanhorse. I opened it. The front of the greeting card had a picture on it of a vine with purple lilacs drooping from it. On the front was printed, "In Deepest Sympathy." Inside was a snapshot of Helen wearing a new blouse over her long skirt and Pauline, arms crossed, legs apart, staring defiantly ahead. In back of them was a neat, modern building with "City of Hope, National Medical Center" on the front of it. Inside, the printed message continued: "To express sincere and heartfelt sympathy in your hour of sorrow." Under some more drooping lilacs, in familiar handwriting, was written: "Mr. and Mrs. Jo Cooney. I hope you are enjoyed it our picture. Pauline Roanhorse." And I knew she would be all right, that girl.

Summer is the time for visiting with friends and relatives. Every summer, Aunt Zone, Mother Jeffers' sister, would come to visit her. At ninety, Aunt Zone was remarkably alert and active. Her clear, gray eyes twinkled with spirited humor. Her wrinkled cheeks glowed pink and her bluish-gray hair was pulled back tight in a bun. She was a short, small-boned woman, the anatomical opposite of Mother Jeffers, but she had raised a big family and worked hard all her life. She was so small and plump that I felt like squeezing her, the way you do a child, whenever I saw her.

She stayed with her youngest daughter most of the time but visited relatives all over the country. "I won't stay by myself, El," she would say to Mother Jeffers. "I don't know why anybody'd want to."

El sat in her hard-backed rocking chair, arms folded and legs askew. She sat like a child or like a man—prepared to leap up any minute—never entirely relaxed, as if hidden dangers were imminent. "Well, maybe nobody wants you, did you ever stop to think of that?" said El.

Aunt Zone chuckled. "I don't care if they want me or not. I'll go stay with them anyhow . . . until they run me off. Then I'll go and stay with somebody else."

"Yes, and you'd jump in any car that's a-going some-

place. We'd just heard that you were down in bed with
all that back trouble and next thing we knew you were
off to Florida with Mabel."

Aunt Zone sat in the vinyl-covered armchair opposite
El, her feet scarcely touching the floor. Her knobby hands
worked nimbly on the yarn slippers she was crocheting.
"I wish you'd throw those old house shoes away, El. They
look worse than some old tramp's," she said.

"I can't help how they look. They feel good. Shoes never
get comfortable until they are wore out. And you'd better
not be throwing anything out like you did the last time
you were here."

"I just got tired of looking at that nasty old dress.
Never did like it anyhow."

"You and Jo will be sorry if you burn up any more
things, sister. I believe I could whip you both if I had
to."

"I'll do as I please. You talk loud but you don't scare
me a bit. I'm still the oldest, remember."

"You may be the oldest, but you're not the biggest.
Sometimes I feel as if I don't own anything around here
any more. I rather thought this was my house, but I guess
it isn't, by damn."

"I wish you wouldn't talk so ugly, El. I don't know
where you got that from. Mama and Papa both would
whup us for talking ugly. Joe and I never did swear
around the children when they were growing up."

El poked me in the ribs and winked. Why, yes, you
can tell that very easy . . . that none of your kids ever
heard any swearing."

"I only remember hearing our papa swear once. It was
a real cold, frosty morning and he went out to saddle up
an old horse he used for plowing. The horse wasn't much

used to a saddle, anyhow, and he was all humped up because of the cold. When Papa cinched him up real tight that old horse twisted his neck around and bit Papa right on the seat of his britches. Papa kicked him in the belly and said, "Goddam you, you son-of-a-bitch!" It like to scared me to death . . . I always was the biggest coward in the world, anyhow . . . I'd heard the preacher say in church that if you took the Lord's name in vain the devil would come and fetch you. Well, I didn't know he meant wait until the day of judgment. I thought the devil was a-coming right then to get Papa and I was looking all around for him. That's the only time I ever heard Papa talk ugly."

"I don't recall ever hearing him or Mama cuss. I'm going to town to buy a new coffeepot. I guess I'll have to, since you put a butcher knife through the bottom of that old enamel one."

"I just hated that old coffeepot. It never did make good coffee," said Zone.

"That's the first time I ever heard of anybody pulling a stunt like that," said El.

"Well, I knew you'd never throw the nasty old thing away," said Zone.

One night when Aunt Zone was staying in Holbrook there wafted through the door a familiar essence from the direction of the pumphouse. El sat straight up in bed. "I smell a skunk," she said.

"Go back to sleep," said Aunt Zone. "It'll go away by morning."

"Yes, and it'll kill all my banties by morning, too. I'm a-going out there and blow the head off that thing, if I can see it."

"Well, let me go with you and hold the flashlight so's you won't kill any of the neighbors," said Zone.

El grabbed her .22 rifle and Aunt Zone held the light. They tiptoed out in their long nightgowns and caps to the back porch and out the door. "Shine it over here," said El. "This way!"

"I don't see any skunk," said Zone. The white light bobbed up and down against the side of the pumphouse.

"For land's sake, can't you hold that light still?" said El. "It's going thisaway and thataway and I can't see a thing. What's the matter with you anyway? Are you afraid of a skunk?"

"No," said Aunt Zone, "But I'm sure afraid of a fool with a gun." While they argued, the skunk made good his escape and the two sisters went back to bed.

Aunt Zone brewed coffee that would make your hair stand on end. She still drank a lot of coffee even though, when she was ninety, the doctor said it was bad for her health. They had wonderfully wild Irish fights, she and El. Somehow, nobody ever seemed to have the last word and never will, I suppose. Now they are the only two left of Grandma and Grandpa Lewis' children.

Every summer the Lewis family holds a reunion at the old log cabin in the mountain valley near Weed, New Mexico. All night long men hover over a pit keeping near the fire for warmth, while they baste and turn a whole beef. On the closest Sunday to the anniversary of the August day when Mama and Papa Lewis came from Texas to settle there, the whole clan gathers for a barbecue and dance. Aunt Zone's and Aunt El's children are no longer young themselves, but the two sisters still have the hearts of girls and a youthful exuberance fed by their dauntless humor and a consuming love for life.

Near the log cabin, boards are placed on saw horses to make the long tables on which are placed barbecued beef, potato salads, hot rolls, homemade pickles and preserves, thick slices of white onions, and black iron kettles of steaming pinto beans. At the end are paper cups and a big blue enamel coffeepot. Aunts, uncles, cousins, in-laws, grandchildren, and great-grandchildren line up to fill their plates; then they spread out over the grass and weeds to eat and talk in the low soft twang of the mountain people.

Over at Eldo Lewis' ranch house the fiddling begins. All day and long into the night the fiddlers play, even when all the dancers drag their feet and go to bed at last. Totally absorbed in that music which outsiders cannot really feel or understand, they play on. Foot-stomping, heel-kicking music—country tunes as venerable, doughty, and irrepressible as the Irish, Scottish, and English ancestors who brought them to America so many years before. It is not written down, this music, any more than the elusive character and temperament of their family traits can be written down. The long Lewis faces of the fiddlers and guitar pickers are wrapped in the same expression you might find on members of a string quartet playing fugues.

While the fiddlers play in one corner of the room, children and old people dance, dance with all the spirit in them, swinging each other lightly, precisely, in the country dances they grew up with. Sweaty faces concentrate on the dance steps. The only smiles are on the ruddy, weathered faces of the men grouped around the deep freeze full of canned beer on the side porch. In the kitchen, the womenfolk who don't dance sit and talk about the ones who do. The coffeepot simmers on the stove.

About midnight, the fiddlers are playing strong and
hard with a rhythm which comes from the soul of the
mountains. Aunt Zone and Aunt El come out of the bedroom, down the hall, where they have gone for a short
rest. "I wasn't tired," says Aunt Zone, "but everybody just
pushed me in there and told me to lie down."

"It's getting to where everybody tells me what to do,
too," says El.

The two of them step out onto the hardwood floor and
inform everyone that they are going to dance a jig. Tough
and hardened men step into the kitchen for a cup of
coffee to steady their nerves. The fiddlers strike up. The
sisters begin to dance. Faster and faster their feet move
in the half-grieving, half-singing, wailing, shrieking, laughing, living strains of Irish music. Around and around they
dance while the relatives stand back to watch. "Land,
pull your skirts down, El," says Aunt Zone, breathlessly.
"Pull your own down," says El. And they dance with all
the high spirits and strength and brash humor of the clan.

In August the clouds start building up—huge, billowing
clouds, row upon row they move ponderously across the
sky from the west. That is when we start cloud-watching.
As the cattle grow weaker and hungrier, all the ranchers
in the country watch and hope and pray for rain. The
parched earth lies still, waiting.

Then, one day, the restless cattle lie down, their backs
to the west, as cumulus clouds bank up across the southwestern sky and there is a faint, damp smell in the air.
By noon, the sun is darkened and faint rolls of thunder
echo and re-echo. A calm settles over the land. Then,
gradually, it begins to rain and the awful tension, the
lump in your throat, and the ache in your muscles suddenly disappear. Cooney and I, Sam and the young Nav-

ajo boys all stand out in the rain until we are soaked. Curtis Roanhorse grins and jumps over the fence. "It's sure a good rain over at West Camp," he says. The horses begin to run as fast as they can, kicking up their heels and playfully chasing one another out in the horse pasture. No words can ever express the elation in a rancher's heart when a long dry spell is finally broken by a good rain. I can still remember how I felt one summer day, after our first rain of the year, standing out in the corral when it was over, smelling the strong, pungent earth and watching a bunch of young bulls we had just bought run across the pasture, throwing up their heads, while behind them, from one end of the ranch to the other, stretched a double rainbow, unspeakably beautiful.

The rain does not always come. There are years when one longs desperately for rain—when the clouds build up thick and heavy only to be dispersed by a strong wind. Then the cattle must be moved to grass somewhere or, at worst, all of them sold along with the ranch, because few ranchers can afford to sell off their cattle and re-stock the following year after paying taxes and leases. This has happened to most cattlemen at some time or other.

The Hopis say that the Katcinas, the spirits who live in the San Francisco Mountains, are borne eastward by the great-bellied clouds. In August they come, bringing rain. Aloof from the world, on their high mesas, the Hopis hold their ancient and complex ceremonials as a supplication for rain. For days beforehand, the priests tend to their sacred rites. At night, down in the kivas, the preparation continues. Sometimes you see the men, days before, scouting the surrounding country in search of the snakes—bull snakes and sidewinders. The snakes will convey the messages of the Hopi people to the gods of the underworld. Then, on consecutive weekends, the chosen villages will hold their "snake dances" in the plazas.

One very dry summer we decided to go, once more, to a Hopi dance. It had been years since I had seen one. I could go back year after year, each time being more absorbed in the pageantry, the ritual chants and dances. The road to the Hopi mesas is paved, now. There are pickups, washing machines, electric lines, television antennas, even sewage facilities among the ancient rock and mud houses on the tops of the mesas. But the Hopi religion, language, and customs have changed surprisingly little over the centuries. The mesas remain some of the oldest continuously inhabited settlements in North America.

These dances are happy, festive occasions and I can't help thinking that the gods must be more pleased with them than they are with some of our solemn and dolorous ceremonies. Hopi religion is not a once-a-week matter, but encompasses the whole of their lives. Hopi people come from all the villages and from their jobs off the reservation. There are curious tourists, government workers, ranchers, an anthropologist or two, friends, relatives, and even a few Navajos.

On top of the mesa, the air is clear and thin. An eagle, chained to one of the rooftops, flags his great wings. The smell of cedar smoke mingles with the odor of corn and meat stewing. An old woman is making piki bread on a hot griddle. She smooths the thin batter with her bare hands while it is cooking until it is tissue-paper thin, then rolls it up, like papyrus. The rolls are different colors—blue, yellow, pink—made from the various colors of Indian corn, finely ground by hand on a metate rock. Another woman sings a corn-grinding song as she works inside a house somewhere. Across the plaza, a radio is blaring rock 'n' roll music.

The Hopi children seem ubiquitous. They climb and jump like young goats over houses, rocks, and along the sheer sides of the mesa. The little ones take hold of your hand, content to go wherever you go and wonder what tempting morsels might be hidden away in your pockets. They are chubby-faced and healthy, with clean, straight, black hair.

Sometime during the afternoon the dances begin. People align themselves on the housetops and along the mud walls around the plaza. Slowly, imperceptibly, a few dark clouds have begun to gather in the west. The chorus comes in, dressed in their buckskin moccasins, leggings, white skirts, handwoven belts, and carrying their drums and gourd rattles. Then come the dancers—faces, torsos, and arms painted with religious symbols. Furs and different kinds of shells hang from their belts and decorate their buckskin skirts. From their mouths dangle the squirming, deadly serpents. Beside each snake-bearer is another dancer carrying a feather with which he touches the snake now and then, lightly.

As the chants proceed slowly, rhythmically, hypnotically, the other world, the white man's world, recedes farther into the distance. The dancers perform, in a circular direction, around the cedar-covered enclosure in the center of the plaza. The intricate, precise songs and dance steps continue from out of the dark recesses of pre-history until all sense of time is lost. Time no longer exists. It is now and was now and will be now forever and ever.

After a while you feel yourself nodding slightly with the rattle of the gourds, the deep, self-assured male voices of the chorus, the beating of the drums. Then you notice, suddenly, that the sky has become dark and threatening. A clap of thunder shakes the heavens. On and on the dancers circle. The rhythm has changed slightly. Now there is a feeling of quiet excitement . . . urgency . . . expectancy . . . in it. Lightning flashes across the sky and another long roll of thunder drowns out the chorus. Still the dance proceeds. It is almost finished now. One by one the dancers turn their snakes loose, with prayers, in the four directions. The snakes slither and scurry off toward the edge of the mesa . . . blessed snakes . . . those ancient symbols of the lightning, which brings the rain, and the male part which insures the continuation of life.

And now the rain comes down . . . harder and harder it beats down on the people, the houses, the metal roofs of automobiles. Fresh and clean and hard it comes, trickling down the sides of the houses, running in rivulets down the ruts in the dirt streets, pouring in streams off the sides of the mesa. The cloudburst opens over all the country, making the Hopi corn grow and giving green life to the barren range. The fierce male lightning strikes and the female rain comes in a release of joy and re-creation. For the Hopis and for us and for all people who live by the seasons it comes.

And when you are immersed in the timeless ritual of a Hopi ceremony, and when you have felt the cold wet rain on your sunburned face, you know that there is nothing on earth more powerful than sex . . . sex in its broadest sense . . . the maleness and femaleness of all things on earth. That force which makes the golden corn ripen, the green grass spring up, which forms the young animals and a baby in its mother's womb. That overpowering and mystical force which unites human beings with all of Creation. The everlasting natural cycle of birth, death, and the rebirth of life. The beauty and order and reason which is Creation. The blackness of death and despair; the brilliance of joy and life are one. And there is no time except now, which was and is and always will be.

12

Enemies

The cattleman has always had two kinds of enemies—
natural and manmade. Of these, the natural enemies have
usually proved the easier to cope with. They have been
with him since the beginning of his industry, which is one
of the oldest on earth.

From the 1860s to the early 1900s, the American West
was the domain of the cattlemen. These men—tough,
shrewd, stable, hard-working, rough-talking, and fearless
—gave their lives to the amassing of fortunes, the development of the land, and the improvement of cattle.

The great conflict of nineteenth-century cattlemen was
that of Man, with his reason, ability, and foresight,
against the overpowering forces of a hostile Nature. The
concept of Man against Nature was a product of Western
civilization. The Indian, on the other hand, was a part of
Nature, accepting it as it was; evolving his religion and

social structure in accordance with natural forces; living within the perfect balance of Nature.

The early-day cattlemen battled drouths, floods, blizzards, windstorms, and Indian attacks the best he could. There was no such thing as supplemental feeding in those days. When the range dried up, the cattle starved and died. The carcasses of cows and calves lay over thousands of square miles of bone-dry, cracked earth, rotting and burning in the heat of the sun. Year after year of drouth in the twenties, besides overgrazing, caused the violent wind to whip clouds of fine dirt a mile high into the atmosphere, carrying it with fury across the nation, finally depositing it in a thick layer of dust which settled over all the land, choking out the remaining vegetation.

Cooney has told me of such drouths and of violent thunderstorms in Texas and New Mexico when, as a boy night-herding cattle, he would watch the dark thunderheads roll over the moon and the air become still and threatening. Some of the men would keep up a continuous noise by singing or whistling, to avert an uncontrollable stampede caused by a sudden blast of lightning. He would shiver in his saddle when the cold rain came and watch the blue lightning flash back and forth between the horns of the cattle. He has made long drives during which cattle herds had to cross roaring rivers—in which cowboys spent the good part of a day trying to start the herd across the rushing, rain-swelled Rio Grande, the cowboys who couldn't swim hanging on to their saddles in the swift current, trusting to their horses to get them safely across. When Cooney first moved his cattle onto the ranch southwest of Holbrook, he had to trail them in to the railroad every fall. In crossing the Little Colorado River, he always lost a few head in the quicksand before a safe crossing was found. And Cooney has seen blizzards in which entire herds would bunch up in the corner of a fence and smother to death in the howling, blinding snow.

Severe weather conditions are still with us, but now cattlemen who can afford it are able to feed during the winter months and dry spells. In extreme cases, sometimes hay is dropped from airplanes to save isolated cattle from starvation. Long drives are rare in these days of good roads and cattle trucks. But in the Southwest, the most formidable and toughest natural enemy remains drouth.

One unfortunate result of the nineteenth-century battle of Man against Nature was, in many instances, a violent disruption of the balance of Nature, causing irreparable loss of wildlife in some areas. Where the deer, antelope, mountain sheep, and buffalo were destroyed to make room for cattle, the cougars, bears, jaguars, and wolves began preying on cattle. These predators were no match for the traps and firearms of human beings. The animals had the alternative of being exterminated or moving to ever-higher, ever-wilder country.

These days one scarcely ever sees a cougar or lobo wolf except in remote wilderness areas, although we have come across the track of a bear or lion crossing the ranch on its way to new hunting ground. Recently, a pair of enormous, beautiful spotted jaguars were shot in the mountains near here, but not before they had killed about thirty head of cattle belonging to the White Mountain Apache Tribe.

Elimination of these large predators resulted in an increase, once more, of the deer and antelope population. This increase is now being controlled by government and state wildlife regulations. Ranchers today contribute to the increase of game animals such as deer, antelope, turkey, and elk by providing them with feed, salt, and mineral. Water development, road improvement and maintenance, and ice-free water in winter all benefit wildlife as well as cattle.

Cooney and I do not hunt and have no other interest in the herds of pronghorn antelope that roam our range than to race them sometimes in the jeep, just to watch their grace and agility. Antelope, for some reason known only to them, try to run in front of a moving vehicle instead of away from it. We sometimes see a herd of twenty or more, perhaps a quarter of a mile away. Frightened, they begin running, coming closer all the time, until they are parallel to the jeep. We have been driving as fast as sixty miles an hour side by side with the antelope when they leap suddenly across the road in front of us. Even a two-day-old antelope has unbelievable speed. That is their only defense, save for the horns of the bucks. In a way, antelope are enemies. They share with our cattle the grass we are paying for and they tear up our fences when they run under them. But they are beautiful enemies and the pleasure of watching them is worth the trouble of mending a few fences now and then.

The demolishing of coyotes by government poisoners often leads to an overabundance of rabbits, who are far more destructive to the range than coyotes. Still, coyotes must be controlled or they would overrun the country, killing small calves and lambs when the rabbit supply diminishes. We have come across coyotes eating the carcass of a small calf. Whether the calf died or whether the coyotes killed it, we cannot be sure. In the cool of the morning, just before dawn, they bark. Two coyotes sound like a dozen. Coyotes are playful and affectionate with each other. The young ones, who have never been

frightened by a gunshot, are curious at the approach of
strangers. One day we were bringing in some cattle from
a dry tank. Two young coyotes stood, not more than fifty
yards away, watching us. When they decided that no one
was going to harm them, they began following us, watching Bess work cattle all the while. They tagged along, for
all the world like a couple of dogs, for about four miles
until we came within sight of the house.

The Navajos say that Coyote is their brother. He is the
chief character in many of their stories, playing the part
of the crafty, lecherous prankster, much as Reynard the
Fox did in medieval French folklore. Raymond told me
one time that the old people said it was bad luck for
Coyote to cross your path and you had to sing a song to
him to avoid trouble.

I was always fond of coyotes, although we would chase
them horseback or shoot at them often to run them away
from the house because of the poultry and sheep. Then,
one night last fall, a frightening thing happened. About
chore time, Sam came into the house to tell us that two
of the ewes hadn't come in with the rest of the sheep.
We supposed that they were lambing out of season and
feared that a coyote would pick them up. We jumped
in the jeep and searched for them until long after dark,
to no avail. As we drove up to the yard gate, I heard
Annie, then just a small pup, yipping violently at something. Her hair bristled like a razorback hog's. Not twenty
feet away from her was a coyote. It looked up at us,
blankly, then began wandering around just outside the
yard fence with its head down. "Cooney, there's something *wrong* with that coyote," I said.

"There sure is," he said. "I believe it has rabies."

The word sent a chill through me. I thought about Annie

and the sheep and wondered if any of them had been bitten. It was too dark to get a good shot at the sick coyote, so Cooney decided to run over it with the jeep. It didn't run fast, but it managed to dodge crazily back and forth. At last we felt a thud and knew we had hit it. Cooney put the body into a gunny sack and we drove to town to see the state veterinarian, Dr. Carl Thompson. Dr. Thompson and Cooney packed the animal in ice and sent it on the bus to the Animal Disease Laboratory.

The next morning, one of the lost ewes showed up down in the arroyo with a newborn lamb. Ceph drove her back to the corral. The men were loading cattle that day, so I saddled a paint horse and trotted off in search of the other ewe. About half a mile from the house, I picked up her tracks and began following them. A short distance from there, I found the body of a lamb that looked as if it had died at birth, or right afterwards. Then I noticed coyote tracks alongside of the ewe's tracks. I followed them up on top of the ridge. The paint pricked up his ears. Just over the hill, I could see the coyote watching me. I spurred the paint and we charged the coyote until he disappeared into the cedars. Back in a narrow, grassy draw below the ridge, I found the ewe with a tiny lamb. She had given birth to twins. The coyote had been following her since early morning, but she had managed to fight it off and save her remaining lamb.

Slowly, I began to drive her back toward the house. When I got her onto the main cattle trail, within sight of the ranch, I decided to lope over and find the whole sheep herd and bring them back where they would be safe until we could get the coyote. A quarter of a mile away I found them grazing peacefully, and drove them down toward the ranch until they were with some cattle on their way to water and I thought that they would go in by themselves.

When I turned to go back to my ewe, she was nowhere in sight. I kicked the paint out again and we took off in pursuit of the ewe. Then I saw them. The coyote had sneaked back, figuring it was his last chance to run her down and kill her. I rode as hard as I could until I had caught up with them, pushed up between the ewe and coyote and, at last, he ran off, reluctant to give up his meal. The lamb's tongue was hanging out, so I stopped to let it suck the panting ewe and give them time to rest before driving them on in.

When the report on the sick coyote came back it was negative, but rabies in its early stages cannot always be detected, so we were never entirely satisfied.

Many forms of wildlife are enemies. Badgers are a menace to horses. A horse can easily stumble and fall in a badger hole and break his leg or a cowboy's neck. Badgers look like clowns in baggy pants. Broad-backed, loose-skinned, they seem to roll across the country. They have powerful forepaws, sharp claws and teeth, and it takes a brave dog to tackle one.

Porcupines are a nuisance, too. Cooney's old cutting horse, Redman, let his curiosity run away with him one day and came in with the saddle horses, his nose full of quills, looking chagrined. Cooney cut the tops of the hollow quills off to let in the air and make them easier to remove, but the process was still painful. Porcupine quills lodged in the nose and mouth of cattle and horses prevent them from eating or drinking and can cause eventual starvation.

One of the most destructive of all enemies is the insipid gopher, who burrows around in the loose dirt

around the edge of dirt tanks. Proof of this came one
year when we were desperate for water. Finally, a cloudburst hit directly over our largest tank, which is really
a small lake, and filled it to capacity. Unnoticed, gophers
had so undermined the dirt that the side of the tank gave
way and we lost all of our precious water in a flood that
ran all day and all night.

Some ranchers have serious trouble with rattlesnakes,
but we seldom see them and, to my knowledge, have
never had a horse or cow struck by one. Most of the
rattlesnakes in northern Arizona are sidewinders, slim
and seldom over two feet long. They do not coil before
striking, but if they are disturbed, fling their bodies sideways in a lightning-fast movement. They are beige or
gray, difficult to see unless they are moving, but they do
give a warning rattle at the approach of an enemy. No
other noise is quite like that rattle. It gives one an immediate and chilling sense of danger.

One fall I rode right over the top of a sidewinder, who
must have been napping in the sun. Neither my gentle
horse nor I realized it until Matthew got down off his
horse and killed it with a rock. Another day, Cooney and
I were riding in the horse pasture. We jerked up our
reins simultaneously when we heard the rattle. Cooney
got down and killed one small sidewinder, then we
looked until we had found its mate. In the summer
months they shed their skins several times and are tem-
porarily blind, so that they will strike out viciously at any
body heat. That is the only time they are very dangerous
and I always wear boots when I am walking around over
the country, because most snake bites are on the ankle or
calf of one's leg. Like most wild things, snakes prefer running away to encountering a human. I don't worry about

snakes near the house, because we have so many cats. Since cats keep all the rodents killed off, there is nothing to attract snakes and they tend to stay away.

Other enemies are lynx cats, foxes, swifts, owls, and hawks. These animals occasionally scent the ducks, geese, chickens and guineas, and try to catch them at night. Of all the hawks in the Southwest, the only one I know to be a real threat to domestic birds is the small, swift, cunning goshawk or, as we call him, the Blue Darter. One summer a Blue Darter caught fourteen of my guinea chicks, one each day for two weeks. We all watched for him, but he managed to sail in when we were eating or otherwise occupied. Several times we attempted to shoot at him, but he kept low to the ground, gliding in and out among the cattle so that we didn't dare take a shot at him.

By far the worst of animal enemies are the product of civilization—wild dogs. Nobody could love dogs more than I do, but the first time I ever saw a yearling heifer with her ears chewed off, her nose lacerated, and her legs so raw, bloody, and swollen that she couldn't walk, I declared war on the wild dogs. Vicious, senselessly destructive, they roam the open country in packs, leaving town at night, one by one, to meet on the outskirts and go about their bloody business. Some are family pets who wouldn't dream of harming a child. Some have turned completely wild and raise their pups in caves and rocky canyons. More destructive than lobo wolves, who killed because they were hungry, the wild dogs hunt down old poor cows and bulls, running them and cutting them down for the thrill of it.

One day when Sam Roanhorse and I were home alone, he shouted at me to get Cooney's rifle. I ran outside and

saw about ten dogs, just outside the corrals, attacking
two young heifers and their calves. One heifer was down
on her knees, fighting desperately to save her calf. So en-
grossed with their victim they paid no attention to our
shouts, they finally scattered when I shot at them. Because there were a lot of cattle around, I couldn't get a
good shot, so Sam rode after them on horseback, but they
were well on their way by then.

The next day Cooney made a "drag" of an old carcass and laid bits of poisoned fat along the trail. We put
out cyanide in most of the pastures as a last resort. I hate
to put out poison for fear of killing wildlife or good dogs
or even children who are out with their parents rabbit-
hunting, but we post notices on all the gates to warn anyone who ventures in.

Until last fall we thought that we had killed most of
the dogs. Gathering cattle in our Woodruff pasture, I was
coming in to the well with four wild cows and their
calves. I had been having trouble driving them, but at
last had started them over the hill toward the well. No
sooner had I gone back after some other cows I had
spotted in the cedars than the four wild cows ran back
past me as fast as they could go. For a long time I loped
after those cattle, working around them until I had them
together again. We reached the hill above the well and
once more they broke away from me and turned back.
Then I heard the dogs and knew what had made the
cows so wild. When I topped the hill, I could see ten of
them, all sizes, shapes, and colors. All told that day we
saw fourteen wild dogs. Bess hates them passionately. If
we come across a pack of them when Bess is in the jeep
with us, we say, "Bess, there are some *bad dogs*." Her

eyes grow wild and she bounds after them in hot pursuit until they are safely headed back toward town.

Predators, drouth, blizzards, windstorms, and lightning are not the only natural enemies we face. There are many poisonous plants and flowers. Turpentine weed causes cows to "sling" (abort) their calves. Wild mustard paralyzes cattle's tongues. Worst of all is loco weed, with its lovely purple flowers. It is a noxious, habit-forming herb. Cows and horses start eating it and soon become addicted to it, refusing to eat anything else. Since it has no food value, they eventually die if they are not found and put on feed. Loco, a Spanish word meaning "insane," makes animals groggy and induces hallucinations. Locoed cows are difficult to handle. They stand looking at a person, shaking their heads, stumbling and falling. Often they go through the motions of drinking long before they get to the water. Horses which have been locoed are virtually impossible to break for working.

One year, when loco was beginning to spread over the range in a rapid and dangerous manner, Cooney noticed that some tiny black insects had appeared in the horse pasture on the loco leaves, causing the plants to wither and die. Although they felt a little foolish doing it, he and a Navajo cowboy gathered up thousands of the minute insects in a Mason jar and deposited them on every patch of loco they could find. It worked. In a few days the insects had destroyed most of the loco on the ranch.

Disease is another omnipresent enemy. Hereford cattle are particularly susceptible to pink-eye and cancer-eye, perhaps because of the reflection of the intense sun on their white faces. The greatest success Cooney has had treating pink-eye has been painting black circles around their eyes to shade them from the glare. The cows' appearance is rather startling, but the treatment works. Cattle have many of the same diseases humans have. Brucellosis in cattle is the same as undulant fever in human beings. In recent years, the disease has been well controlled. Cows also develop cysts and tumors and have numerous calving problems.

The once-menacing screwworm is being eradicated rapidly in many southern and western states. Male blowflies are sterilized by radiation and turned loose to mate with females who then lay their eggs under the skin of cattle. The eggs do not hatch and the species is gradually breeding itself into extinction.

Even more dangerous to cattlemen than natural enemies have been human enemies. After each Homestead Act that Congress has passed, the western states have filled with hopeful farmers and laborers from the South and East, seeking to stake out their small claims to part of the wide country. Unfortunately, most of the West is not and never will be suitable for farming. There were disputes over boundary lines, water rights, grazing, and the use of the soil. Plowing up the dry earth only made it more vulnerable to the ravages of wind and water and destroyed all the native vegetation. In the end, most of the small homesteads were bought up by the ranchers whose cattle had grazed the country for years before they came.

Disputes between cattlemen and sheepmen are as old as the beginning of stock raising, and are traditionally engendered over disputes about grazing rights to certain territory. There is also a universal and deeply rooted arrogance on the part of accomplished horsemen, from the Mongols to the Cossacks, to the Comanches and the American cowboy, who look with disdain on the humility of the farmer and sheep herder who toil with their hands. In this more enlightened age, cattlemen and sheepmen are the friendliest of enemies, hurling an occasional barb at each others' businesses, but helping each other out if the need arises. The National Cattlemen's Association and the National Wool Growers Association co-operate with one another for their mutual benefit. Many ranchers these days raise sheep as well as cattle, letting the animals forage side by side, getting multiple use from their land.

Human enemies in these times take the form of cattle thieves, trespassers, and vandals, who remain difficult to apprehend on the large spreads of the West, and even more difficult to convict because of lack of concrete evidence. Trespassers unwittingly leave gates open, not realizing that an entire month's work at roundup time can be lost by the simple act of forgetting to close a gate. Vandals have shot holes in our drinking tubs and windmills, and have dumped garbage on our property, causing the death of any cow who happens to pick up a tin can or wire and get it lodged in her throat. Misguided urban hunters have been known to shoot cows, mistaking them for deer and elk. Many a cowboy has had a horse shot from under him during hunting season.

More elusive, far more difficult to understand or cope with are the unseen enemies of a changing social structure. They may take the form of strict government controls, deadly to any form of agriculture or ranching. Price supports for farmers make feed costs so high that only the best-organized and knowing rancher can afford to feed during periods of drouth or cold spells, without depleting his entire income. If we supplement our feed with protein blocks or similar feed over the winter, the cost may run as high as thirty thousand dollars, not including hay, mineral, and salt. The government's emergency drouth feeding programs usually consist of "cheap" feed which is surplus grain that cannot easily be fed to cattle on the large ranges of the West because the wind blows it out of the feed troughs, wasting most of it.

Cattlemen have stubbornly resisted government aids and controls over the years. Most of them have the attitude an old cattleman once expressed when he said, "I've made it alone so far and I'm damn sure not going to take the government's tit now." In the past few years, foreign imports from Australia, New Zealand, and Argentina, plus rising beef production in this country, have created a surplus of beef which has seriously lowered prices.

Because of recent land speculation and real estate promotion in the sparsely populated western states, land prices have skyrocketed, even when there is insufficient water to support an increase of population. While ranching country that sold for fifty cents an acre eighty years ago is selling for thirty-five to forty dollars an acre now, one cow still requires the same amount of grazing land it did then. In most of northern Arizona, ranchers can only graze five to ten head per section because of insufficient rainfall over the past twenty years. Consequently, a man who is making a living from cows is, in spite of higher prices than he received eighty years ago, not much better off financially.

With the increase of land values, the leases and land taxes have gone up out of proportion to the rancher's value of his land. Most of the land is owned either by the state, the Federal Government, or large corporations. Privately owned land is at a premium and is rapidly being bought up by companies who use it as an income tax deduction and are willing to speculate on it for a period of thirty or forty years. It is virtually impossible for a young man starting out in business to buy a ranch and pay it off in his lifetime with an income from cattle alone. He must have backing from some other source or find a good ranch to lease.

In short, I doubt if there is another business in which a man gets less return from his investment in money and in time. It is not unusual for a rancher to hold a million dollars' worth of land, equipment, and cattle and owe money. A few years ago, a rancher could save the profits of a good year for the bleak times ahead, but in these days of high income taxes that is becoming more and more difficult.

Many cattle ranchers could improve their incomes considerably by selling their land to a speculator, paying off the income tax, investing the rest in securities, retiring on the interest, and not have to work a lick the rest of their lives. Then why, you ask, stay in the cattle business?

That is like asking an artist why he prefers to paint and starve than go to work in his grandfather's tool factory . . . because he is doing what he was born to do and what he does best; because he likes being around cows and working for himself eighteen hours a day, knowing that nobody is pushing him around, telling him what he has to do or when he has to do it. Because he is glad of the opportunity to raise his children in the sun and fresh air and space of a ranch. He knows that if he makes a mistake it is his own fault and if he has one good year out of ten when it rains, the calf crop is about 75 percent and the market price is up, then it is worth the other nine bad years.

For the past one hundred years, the percentage of people making a living from farming and ranching has decreased. It is now less than 10 percent. Large ranches are surviving, even prospering; small ranches are disappearing. Fewer people are needed to operate a ranch nowadays. And yet this relatively small percentage of the total population has an importance out of all proportion to its influence in the government. The producers of the nation's food supply are the backbone of this and any nation. Without food, science, art, military programs, and industry cannot survive. While the rancher's way of life and way of thinking are in opposition to the whole trend of our society, he has virtually no voice in government with which to defend his views.

Combating the rancher's enemies are certain encouraging factors. One is scientific progress. Every year, more means are discovered by which to prevent disease, destroy insect pests and harmful weeds, to raise healthier and heavier cattle, and to fight adverse weather conditions. Engineers and scientists are exploring the problem of drouth and the ever-lowering water table in the western states. Great new dams have been built; new ways to stem evaporation and transpiration of water have been discovered; bold plans are being considered for bringing in converted salt water from the ocean and fresh water from the rivers and lakes of the Pacific Northwest. And, every year in the United States there are about three million more mouths to feed. Because Americans have traditionally preferred beef to any other meat, the cattle industry will probably survive.

The cattleman is still standing on his own two bowlegs, wearing his battered stetson and run-down boots, cussing

at everything from the weather to the lack of good cowboys to the Department of Internal Revenue. But as long
as people eat beef, somebody has to raise it on the hoof.
And as long as somebody has to raise it, he's willing to
try.

13

Roundup

There is always a day in August with a fleeting touch of fall in the air. The weather will have been hot and oppressive for several weeks and then, one day, a fresh wind out of the north sweeps briefly over the land, carrying with it that sharp, earthy smell of fall. Often I have been down on my hands and knees in the yard, digging around the rose bushes, my forehead damp with perspiration, when this sudden and exciting chill came in the air and I knew that, before long, it would be time to round up cattle.

Autumn has always been my favorite season. Something about the damp, leafy smell of it intensifies all my emotions. The clear, sharp air, coming after a drowsy summer, arouses sleeping senses and startles them into awareness. Fall colors are the colors I love. I revel in the warm yellows, ochers, siennas, and vermilions of the as-pen trees, scrub oaks, manzanitas, and sumac of the nearby mountains. In the midst of all this vibrant beauty is that ephemeral quality without which there is no beauty. The very urgency of fall—the blaze of life and color that rebels against the inevitability of coldness, death, and winter—makes me love it all the more.

In northern Arizona, the autumn winds are gentle. After the late summer rains in August and September, the whole range, at long last, turns from terra-cotta to green. Almost overnight, after a good rain, the grass pushes up through the reddish earth and begins growing rapidly. If the rainfall has been consistent and no early frost has stunted it, by mid-October the grama grass has headed out and waves like wheat in the areas where it thrives. Grama, a Spanish word meaning "grass," is the best natural feed we have. Through September and October, the yearlings graze on grama, putting on the additional weight that means the difference between profit and breaking even for the year. Down in the protected canyons grow wild oats and aromatic herbs and bushes. Other grasses are fescue, needle grass, and sacaton, the coarse, tall bunch grass. The grasses that come after the late summer rains are the only feed the cattle will have for the winter, except for browse. When there is no rain, there is no grass, and cattle must survive the best they can on white sage, buck brush, chamise, and other browse, plus the protein blocks we put out.

Cooney usually contracts for sale of the cattle early, in June or July. In the old days of ranching, a cattleman's word was as good as everything he was worth. These days, most agreements are written down in the form of contracts to avoid later disputes. If a cattleman says that he'll sell his cattle at a certain price, then the market

rises and he rejects the first price in favor of a higher
one, he loses the respect of most buyers. Similarly, if a
buyer contracts for cattle, putting a small percentage
down as a forfeit, then the market breaks and he gives up
the forfeit rather than take the cattle, his reputation suf-
fers. There is nothing wrong with letting the forfeit go,
but cattlemen will remember it the next year, wonder if
they are going to be left once more with all their cattle,
and trade with someone else. Most cattle buyers prefer
to go deeply in debt than refuse the cattle and lose pros-
pects of trading again in a certain area.

The cow buyer is not quite like any other man on
earth. He is, often as not, a free-wheeling, fast-dealing,
fun-loving, high-paced, shrewd man, able to take life
with a grain of salt. His business is one of the greatest
gambles there is, short of having a permanent seat at a
roulette table in Reno. His credit stretches farther and
farther as his reputation increases. He lives from one
year to the next, never knowing if he'll make a million
dollars or lose the mortgage on his house. His family
survives, somehow, with the good management of his
wife, a warm personal relationship with his banker, the
trust of cattlemen, and a certain amount of luck. We
know a buyer who has what he calls a "hanging tree" in
the backyard in the event all else fails.

Most cattle buyers cannot resist the temptation of
practical jokes now and then. We heard a story about a
buyer who called a rancher friend in California and
asked, "Say, could you use a few bulls?" "Sure, send 'em
on," said the rancher. Two days later at the railroad depot, he received fifteen carloads of Mexican *corriente*
bulls, of doubtful breeding.

An example of the way people used to feel about cattlemen occurred when we were in El Paso one winter. Cooney had bought some badly needed dress clothes and found it necessary to cash a check. The clerk who waited on him said, "Excuse me, sir, but all personal checks have to be approved by the manager."

The manager walked up gravely, shook Cooney's hand, and then smiled. "You know, Mr. Jeffers," he said, "my father worked here before me and he told me something I never forgot. 'Always shake hands with a man,' he said, 'and if he's got calluses on it, cash his check.'"

By the first of October we are ready to start the roundup. There is a feeling of expectancy, mingled with excitement and anxiety before we start. For the next month, we will be working every day from sunup to sundown, rushing to town to make phone calls at night, trying to settle on a delivery date satisfactory to us and the buyer, who will be receiving thousands of head of cattle the coming month; ordering railroad cars from the Santa Fe; trucks to haul the cattle from the ranch to town; notifying the cattle inspector, who must be there to inspect the brands before the cattle are shipped; and arranging with Bill Jeffers, Cooney's cousin and business partner, to have his cattle driven in from the ranch north of Holbrook at the same time.

During fall roundup, there isn't time to think about anything except getting the cattle delivered. I found a sign once that I felt was expressive of the general mood, and tacked it up in the kitchen during roundup. It read: "Anyone who remains calm in the midst of all this confusion simply does not understand the situation."

When we begin working, the tension disappears. It is replaced by physical work, exhaustion, and a sense of accomplishment. We usually begin working at the West

Camp. About daylight, the men begin doing their regular chores while I cook breakfast. When we have eaten, Cooney sometimes washes the dishes, giving me time to pack the dinner we take to the West Camp. The men throw our saddles and other gear into the back of the jeep pickup and we start out. Cooney and I and the two dogs crowd into the cab. Sam and the other cowboys ride in the back, their collars buttoned up and their hats pulled down low against the chill in the air. Bess is still groggy, somewhat grouchy and disagreeable from having been rudely displaced from her warm quilt at an unreasonable hour. Annie sits precariously next to Bess, doing her utmost to stem her excitement. Her ears are alert; her nose quivers with anticipation. Whenever we hit a dip in the road, Bess lurches forward, bumping her nose against the dashboard, then turns to look daggers at Cooney. "I think we ought to have a seat belt installed for old Bess," I say. "You'd think that after all these years she'd learn to brace herself," says Cooney. Bess never learned to ride in the back of the pickup like other dogs. We tried it a few times, but she just fell out, and we would look back to see if she was all right and she'd be running after us as hard as she could to catch up.

Sometimes Annie spots a herd of antelope running across the road a hundred yards in front of us. Abandoning her manners, she throws herself across my lap, knocking off my hat, sticks her head out the window and sniffs desperately, making low, imploring whines and growls in her throat. She is reprimanded severely by Bess's snarling upper lip and reluctantly settles down again until we arrive at West Camp.

I take the food out of the boxes and arrange it so that all we have to do is heat it up when we come in from

the drive. The man who stays at the West Camp has gone
out to wrangle the horses. As I put on some more coffee,
the horses run into the corral, pushing and kicking each
other to be the first fed. The gentler horses shove their
noses down in the morrals (feed bags), eager to get at
the oats or barley in the bottom. Sam coaxes the broncs
to come to their morrals, then slips the straps up over
their sensitive ears. When the horses have had their grain
and we have finished our second cup of coffee, Cooney
and the cowboys catch the horses. If the horses are young
and only "half-broke," they must be driven into a corner
of the corral and roped. Once in a while a bronc will
fight the rope, rearing up, pawing, and biting, trying to
kill the man who caught him. This happened one year
with a young, white-faced roan bronc we got out of
Mexico. His eyes were light blue and wild-looking and
we called him "Eagle." The minute he felt the rope
around his neck he began pawing and attacking Cooney
in an attempt to kill him. As a last resort, he was heeled
and brought to the ground.

Cooney held him down on the ground while the horse
squealed and snorted, kicked and pawed, bit and foamed
at the mouth. The men choked him with the rope until
the fight had left him. At last he got up, staggered
around, and allowed himself to be saddled. He tried to
buck a few times that day, but finally gave up. After
that, all Cooney needed to do to catch him was show
him a rope. Eagle would look at it out of the corner of
his eye and stand still.

Since Bess's retirement, she has been content to lie in
the shade of the house, snap at flies, watch the progress
of a troop of ants as it parades before her, and guard
the chickens until our return. Annie trots along beside us,

sniffing at everything, thinking that this surely is the most
interesting world imaginable.

For about two miles we ride in silence, shivering with
the cold, penetrating breeze. Cooney sits relaxed and
easy in his saddle, looking as if that were the only place
on earth he really felt completely at home. He makes his
little roan travel in a fast, steady walk. Sam, on a buckskin horse, trots to the side of Cooney, his back straight,
his knees pressed tight against the horse's sides, his arms
flopping up and down, sitting firm in the saddle, sure of
himself. I am riding a Mexican cow pony, a well-muscled
pinto who moves smoothly, gracefully, over the rocks. I
ride in an easy trot, putting all my weight on my legs, so
as not to tire myself too soon. At some distance behind
us is the big, barrel-chested man who took Ceph's place
at West Camp. He has kept his big horse fat and sleek,
to carry the burden of his weight. He rides heavily, hum-
ming to himself in a deep, gruff voice.

At last we split up. The men go in opposite directions.
I follow Cooney until we have found some cattle. Then
he leaves me to drive them while he scouts a mile or so
on either side for more. We make our drives and meet at
Post or Lost Tank, let the cattle water and settle down,
then drive them back to the camp.

One day, when Annie had stayed at the camp with
Bess, Cooney and I rode up on a large buck antelope
watering at a remote water hole. He stood there drinking
and looking at us cautiously with his golden-brown ram's
eyes. It was then I thought of what it was Cooney reminded me of: he moved with the same graceful caution
as this great buck, as one who is accustomed to danger,
to having his own way, to walking alone. The buck and
Cooney looked at each other in passing with their steady

hazel eyes, perhaps feeling a common fleeting emotion.

That same day, Cooney and I covered miles of country without seeing any cattle or cutting any sign of cattle. Coming off the wide ridge between Post Tank and the West Camp, we picked up the tracks of a cow and calf and began following them over toward the rough, rocky country where the huge fissures in the ground start. Our horses' ears twitched when a calf bawled somewhere. The ground was so cut up and rocky that we had lost the tracks. "Now where would I go if I were a cow?" said Cooney to himself. He noticed some brush that had been broken by a passing animal and started off on a narrow, zigzag trail that led between great slabs of red and buff sandstone. We heard a crackling noise and opposite us, on a narrow ledge, stood an old, stout, long-horned cow with a steer yearling. She looked at us fiercely and defiantly. "I've been trying to bring that old Nelly in for the last two years," said Cooney. "She's as old as I am and she's got a steer yearling, too."

The cow took off in a run. Cooney watched for a moment to see which way she headed, then started off in a high lope after her. For fear of getting in the wrong place, and because the country was too rugged to run beside him, I tagged along behind, spurring my horse, holding onto my hat, and doing my level best to keep up with him on what I knew was going to be a wild chase to the finish.

The old horned cow ran into the cedars where they were the thickest. We stopped abruptly to listen, having lost all trace of her again. I went one way and Cooney another in an effort to roust her out of the brush. I wove in and out of the cedars, straining my eyes and ears for a sign. My head was down, scanning the ground for tracks, when I rode under a cedar limb and startled a sleeping owl who suddenly flew up in front of me with a terrible screech and flapping of wings. My horse jumped and I nearly fell off.

I had just regained my balance and composure when I heard Cooney whoop and saw him dashing recklessly through the cedars after the old cow and the yearling, who were running for all they were worth. About that time one of my bridle reins which had been patched broke and Cooney's hat was knocked off by a limb. When we had recovered his hat and fixed my reins, the cow was gone again.

We had been after her too long to give up now, so we tracked her down once more. Silently we moved through the trees and then saw the yearling in front of us, looking back and bawling. "That big devil's still sucking his maw," said Cooney. Behind the low, thick branches of a cedar a few feet away we heard a low rustle and saw the tip of a horn. The old cow, hot and tired from running, had hidden behind the tree and was lying down, her head held close to the ground. We went around the tree. She got up when she saw us and began to sling her head and charge the horses. Cooney untied his rope, leaned over, and hit her on the nose with the double of a rope. She stood there a long time, snorting and panting. He hit her again. Then, suddenly, the rebellion went out of her eyes. She had lost her battle and knew it. She trotted carelessly over to her yearling, bawling to it, then turned to look at us as if to say, "I've had my fling and I'm ready to go now."

In about ten days the work is finished at West Camp and we are ready to roundup the holding pasture on the west side and bring the cattle across to our main ranch.

One of the men brings the saddle horses, the others move the herd, and I drive the jeep over to pick up the men at the halfway point, where we keep the herd in a small holding trap overnight. Before Sam and Ceph fenced off the trap, the men had to night-herd the cattle coming across. A few steers usually broke out at night. With the trap, we don't lose any cattle. Modern cowboys, used to a warm bed, don't relish the idea of sleeping under the stars or huddling around a campfire all night to stay warm. Sleeping may be more romantic the old way, but it is also colder and harder.

For about two and a half more weeks, the drives continue every day until all the ranch has been covered. We make the drives in a circular direction, starting from the Woodruff pasture east of the highway. Then we cover Five Mile Wash, the microwave tower, Porter windmill, Candalaria Tank, the open country around Red and Coyote tanks, and at last, the farthest reaches of the ranch, back in the deep canyons and cedars against the west and south fence lines.

I go with Cooney every day unless I am too tired from an especially strenuous ride the day before. I am older and stronger now, and every day the drives seem easier to me. I think back sometimes about that first happy, miserable year as a ranch wife amidst all my aching muscles, trials and indecisions, embarrassments and mistakes, and wonder how I made it. I am still no skilled equestrienne, but I can handle a horse better, get in the way less often, and seldom lose my directions more than once a day.

When we finish working the cattle late in the evening, I fix a light supper of leftovers. Then, when the men have gone to bed and our ranch house is still, I start cooking a pot of beans, a beef stew, or a roast for the next day's dinner.

About the end of October, the climax of the year's work arrives: the day we round up perhaps a thousand head of cattle from the buck pasture, put them into the run-around, and work them. I remember, particularly, rounding up one day after we had had a good shower during the night. The rain had washed the dust off the grass and trees, making their greenness more vivid than ever. The cedars were strongly aromatic. There were little pools of water everywhere on the rocks, which, being wet, were intensely colored. All this land which, millions of years ago, had been sediment deposited on the bottom of a warm, shallow, inland ocean, had a strange, faint salty odor of the sea about it. The pools of water looked and smelled like tide pools.

We crossed the canyon, wading through the shallow, rushing, rust-colored water. It was one of those fine brisk fall days when the white clouds pass swiftly and lightly across the blue sky. A shiver would run up my back as clouds concealed the sun. The next moment, my forehead would perspire around my hatband as the sun shone down warm and strong. It reminded me of the old fable about the argument between the sun and wind about which one could make the man remove his coat. I looked around over the wide, moody stretches of northern Arizona and thought that nowhere on the face of the earth could there be a country with so much cruel, intemperate beauty—almost too much beauty to bear.

All afternoon we hold up the herd at the back of the run-around while Cooney, mounted on a fresh horse, moves through the herd quietly and swiftly cutting the cattle to be sold. He handles his horse with the sureness

and authority of a man born and raised with horses. He and the compact roan work together, the way no man works cattle unless he has done it all his life. There is a minimum of effort in his movements one never sees except in a real cowman.

The cattle in the corrals mill around and bawl all night long. Sleep would be impossible except for the complete exhaustion following the day's work.

Early in the morning, when half of the orange sun shows above the horizon, we drive the cattle out of the corrals and move them slowly up the fence line to a corner where the grass is thickest. They spread out and begin to graze. The cowboys stay with the cattle. Cooney and I lope back to the house, then drive to town to make last-minute checks on the buyers, railroad cars, and trucks. When we return, I take dinner out to the men who are day-herding.

About four o'clock that afternoon we get on our horses again and ride out to help the men bring the herd back to the corrals. The cattle inch along, reluctant to quit the tall grass. Nearing the house, a few of the steers and cows make one last attempt to break away. The old long-horned cow has her eyes fixed, longingly, toward the West Camp.

It is dark by the time the cattle are penned. I start supper while the cowboys bail out the remaining water in the drinking tubs, and tie off the float valves. Buyers usually take a 4 percent "shrink" off the price of the cattle or agree that the cattle stand in a dry corral all night. This is to prevent unscrupulous ranchers from letting their cattle fill up on water before they are weighed.

Once again the cattle mill and bawl all night long. Before sunup, I get up to make breakfast and put on my biggest coffeepot to boil. Cars drive up in the semi-darkness. Bill Jeffers has come out to look over the cattle. The buyers arrive to receive the cattle. Then the cattle inspector comes in. They gather in front of the fire, warming their hands, drinking hot, black coffee.

As dawn breaks, Cooney gets his cow whip, mounts his horse, and begins cutting the cattle from the alley into five different corrals, with a man on each gate to let the cattle in. He separates the steer yearlings, heifer yearlings, steer calves, heifer calves, and cows. The calves and yearlings must be of uniform size and age. The cows are carefully culled again for lameness, blindness, or signs of cancer. The "dry" cows and barren cows are separated from the "wets," ones with calves, because they all bring different prices.

I man my station at the scales and begin weighing the cattle as fast as Cooney cuts them. The cattle inspector, the buyers, and I stand around stamping our feet, blowing on our cold hands. We weigh the cattle, mark down the weight, and count them as they come off the scales. "Get that cat off the scales!" somebody yells. Mehitabel, in spite of the noise and confusion, is strutting back and forth on top of the scales, adding her few pounds to each draft weighed. "It took me weeks to teach her to do that," I say. Nobody thinks it is funny.

About the time the men are ready to load the trucks, a singular occurrence, understood only by the gods of Nature, disrupts the whole process. Every fall on the day we ship cattle, one of my game hens has come off a well-concealed nest with a flock of small, peeping chicks and has invariably led them straightaway through the alley-ful of stamping, pushing, crowding cattle, while grown men hold their breaths until she is safely on the other side, with her family.

By late afternoon, the cattle have all been trucked into Holbrook. All but the culls, which are usually sold separately. Cooney and the men have taken their whips and warm jackets into Holbrook, where they will be up most of the night at the stock pens, waiting to get the brands inspected, the cattle divided into carloads, and at last loaded out on the Santa Fe.

I am perverse about going down to the stock pens to see the cattle loaded—not because I mind standing around in the cold, but because I do not want to look at the old cows again. Every year we sell about fifty "hulls," the old "shelly" cows who have lived a long, wild life in their chosen canyons and cedar brakes, free except for the journey to the corrals twice a year when their calves are branded, and in the fall, when their calves are sold.

They have produced calves every season for nine or ten years and raised them through the bitter cold of the early spring snows. Now the cows are old and swaybacked, sometimes half-blind. Their ribs protrude from their sides and their flanks are hollow. Their faces and necks are wrinkled. Their hooves have grown long and spread out; their teeth are worn down to the gums from sand-covered feed. All their remaining strength has been sapped by the calves which tug at their flabby bags.

Their horns are long and sharp. With them, they have fended off coyotes, wild dogs, and the shrieking eagles who try to seize the newborn calves with their talons. Now these brave and truculent old cows are being herded up the ramp into the cattle cars, for the long ride to wheat in Colorado, Kansas, or Texas. Some of them will perish on the way. When they get off the train, their tired, sore eyes will brighten to see more feed than they have ever seen in their lives. They will push and shove and hook at each other to get to the feed. And when they are fat for the first time in their lives, they will be killed. They have never stopped serving man from the hour of their births to the moment of their deaths.

This year, I didn't want to see them go again, and so I stayed alone at the ranch. It was quiet, except for a few dogies who stood around bawling for the old cows. I felt very tired and stood, leaning against the yard fence, letting the wind blow my hair, looking at the crimson sun in the west.

Somewhere in the dusk a mourning dove called out sweetly and sadly. I thought of a Navajo cowboy who had worked for us once. He had been all through the Pacific campaigns in the Second World War, and when he came back they had a lot of ceremonies for him because he had artillery shock from seeing so much death. His face was wistful and preoccupied. He used to say, when the doves called, "I don't like to hear those doves. They always make me feel lonesome."

Listening to that dove I thought about Raymond and Matthew, about Sam and Helen, about Grace, and, especially, I thought about Lizzie S'Nez. Then it was dark. Bess and Annie and Mehitabel and I went in the house. I built a bright fire in the fireplace and brought my supper into the living room. Drowsy and peaceful from the warmth of the fire, I threw a blanket over me and lay there on the sofa, listening to the logs crackling and waiting for Cooney to come home.

Postscript

Jo Jeffers Baeza

I wish I could say that Cooney and I lived happily ever after, but we didn't. Perhaps some of our problems were foreshadowed in the book. Enough to say we tried to change each other and couldn't.

The story has a happy ending, though. I moved to the White Mountains south of Holbrook, remarried, and raised two beautiful stepchildren. Cooney remarried, had a beautiful daughter, and lived long.

When I was about 50 I started living my own life as a single grandma. The same year my first grandson was born, I began a career in journalism. For the past eleven years I have been a newspaper reporter and editor, college English teacher and free-lance writer. I've not strayed far from Navajo County or the mountains I have come to love so much.

Most of the principal characters in *Ranch Wife* are gone. Nearly everything about ranching has changed in the thirty years since I wrote the book. Only the female bonds from those years endure. My dearest friends are still ranch women and their daughters.

I am an elder now to my Navajo friends. We have kept in touch through many weddings, births, and graduations. Last year when Pauline and Helene Yellowhair (Roanhorse) brought their mother to visit me, Helen said, "Make some biscuits like you used to make on the ranch." I hadn't made biscuits for a long time, but you don't turn down a Navajo Grandma.

To Ann and Bill Jeffers, I'm still "Aunt Jo." They let me come out to their ranch and play cowboy, even though I'm so stove-up I sometimes need a boost onto a horse. Last summer Ann and I made a pilgrimage to the old log cabin in Weed, New Mexico, where her dad and Cooney were raised, and found the Drag A headquarters near Datil where they once ranched.

I have never been out of animals for long. When my old dogs got shot last year, someone gave me an anti-social Border collie named Duke, and my grandsons gave me a hyperactive puppy named Emily. I almost drowned saving her when she fell through the ice. One morning I found a little Apache mustang covered with brands on my front porch looking in the window. She's mine now, and foaled this spring.

What a wonderful life I've had. If I had to do it over again, I would probably do it over again, because I've always followed my heart. As my daughter once said, "You just close your eyes and jump in and heal up afterward."

I have loved my mother-in-law, most of my relatives, and all the children I have helped raise. I know, now, what

Mother Jeffers meant one time when she was very ill and in a coma. She opened her eyes, looked at me, smiled, and said, "I think the little children loves me."

I would hope they love me, too. That's all that counts.